The Beginning of the Gospel of Christ

A Commentary on the Gospel of Mark

By W.J. Sturm

Text copyright © 2018 William J Sturm All Rights Reserved

Scripture quotations are generally taken from the New King James Version®, Copyright © 1982 by Thomas Nelson, Inc. (and those few out-of-sequence footnotes in those passages are particular footnotes retained from the NKJV.)

To my dear grandmother, Lois Mae Sturm, the first born again believer that I know of in my lineage; a Bible believer, an evangelist to friends, neighbors, strangers, rest homes, and most importantly—family; a lover of Christ's church and charter member of the Calvary Baptist Church of Sun Prairie, Wi which I attended through my 19th year; a godly wife to my dear grandfather, Robert (who still lives in his 96th year); a nurturing grandmother who never missed an opportunity to nurture and admonish in the Lord.

How fitting to be named "Lois" (2 Timothy 1:5).

Reunion will be sweet.

Preface

This is a labor of love. I love the folks I get to teach and challenge each week. I wanted them to have sermon notes without trying so hard.

These messages were preached on primarily Sunday mornings. Most of Mark 13 was taught/preached on Sunday evenings as the subject matter was a little challenging and I didn't wish to lose some of our younger folks in the faith with this type of material.

Maybe you will have the opportunity to have my commentaries on Ruth, the Minor Prophets, and the Psalms. Much of the materials in Hosea, Ruth, and the Psalms were taught on Wednesday nights and Sunday nights with special attention to their salience on the Gospel of Mark. I am afraid you won't get much of that in this commentary or those, but it is a challenge for the pastor to make sure the handles with which the folks leave the fold each week are few and large. This is accomplished by making sure the emphases are clear, concise, and…well…for lack of another "c"…bombastically and energetically beat like a stubborn nail by a weak man with an over-sized hammer.

….so there…I am thankful for the "three to thrive."

Table of Contents

Chapter 1

Chapter 2

Chapter 3

Chapter 4

Chapter 5

Chapter 6

Chapter 7

Chapter 8

Chapter 9

Chapter 10

Chapter 11

Chapter 12

Chapter 13

Chapter 14

Chapter 15

Chapter 16

Appendix 1: Review of E.M. Bounds' "Necessity of Prayer"

Appendix 2: Some thoughts on Suicide out of Mark's Gospel

Appendix 3: A Study on the Scriptures in Mark (Bibliology of Mark)

Appendix 4: Israel, the Church, and Dispensations

Introduction
Regarding Date of Writing, it seems that Mark was at least in Rome at one time based on his presence with Peter in Rome in 1st Peter 5:13.

Chapter 1

1:1-3

The beginning of the gospel If Mark is using **gospel** in the sense that Paul is (1 Corinthians 15:3-4), it is certainly an expansion on Paul's truncated version and goes on the vein of thought that if Jesus was able to die for our sins, then he must have lived a perfect life—otherwise there would be no resurrection. We are, therefore, reading of His perfect life.[1]

> "The "gospel" is an important subject in Mark. The word *euangelion* appears seven times (also 1:14–15; 8:35; 10:29; 13:10; and 14:9. Cf. also 16:15) versus only four times in Matthew and none in Luke and John (but Matthew has the cognate verb once and Luke ten times)."[2]

of Jesus Christ, the Son of God. 2As it is written in the Prophets: There are some variances in the manuscripts here: Some versions drop "Isaiah the prophet." Without getting into manuscript evidence and translation philosophy, let's address two arguments:

1. It was an addition by some scribes to clarify where the crux of the quotation is coming from, but it was not given by the original writer as he would have known it wasn't correct.

---

[1] On the other hand, maybe Mark is just using the "Good news of Jesus Christ" in a different way than Paul did. This leads to another question, though: "Would Paul declare Mark as 'damned' in light of Galatians 1:8-9?" It rather leads to another question, which version of the Gospel will the end-times angel be preaching (Revelation 14)? It is my opinion, then, that Paul gave a truncated version of Mark's Gospel.

[2] James A. Brooks, *Mark*, vol. 23, The New American Commentary (Nashville: Broadman & Holman Publishers, 1991), 38. Knowing that Matthew uses the word Gospel only four times and: 1. Virtually none of them are other than what one finds in Mark (Other than Matthew 9:36, perhaps—which could be easily attributed to Matthew's thought pattern from 4:23 and a handy way to summarize), and 2. Matthew lacks the thematic flow of Mark…one could argue that Mark is the original document while Matthew is a sort of enlargement/development (otherwise, Matthew would have been more concerned about the thematic flow of the word "Gospel").

2. It was dropped by later scribes who assumed the original writer would have never given a "faulty reference."[3]

"Behold, I send My messenger before Your face, Who will prepare Your way before You." This, along with his description found in verse 6 and its implication of the prophecy concerning the "coming Elijah" in Malachi 4 make the 1st and 2nd references to Malachi found in this book. **3"The voice of one crying in the wilderness: 'Prepare the way of the LORD; Make His paths straight.' "** So, two prophets are quoted here: Malachi (3:1, to be exact); and Isaiah (40:3, to be exact).

1:4-8

4 John came baptizing in the wilderness and preaching a baptism of repentance Repentance is big, and whatever it means at this junction one comes away understanding that it was huge from the perspective of Jesus as well (1:14-15).

for One should point out that if you "take an aspirin <u>for</u> a headache, it is because you already have one; not because you wish to have one. So also if you are baptized **for the remission of sins** it could be understood that you are being baptized because "you already have" **remission of sins**, and so you wish to partake of **baptism.**[4]

5 Then all the land of Judea, and those from Jerusalem, went out to him and were all The comprehensiveness of these two "all" statements of verse 5 should strike the reader with the effect of an entire population

---

[3]However, they unwittingly allow a clear conglomeration of Jeremiah and Zechariah to exist without similar argument in Matthew 27 where we read of Judas' place of death. Jeremiah was given the credit for the bulk of the conglomeration, perhaps, because he was the better known of the two, or because the books were in a different order at the time and his was first (the entirety of the group being labeled "Jeremiah" because it was the front book), or because the bulk of the material making the point of Matthew came out of Jeremiah.

[4]Alvah Hovey, ed. *An American Commentary on the New Testament, Mark & Luke* (Valley Forge: Judson Press, 1881), 16; This commentary offers a lesser-known argument that sounds quite nice: "Pardon was not then promised or expected upon submission to baptism, in itself regarded; but this act, in which repentance was confessed and reformation of life was promised, was evidently a suitable act for one who wished to forsake his sins and be forgiven."

being baptized, and giving the credit for it to this very unorthodox man. **baptized by him in the Jordan River, confessing their sins.**

8 I indeed baptized you with water, but He will baptize you with the Holy Spirit." This is the second reference to Isaiah (44:3).

1:10

10 And immediately, Used 40 times by Mark.[5]

coming up from the water, He saw the heavens parting a clear third reference to Isaiah 64 and a wonderful fulfillment of the God of Heaven coming down through "rent" Heavens in the Person of the Holy Spirit.

1:11

Then a voice came from heaven, "You are My beloved Son, in whom I am well pleased." There are three things which were our observation as to the details the Holy Spirit includes within the record:

1. There are three distinct persons within what is normally called "the Trinity" (verse 11).
2. There is at least a necessary consideration as to the mode of baptism (with the "coming up from the water" (verse 10).
3. The very curt beginning to a ministry full of urgency and intent ("immediately", verse 10). Before one feels like they can finally put their hands on their knees in 2:13, they are moved quickly and often through 1:10, 18, 20, 21, 29, 30, 31, 42, 43 and 2:2, 8 & 12.

We are not saying that these were teaching points for Mark's agenda, but we are saying they were not, at least, excluded by the Holy Spirit, and did occur.

---

[5] "G2112 - eutheōs - Strong's Greek Lexicon (KJV)." Blue Letter Bible. Web. 16 Jan, 2017. https://www.blueletterbible.org//lang/lexicon/lexicon.cfm?Strongs=G2112&t=KJV; The author that uses it the most after that is Matthew with 15, and then Luke with 8.

But Having now read the account of the baptism of Jesus; and having observed that Mark called it "the beginning of the Gospel of Jesus Christ, the Son of God," let us answer the question of "why did Mark begin with Jesus' baptism." The short answer is: "to show us the beginning of the good news of Jesus the Christ and Son of God." It means, then, that Mark knew the story began here with this episode of Jesus' baptism.

Having given, now, the short answer, here are the reasons that apply to Mark's agenda[6]:

1. <u>To show a proper reception to an approaching King (verses 2, 3, and 15).</u>[7] In that time there would be a forerunner for a King to "clear the way" and get people's attention.
2. <u>To show us when Jesus received Who it was that drove Jesus to temptation (verse 12).</u> All one must do is see how little is mentioned of the temptation of Jesus in Mark compared to Matthew and Luke to see that the temptation was not the point of baptism, and was certainly not a big deal in proving that Jesus was the Christ or that Jesus was the Son of God (Mark 1:1).
3. <u>To show us how Jesus became the Christ.</u> Jesus was always known as the "Christ" (1:1), but that was proleptically. The Holy Spirit came upon him and anointed him at his baptism so though he has always been Jesus the Christ, he was actually in real time "Christed," at his baptism. Some have asked whether Jesus' identity as "the Christ" (verse 1) actually occurs here. In other words, was Jesus "the Anointed" ("the Christ") before He was "anointed" ("christed")? Since we're dealing with Isaiah language four times already in this passage, it seems reasonable that Isaiah 61:1 is at least being recognized:

   *The Spirit of the Lord GOD is upon Me, Because the LORD has **anointed** Me to preach good tidings to the poor; He*

---

[6] This is not a Gospel harmony. I will only consult the other Gospels to keep me from error in interpretation of this Gospel. To do anything else would be little more than undervaluing the agenda of Mark. Some of these reasons are already listed in my Matthew commentary and applied to his agenda.

[7] *Life Application Bible, NIV Edition* (Tyndale House & Zondervan Publishing, 2001), 1725.

has sent Me to heal the brokenhearted, to proclaim liberty to the captives, And the opening of the prison to those who are bound;

Here, then, is the verb form of "Messiah" (O.T.) or "Christ." Luke 3:21-4:21 leave no almost no doubt—placing Jesus' quoting of this Scripture almost immediately after His baptism with Jesus saying "today this Scripture is fulfilled."

We are absolutely <u>not</u> saying that there was an eternal Christ that came upon Jesus. This is the perspective of most eastern religions and those American offspring spawned primarily in the 1800's (such as Christian Science.[8]

> <u>The earliest heretics took advantage of this statement to represent this event as the descent of the eternal Christ upon the man Jesus for personal indwelling.</u> Later critics have adopted this view. But it need hardly be said here that such an opinion is altogether inconsistent with all that we read elsewhere of the circumstances of the Incarnation, and of the intimate and indissoluble union of the Divine and human natures in the person of the one Christ, from the time of the 'overshadowing of the Virgin Mary by the power of the Highest.' The Spirit descending upon him at his baptism was not the descent of the eternal Christ upon the man Jesus.[9]

4. <u>To show us how Jesus became the Son.</u> Did you notice that the voice from Heaven declares Him to be "my Son?" There is good reason to see that, as "Christ", "Son" is a term that was given to Jesus at His baptism. Furthermore, as will be seen here, "Son" is related to "Christ"/"anointed One" and to the idea of "kingship" (discussed under #'s 1 and 3).

---

[8] For more information on this theory listen to http://www.sermonaudio.com/sermoninfo.asp?SID=123141240368 [accessed 1/18/17].

[9] H. D. M. Spence-Jones, ed., *St. Mark*, vol. 1, The Pulpit Commentary (London; New York: Funk & Wagnalls Company, 1909), 2.

> *Psalm 2:1-7 Why do the nations rage, And the people plot a vain thing? 2 The kings of the earth set themselves, And the rulers take counsel together, Against the LORD and against His **Anointed,** saying, 3 "Let us break Their bonds in pieces And cast away Their cords from us." 4He who sits in the heavens shall laugh; The LORD shall hold them in derision. 5 Then He shall speak to them in His wrath, And distress them in His deep displeasure: 6 "Yet I have set **My King** On My holy hill of Zion." 7 "I will declare the decree: The LORD has said to Me, '**You are My Son, Today I have begotten You.***

It is immediately observable, then, that Jesus was "begotten" or became "the begotten Son of God" at His baptism.

5. <u>To show us where Jesus has been (verse 9).</u> Why is Mark taking the time to use those words other than the simple fact that he was inspired by the Holy Spirit to do so? Because it is to draw in contrast to the other folks (1:5).
6. <u>To show us the impeccable character of Jesus (verse 11).</u>
7. <u>To show us Jesus' identification with sinful people (verse 4).</u> Okay, here is Jesus taking part in a baptism that symbolizes repentance from sin. Jesus did not have any sin to confess, but he was still taking part in a baptism of repentance from sin. How do we justify this? Consider this fifth reference to the prophet Isaiah:

> *6:1...I saw also the Lord sitting upon a throne, high and lifted up, and his train filled the temple 2. Above it stood the seraphims: each one had six wings; And one cried unto another, and said, Holy, holy, holy, is the LORD of hosts: the whole earth is full of his glory. And the posts of the door moved at the voice of him that cried, and the house was filled with smoke. Then said I, Woe is me! for I am undone; because I am a man of unclean lips, and I dwell in the midst of a people of unclean lips: for mine eyes have seen the King, the LORD of hosts. I am a man of unclean lips. **I dwell in the midst of a people of unclean lips.***

1:14-15

17. From that time Jesus began to preach, and to say, Repent: for the kingdom of heaven is at hand. Now look, that word "**repent**ance" is actually related to the rest of the directions Jesus gives. Repentance, then, is related to "the Gospel of the Kingdom" and "**believ**ing."

"Repentance is a sort of John the Baptist thing"

No, it's actually kind of a "Jesus thing" too which means that it was "a God thing." We're supposed to be repenting. Why? We have naturally unbelieving hearts that are naturally not ready for the King.

In the context of John's baptism of confession and repentance of sin, repentance means to turn from that wicked sin that is keeping one from being ready for a coming king.

and believe in the gospel." So, the talk we're about to see about "fishing for men" is connected to the message of Jesus and John the Baptist.

1:16-20

And as He walked by the Sea of Galilee, He saw Simon and Andrew his brother casting a net into the sea; did you notice He found them employed?[10] **for they were fishermen. 17 Then Jesus said to them, "Follow Me,** The last time anyone did that was in 1 Kings 19 with Elijah calling Elisha. The disciples respond much like Elisha: Elisha burned the plows and offered a sacrifice of oxen and there hasn't been another prophet who has come by since that time and said, "Hey, come with me. You're going to take over for me eventually." Well, in Mark 16:18, the disciples "take over" in what we call the "Great Commission."

---

[10]Perhaps Matthew 20:1-11 allows for Christ to employ the "idle." This, of course, involves soteriology.

Let us also consider that Mark also records Jesus being surmised as a resurrected Elijah by those around Herod (6:15)[11] and by those around Jesus' disciples (8:28);[12] He furthermore records the appearance of Elijah on a mountain with Jesus (and Moses and Peter, James & John) (9:4),[13] a discussion occurs in which Elijah was promised (9:11),[14] and of course we remember when Jesus was mistaken for calling on Elijah for deliverance (15:35).[15] Since all three Synoptic Gospel writers appear to give virtually equal weight to Elijah, it seems as though the early Christian belief was that Elijah was to be closely associated with Jesus, yes, but also with John the Baptist as in this context here before us. See more on Elijah and Christ/John the Baptist in my commentary on 1-2 Kings.

and I will make you become fishers of men." At this point we could continue on about how we need to consider the intricacies of catching souls. We could banter with delight concerning the depth and temperature and season and lure and line weight and particular behavior of particular fish at particular times, and we could consider the speed or reaction of the fisherman. We would certainly admit that not all souls require the same attention or the same effort, but alas!...they all have the same need (they must be caught). **18 They immediately left their nets and followed Him.** Clearly, Mark (nor Matthew) felt it essential to their agenda to explain why they "left immediately." What caused this? Consider Luke 5:2-11 and you'll find Luke adds more detail helpful.[16] In doing this, you will see my desire to reinforce the practice of allowing the other records of Scripture to keep us from making grave mistakes in interpretation—in this case addressing "why did these disciples abandon their work to follow Jesus?"[17] Does it seem strange to consider a "Christian who is not a disciple?" The concept of a disciple who doesn't fish for men is equally as foreign.

---

[11] As does Luke.
[12] As do Matthew and Luke.
[13] As do Matthew and Luke.
[14] Matthew also records this.
[15] As does Matthew.
[16] Jesus had just proven Himself to be the Master of all fish.
[17] It should also be pointed out that Jesus, according to John 1, had probably already enlisted them closer to the location of John's baptism. See comments in my commentary on Matthew (chapter 4) for more thoughts on this.

19 When He had gone a little farther from there, He saw James the son of Zebedee, This was quite probably the brother of Zecharias, John the Baptist's father, while Salome his wife was probably the mother of Mary. This would make James and John first cousins of Jesus. **and John his brother, who also were in the boat mending their nets. 20 And immediately He called them,** undoubtedly in the same manner in which he called the other two.

Ed Stetzer and Eric Geiger, in their book *Transformational Groups,*[18] give five amazing things about the timing of Jesus in his calling of these men, and I have adapted them to our passage here:

1. **He called them before they were believers.** In our understanding of the Gospel, these men were not—in this passage—believers of the Gospel. Think about how God is preparing folks before they even come to full faith. Many were working in a ministry in a church for years before the Lord opened your heart to the truth of the Gospel. Or consider how God takes something you had an interest in before you came to faith and is now using that to reach others now that you have believed the Gospel and have been saved.
2. **He called them before they were ready.** He decided that there were worse things than a lack of perceived readiness: One of those "worse things" was disobedience.
3. **He called them before they could clearly understand the mission:** There's very little chance that these fishermen knew what they were really going to do to "catch....men."

"catch them with what? For what? When? For how long?"

But my! How we are spoiled! We are so thirsty for control we want all the answers about each turn before we say "yes" to something. Jesus is too kind to trick you. I've heard it said that nobody waits until all the lights are green on the route to work before they leave the house, or they'd never leave the house!

---

[18](Nashville: B&H Publishing Group, 2014), 159-166.

4. **He called them before they were worthy of His time.** I don't have much to say about this other than you are worthy of my time. We have a wonderful system in place. It's called membership. That's one of the reasons we maintain a membership list. We have people who need a pastor and one of the chief ways they acknowledge that reality is by joining a church.
5. **He called them knowing some would not be winners.** Let's be honest, we all know somebody we have put time into that we wish we had not…but time spent on behalf of Jesus for somebody that proves to be a real downer for the ministry is no waste of time at all.

and they left their father Zebedee in the boat with the hired servants, and went after Him. Why did these men feel at liberty to leave their dad and why didn't their dad follow quickly behind and say, "Wait just a minute, you get back here and play your part of this family business?" Why did these men feel the liberty or even the compulsion to follow Christ? Maybe there is some historically-contextual demand that they leave when a Rabbi calls, or maybe it was their right to take a leave of absence? We have already addressed the "why", in part, when we discussed Luke 5, but the "why/how" of the possibility of their departure (why they even could depart) remains a textual mystery to me.[19]

We are not allowed to even entertain the idea of being a disciple of Jesus if you do not fish. I'm not saying you're not saved, I'm saying it's an embarrassment for disciples of Jesus to not be fishermen. I'm not saying that you have to be as good of a fisherman as anyone around you. I'm saying that if you don't fish, you probably shouldn't be too rowdy about claiming to be a follower of Jesus. We are not allowed to just finance fishing. We are not allowed to <u>just</u> build big buildings for fish to come to once they are caught. We are not allowed to <u>just</u> have a comfortable place for fish to be. We are commanded to go fishing. We are commanded to fish everywhere.

---

[19]Again, some guessing (albeit educated guessing) is done in the commentary on Matthew 4.

There are reasons to believe these men were not "common hands." They were more fishing bosses. These people were pretty wealthy.[20] You don't get to own boats by being a pauper. You don't get nets and crews by being ignorant peasants. These people are well-to-do and so when you were to say to them, "What is the first thing you were expected to be when you were called to be his disciple?" They would have said, "We were supposed to be fishermen of men."

1:21-22

Then they went into Capernaum "village of Nahum" (the prophet of the O.T.?)[21] So, day one he is at a place of high traffic fishing and trade commerce—a town on the approach from the Sea and on the trade routes between Egypt and Mesopotamia. **and immediately on the Sabbath He entered the synagogue** these were meeting houses that were built to hear the sacred Scriptures of the Old Testament read after the Hebrew people were taken captive and removed from the place of their temple in Jerusalem.[22] **and taught. 22 And they were astonished at His teaching, for He taught them as one having authority, and not as the scribes.** Now a scribe, by definition, is somebody who made their living copying a written or spoken record of discourse. However, in this context, we are talking about those who made their living copying the Scripture…more specifically, the Old Testament Scripture. Let's take it a step further. These folks had developed into a guild of their own. You see, if you belong to a body of tradesmen that own the rights to particular bodies of truth—to be more exact, truth that is absurdly important to both your temporal and eternal well-being—you can have an obvious propensity to use your trade to control the masses. So these scribes soon became "experts"—highly paid experts—in the very writings they were supposed to be simply making more numerable and accessible. You see. The **scribes taught,** but not with **authority.**

Scribes in the day would quote experts before them. These experts usually took the compiled written form known as the "Midrash."

---

[20] They had homes or access to homes in Jerusalem (John took Mary to his own home in John 19). Multiple homes is a sign of wealth.
[21] James A. Brooks, *Mark*, vol. 23, The New American Commentary (Nashville: Broadman & Holman Publishers, 1991), 49.
[22] Incidentally, the temple was also destroyed.

These experts, in turn, consulted the "Talmud", which were very early rabbinic writings of the actual Mosaic text. So the "experts" quoted the "experts" who quoted more "experts." Jesus apparently spoke from the perspective of the author rather than from the perspective of a so-called expert.

1:23-24

23 Now there was a man in their synagogue with an unclean spirit. If I were going fishing, I would have desired fish that were already clean. Yes, I know people who are both dirty and clean, by this world's standard, need catching. I would have preferred the fish that knew how to tithe and respected the Bible and had a sense of morality. Jesus, however, shows us that we get the privilege of catching some not-so-clean fish. And we have a choice: avoid them…or catch them. **And he cried out, 24 saying, "Let us alone! What have we to do with You, Jesus of Nazareth? Did You come to destroy us? I know who You are—the Holy One of God!"** I guess I am not sure if I think this is more of a reflection on the Psalms (16:10) or Isaiah (6:1-3 and 20-some other places). Here again, the main point is not which passage they were choosing, but rather that they believed the witness of the Old Testament Scriptures. Consider how the demons reflect so many of what we see today in many so-called conversions: "From these words, it is clear that they had great knowledge, and no charity. They feared His power to punish, and did not love His righteousness."[23] Notice furthermore how they could discuss His character, yet they had only a natural, survivalist attitude: "How may I keep from being destroyed?"

Several of these themes show up again in the book of Mark:

1. Demons wanting to avoid Jesus (1:24; Mark 5:7)
2. Demons identifying Jesus (1:24; Mark 3:11)
3. Demons convulsing under exorcism (1:26; Mark 9:20)
4. Those things outside human control obey Jesus (1:27; Mark 4:41)

---

[23] Augustine of Hippo, "The City of God," in *St. Augustin's City of God and Christian Doctrine*, ed. Philip Schaff, trans. Marcus Dods, vol. 2, A Select Library of the Nicene and Post-Nicene Fathers of the Christian Church, First Series (Buffalo, NY: Christian Literature Company, 1887), 177.

5. Jesus cannot keep Himself a secret (1:28; Mark 1:45)

Within this text, you'll notice a theme which you have seen before:

Immediacy in Mark's voice (1:21; 1:28; Mark 1:10; Mark 1:18; Mark 1:20). I'll say this again. Not everything is urgent…but something is! Let me say that Jesus "immediately went into the synagogue on the Sabbath". Mark is trying to show us that this ministry of Jesus was marked with purpose. So he went immediately upon the calling of his disciples. He called them to fish and then showed them how to fish! He preaches right and does right. Notice that his "going into the synagogue to preach and do miracles" was his way of showing the disciples how to fish for men! There was not calling, and then a vetting process. I wonder, how many of you felt called to fish last week and you went out "immediately" and met a neighbor to catch? How many of you "immediately" added Muslims and Homosexuals and people with good morals and people of different colors, by name, to your prayer list for salvation? I wonder how many of you immediately started studying your Bible more, practiced telling your story more, spoke the Gospel to your spouse more?

Now, Jesus had enough sense to start where He had the most influence. He's a Jewish man, raised by a Jewish man, who taught him to go on a Jewish day of worship to a Jewish house of worship. I do realize that I could say something along the lines of "Even Jesus knew what day to go to church…and He never needed to pray about it or decide 'should I go to church this week?'" Even though the text teaches this, I don't think it was the intent of the Mark or the primary intent of the Holy Spirit to do so…not the primary intent. So I won't.

I could also say something here that would be equally sharp such as "if the people in the synagogue that day decided to spend the day down at the racetrack, they would have missed Jesus." It's incredibly true. Anybody knows that when Jesus said "He was building His church"[24] and that a "church" is a "called out assembly for the purpose of worship" and that as a church, formed by the Lord, they are "two or

---

[24]Matthew 16:18

three gathered in His Name"[25]—anybody knows that You should expect to miss the presence of the Lord if you miss the gathering of His people. And…though this passage certainly could be preached that way because it is a good application, it is evidently not the primary goal of Mark to say so…let alone the Holy Spirit behind Mark's pen.

So, the clear reality is that Jesus goes to the place where people are ready to hear from God from a learned man. Jesus knows Who He is and Whose He is. Jesus knows His audience, and Jesus knows the cost of speaking to such an audience.[26] He goes to the place where He will be best heard. Everybody knew, contrary to our own culture, that the most important matters were eternal matters, and that eternal matters were discussed around God's law in the midst of a house dedicated to that purpose. Ask yourself: "Does my schedule and my agenda reflect my belief that eternal matters are the most important matters and are discussed around the Word of God around the people of God in the assembly of God?"

Within this text lies a newer theme: Jesus is described as "teaching with authority" twice (1:22 and 1:27). Basically, the passage today is bookmarked by these two almost identical statements. We realize, once again, that we have yet another theme that runs throughout the rest of the book—the Words of Jesus are the life-changer, and the Works of Jesus substantiate His Words (this happens again in the very next chapter, 2:9-10). The immediate proof is that, although they are amazed that demons are afraid of Jesus, they mention, again, His authority and His teaching.

"Can unsaved/saved people cast out demons?" It is not recommended that you see it as a "norm"—unless you are about to reveal a new body of truth. This is, by the way, why the Mormon religion feels the freedom to accept, as a rule, miracles: They have "another Testament." The apostles instruct us to fight these battles with the armor on, standing on our knees (Ephesians 6:10-18).

Now, some considerations:

---

[25]Matthew 18:15-20
[26]Which, oddly enough, was a potentially high cost according to this account in Luke 4.

1. On miracles
   a. There was no miracle, even in those days, if there were established cures.
   b. They exist to bring light to new Scripture. That's what's happening here, right? There is no New Testament.
   c. They were never, ever the focus. Every good Work Jesus did was to bring attention and credibility to his Words.
2. On Demon possession: What do we say to those who say "demon possession" was just an ignorant way of diagnosing physical problems?
   a. "You need to consider that this was a time when overt demon activity was at its peak." It was, after all, the only period of time where God, as "fully man" walked the earth. Whenever Jesus is in the house, demons show their head too. I doubt very seriously there were many demons around in synagogues. I say unto you…the devil need not show up in most houses of worship. And this application follows that since Jesus cannot be present I the flesh we can expect supernatural resistance when those stand in Jesus' stead, teaching His teaching with His authority.
   b. "The spirit world does not get enough activity today." Many of what we see as "evidence" of Satan today are evidences of our flesh.
   c. "Jesus, by His words, confirms that this man was demon-possessed" (1:25). We believe this man was in fact demon-possessed because Jesus said he was.
   d. We are promised that Jesus did, in fact, have a decisive victory over the demons in His day (John 12:31; 16:7-9). Consider Russell:

   It may be objected that if any such event as the casting out of Satan did then take place, it ought to be marked by some very palpable diminution of the power of the devil over men. The objection is reasonable, and it may be met by the assertion that such evidence of the abatement of Satanic influence in the world does exist. The history of our Saviour's own times furnishes abundant proof of the exercise of a power over the souls and bodies of men then possessed by Satan which happily is unknown in our days. The mysterious influence called 'demoniacal possession' is always ascribed in Scripture to Satanic agency; and it was one of the credentials of our Lord's divine commission that He, 'by the finger of God, cast out devils.' At what period did the subjection of men to demoniacal power cease to be manifested? It was common in our Lord's days: it continued during the age of the apostles, for we have many allusions to their casting out of unclean spirits; but we have no evidence that it continued to exist in the post-apostolic ages. The phenomenon has so completely disappeared that to many its former existence is incredible, and they resolve it into a popular superstition, or an unscientific theory of mental disease,—an explanation totally incompatible with the representations of the New Testament.[27]

1:29-31

29 Now as soon as seen in verses 10, 18, 20, 21, and 28, this same word for "immediately" is used in the next verse ("at once"). **as they had come out of the synagogue, they entered the house of Simon and Andrew, with James and John.** This gives us the reality that these little segments really occurred in close succession one with another. Taking

---

[27] James Stuart Russell, *The Parousia: A Critical Inquiry into the New Testament Doctrine of Our Lord's Second Coming* (London: Daldy, Isbister & Co., 1878), 130.

these verses by themselves, it seems we have a group of five at this point.

This hardly seems like another anecdote of "fishing for men." Rather, this seems like an episode of Jesus and what we might call "opportunity targets." He wasn't looking for teaching to do or fish to be caught, but He did rightly because he was living in that home and was to enjoy the Sabbath meal in that home with the four men in this passage.

30 But Simon's wife's mother lay sick with a fever, and they told Him about her at once. We can talk about how it's important to take care of your parents in their twilight years and not ship them off to second-rate homes here and there, and making sure they're well cared for, but I don't think that would be popular so I won't say anything about it.

31 So He came and took her by the hand and lifted her up, This is a detail unique to Mark in both this story and in the healing of the demon-possessed man (9:27).[28] **and immediately the fever left her.** One does not know if Jesus knew Peter's mother in law before this episode.

    a. He knew Peter, we're told, from John 1.
    b. He knew Peter's business associates, James and John through familial connections.

Some of us were "fevered" with addictions, and some were fevered with worries, and some are fevered with the addiction to worry. Jesus saves people. It is His character to save. His Name means "Jehovah saves." We know, then, that when we are healed by the touch of Jesus, we have something eternally significant going on in our lives.

I don't think I need to remind you, do I, that many died this night in the world of fever? Do I need to remind you that not everybody was seen by Jesus? Should we remind ourselves that Jesus was dealing with this woman because Jesus was dealing with her son in law, Peter? Have

---

[28] All three Synoptics say Jesus did this with the Jairus' daughter (to round out Mark's three accounts of "lifting by the hand"). Matthew and Luke say this of no one else.

you considered that Jesus affects people through you or because of you because of their proximity to you? Have you considered that you could be the avenue of blessing or salvation in the lives of others by your mere presence in a place?

And she served them.[29] Here is a scenario where a lady is cured of a malady and it moves her to serve ("wait tables"). Question: Do you find it easier to serve when you have been relieved of something in your life? When you consider the heartache you used to have financially, do you serve others through your generosity? When you consider the health problems you used to endure, do you serve others through your strong arms? The reality, though, is that I don't think this was out of the ordinary for a lady to be hospitable to guests in her home whenever possible. I think the point of Mark is to demonstrate that this woman was cured to pre-fever health. At any rate, this isn't a bad thing for us to learn: we should never waste our good health being selfish—even if it is more culturally than "Christian" to be hospitable.

1:32-34

At evening, when the sun had set, probably, the meal Peter's mother in law had prepared for them was being consumed as it was usually eaten following the setting of the sun. Did He get to sit and enjoy a meal? **they brought to Him all who were sick and those who were demon-possessed.** Now that the Sabbath was over, hard work could be done, and others were free to work at bringing their sick to Jesus.[30] **33And the whole city was gathered together at the door.** Imagine a township, the size of the one we mentioned in 1:21 showing up at Peter and Andrew's home. I am not comfortable with very many people knowing where I live, but here we go... **34 Then He healed many who were sick with various diseases, and cast out many demons; and He did not allow the demons to speak, because they knew Him.** Once again, the reader is left with the question of whether it was the "who" or the "when" of this evangelism with which Jesus was concerned. We are not sure,

---

[29]More on this in the author's commentary on Matthew 8:14-15.
[30]A.T. Robertson, *Word Pictures in the New Testament* (Nashville, TN: Broadman Press, 1933), Mk 1:32.

within this passage, whether it was because it was a demon or because it was a demon early in the life of Jesus' ministry.

1:35-37

35 Now in the morning, A reader is hopefully getting the idea that Mark wants you to have a grasp of this Sabbath day/night as it pertains to the business of Jesus. Are the readers supposed to assume this means that all Christians are supposed to be endlessly serving and healing (so to speak) and traveling to fish (so to speak) and sleeping very, very little? Stay busy…for awhile (with all the "immediately" references)? It seems that our lives our filled with seasons of opportunity. **having risen a long while before daylight, He went out and departed to a solitary place; and there He prayed.** Is this a prooftext to get up early to pray? Perhaps, but Jesus' prayer was of obvious necessity, while the timing may have been because He was alone. Furthermore, He saw that communion with the Father was of greater concern than service to others. We are let in on this concern of Jesus when Simon relays the desire of the people to see Him (1:36-37). If you want to get right down to it: Jesus was concerned about service…to a point. He realized, though, as God's Son, that spending time with the Father was worth avoiding people.

> 6:46 And when He had sent them away, He departed to the mountain to pray.

> 14:32 Then they came to a place which was named Gethsemane; and He said to His disciples, "Sit here while I pray."

If Mark's themes of "urgency" and "prayer" mean anything, they mean that Jesus was at least urgent about prayer (see appendix).

1:38-39

But This word along with "next towns" of this verse help us understand that Capernaum wanted to own the time of this Jesus, but that what ultimately moved Him to those other towns was His mission. **He said to them, "Let us go into the next towns, that I may preach there also, because for this purpose I have come forth."** "According to Josephus,

Galilee was a densely populated district, with upwards of two hundred villages, each containing several thousand inhabitants."[31]

To answer this, one may need to see what Jesus didn't say: "that I may do more miracles there also, because for this purpose I have come forth." Now, I think it should be pointed out that this was not that which we focused on a couple of weeks ago—"teaching with great authority" (mentioned twice in the episode of the demonic man in the synagogue). "Preaching" is a different word—meaning the "heralding of a message." It's more than "conveying truth." Now, in view of the reality that "teaching with authority" was more important to Mark than doing miracles in that episode of the synagogue, it should also be noted that **preach**ing was more important to Jesus than doing miracles, and it was the reason He came to Galilee (1:14; 1:28).

Still, though, why did He need to come there? While there is room just in Mark that it could be "for this cause I came outside of town," Luke 4:43 gives more of the idea that Jesus had been sent out long before and was still on mission (passive voice; perfect tense).

Let us at least be cognizant of the reality that if Mark's theme of "urgency" in Jesus' life means anything, Jesus was urgent about doing the will of His Father. "Let's get moving! I know why I am here!" This was not the encapsulated purpose of Jesus as stated in Mark 10:45, but it is just as required as part of the process. Likewise, we don't need to be as clear on the "big picture" of our lives as we need to be on the steps in front of us.

Jesus showed us that He don't save the world without giving His life as a ransom. He don't give His life a ransom if He didn't preach that Gospel proclaiming your work. He didn't don't preach that Gospel proclaiming that work if He didn't leave Capernaum. He didn't leave Capernaum if He didn't get up early enough to beat the crowd and meet with His Heavenly Father. Or, to say it in a way as a man I admire says

---

[31] H. D. M. Spence-Jones, ed., *St. Mark*, vol. 1, The Pulpit Commentary (London; New York: Funk & Wagnalls Company, 1909), 7.

it when he quoted somebody else: "Everybody wants to change the world, but nobody wants to do the dishes."[32]

Some of you in your middle years, what are you doing here? What usefulness do you have? I may not be able to tell you that, but I can remind you that the most important thing today is that the Heavenly Father has your attention, and that you "abstain from fornication" (1 Thessalonians 4:3) and that you give thanks in everything (1 Thessalonians 5:18). Nothing fantastic, but everything honorable. I cannot tell you that you will be talked about in books, but I can tell you that if you care for your aging parents and pay your bills and cut your grass and be faithful to your church, you will be known as the one taking the step before you on the way to your questions being answered.

You see, you will be known for something at the judgment, and maybe passing your time here on earth as a prayer warrior or a gardener or as a volunteer or as an honorable aunt or uncle or grandparent or parent isn't something you can see being talked about in Heaven…but if you throw off those honorable practices…that will most certainly be a topic when—as we heard in our passage in 2 Corinthians 10—we stand before "the judgment Seat of Christ."

39 And He was preaching in their synagogues throughout all Galilee, Here we see that Jesus is following the newscasters of 1:29. We furthermore see that some come to Him without much work on His own (1:40).[33] In other words, Jesus already had credentials in these other towns from the "fame" of 1:29. **and casting out demons.** as He did in Capernaum (1:34). I really want to continue to press the issue that demonic activity must have been at a frightening crescendo in this part of the nation of the Gentiles.[34] We discussed this in the past passage and I wanted to be sure we crossed that here as well: **Casting out demons** accompanied **preaching in their synagogues.** I do think it is significant, though, that a great deal of fights were started by Jesus. Of all the things

---

[32]Preached by Mark Dever at T4G, 2016 (quoting Mike Borten; http://t4g.org/media/2016/04/endurance-needed-strength-for-a-slow-reformation-and-the-dangerous-allure-of-speed/ (17:33), [accessed 3/13/17].

[33]This story, by the way, comes before the episode of the "fevered mother in law" in Matthew.

[34]I want to further confirm that his works confirmed his words (Hebrews 2:4).

that could have been added to **preaching,** Mark picked out **casting out demons.**

1:40-41a

40 Now a leper I think it would be good for me to read a description of what leprosy is. This is written by a man named Kuizenga in 1927:

> *The disease which we today call leprosy generally begins with pain in certain areas of the body. Numbness follows. Soon the skin in such spots loses its original color. It gets to be thick, glossy, and scaly. As the sickness progresses the thickened spots become dirty sores and ulcers due to poor blood supply. The skin, especially around the eyes and ears, begins to bunch with deep furrows between the swelling, so that the face of the afflicted individual begins to resemble that of a lion. Fingers drop off or are absorbed. Toes are affected similarly. Eyebrows and eyelashes drop out. By the time one can see the person in this pitiful condition is a leper, by the touch of a finger one can feel it. One can even smell it, for the leper emits a very unpleasant odor. Moreover, in view of the fact that the disease-producing agent frequently also attacks the larynx, the leper's voice acquires a grating quality. His throat becomes hoarse and you can now not only now see, feel, and smell the leper, but you can hear his rasping voice. And if you stay with him for some time you can even imagine a peculiar taste in your mouth, probably due to the odor.*

came to Him,

> *Leviticus 13:38 If a man also or a woman have in the skin of their flesh bright spots, even white bright spots; 39 then the priest shall look:...44 He is a leprous man, he is unclean: the priest shall pronounce him utterly unclean; his plague is in his head. 45 And the leper in whom the plague is, his clothes shall be rent, and his head bare, and he shall put a covering upon his upper lip, and **shall cry, "Unclean, unclean."** 46 All the days wherein the plague shall be in him he shall be defiled; he is*

unclean: he shall dwell alone; **without the camp** *shall his habitation be.*

*Leviticus 5:3 Or **if he touch the uncleanness of man, whatsoever uncleanness it be that a man shall be defiled withal**, and it be hid from him; when he knoweth of it, then he shall be guilty.*

We see from this passage the audacity of Jesus in touching a leper—knowing that it was permissible because of the soon to be "clean bill of health" is a distant first, but a first to a respectable "second" to the leper's desperation: "If I die for my transgression in my misery, fine, but if I'm healed, there's no transgression at all."[35]

imploring Him, kneeling down to Him and saying to Him, "If You are willing, You can make me clean." I don't have to have a grasp on "why?" to have a grasp on "who?"

Matthew 13:35 records Jesus saying that He was revealing to the disciples that were "hidden from the foundation of the world." These were hidden since Genesis 1:1. If the Lord owns the world then the mysteries that were hatched before the world was even created belong to Him. Deuteronomy 29:29 says the mysteries belong to the Lord. Even, the mysteries of leprosy.

Why does a God of love would allow leprosy to begin with? No answer changes that He is the One that heals. And each instance of healing, physically or spiritually, is an exceptional act of Christ and is so unrequired that it is absurdly gracious and greatly audacious.

1:41b-42

---

[35] This is as mysterious as Jacob in Genesis 32 where it may have been deemed in appropriate to wrestle with an angel of the Lord or to disobey the angel of the Lord or to demand blessing from the angel of the Lord, but he was going to die at the hands of his brother anyway…so "if I die in my loneliness and hopelessness, let's get on with it…but I might actually be blessed by taking this chance."

Esther ("if I perish, I perish") is another good example of desperation as seen in 2 Kings 7 with the four lepers.

Then Jesus, moved with compassion, stretched out His hand and touched him, we can't imagine this, can we? As soon as somebody gets the bug, "Oh man!" and we're swabbing everything down. With all of our selfishness, it's no wonder we: 1. Don't have compassion; 2. Don't have the courage to touch a sick person. Spurgeon's autobiography relays his time of ministry in London during a cholera outbreak:

> "I recollect, when first I came to London, how anxiously people listened to the gospel, for the cholera was raging terribly. There was little scoffing then. All day, and sometimes all night long, I went about from house to house, and saw men and women dying, and, oh, how glad they were to see my face! When many were afraid to enter their houses lest they should catch the deadly disease, we who had no fear about such things found ourselves most gladly listened to when we spoke of Christ and of things Divine. And now, again, is the minister's time; and now is the time for all of you who love souls. You may see men more alarmed than they are already; and if they should be, mind that you avail yourselves of the opportunity of doing them good...."[36]

stretched out His hand and touched him, and said to him, "I am willing; be cleansed." And the reason? Because Our Lord is compassionate (1:41).

1:43-45

43 And He strictly warned him and sent him away at once, 44 and said to him, "See that you say nothing to anyone; but go your way, show yourself to the priest, and offer for your cleansing those things which Moses commanded, Now, understand that this was going to be unusual. The last time this happened was 600 years ago…and it was under the ministry of Elisha—a protégé of Elijah's. So, remember, the last time a Rabbi or prophet is recorded in Scripture as saying "follow me" was when Elijah the prophet called "Elisha" the prophet and Elisha

---

[36] C. H. Spurgeon, *C. H. Spurgeon's Autobiography, Compiled from His Diary, Letters, and Records, by His Wife and His Private Secretary, 1834–1854*, vol. 1 (Cincinatti; Chicago; St. Louis: Curts & Jennings, 1898), 371–372.

then burned his plows (see notes on verses 15-20). Now, the last time we have seen anybody healed of leprosy was when Elisha was found "performing this miracle" earlier in his ministry. Clearly, then, you can see that Jesus is once again being compared to Elijah.

This man was delayed in his obedience, but for what reason? Perhaps the answer to this is the reason for the parenthetical material to begin with.[37] 2 Kings 7:1-10 finds four lepers who are put in a situation where they placed in a situation of desperation and see death in lawfulness or in seeking the help of those who could kill them and then find it as a sort of crime to keep the news of their fortune to themselves. With all this attention on Elijah and Elisha, I am almost certain Mark wants you to think of that story when you see this one. Lepers who happen upon good fortune can't keep good news a secret and they find such good fortune when they become desperate enough to touch a clean man and become, themselves, helped.

as a testimony to them." Imagine the **testimony** these priests would have beheld when they had not seen a "leper" made clean until this very man walked in among them. Oh, the testimony, portrayed before the priests…how powerful it would have been. Jesus did more than a gaping Moses (who saw his leprous sister in Numbers 12) and a distancing Elisha (2 Kings 5)—He sent a healed Hebrew back to the temple. This is your Jesus and mine: surprising the unimpressed and touching the untouchable. I think that if being cleaned makes me this passionate towards Him, then may I be shown the ways I am yet the leper.

Consider the reality that this man had to take a trip to Jerusalem just to be a testimony to Jesus. Consider the trip. What jovialness he would have felt. This makes the command of verses 43 and 44 so very comical. Certainly Jesus knew what would take place, but to tell a man that has been an outcast for years to simply and secretly take a trip from Galilee to Jerusalem without telling anybody what happened to him is,

---

[37] From Matthew 8:1, it becomes pretty obvious that this episode is recorded out of order from true chronology (More notes in my commentary on Matthew 8:1-4 in the commentary on Matthew.). When you put verse 39's record before 2:1, it becomes pretty clear that this episode is something that Mark wanted conveyed, but that order wasn't as important to Mark as the theme of "immediacy" (used for the 8th and 9th times in these 43 verses; verses 42 and 43).

well, rather strange. The change in condition for this man furthermore makes verse 45 rather expected.

45 However, This man disobeyed the Lord. It seems that "don't tell anybody" and "go to the temple" were contrasted here with **However.** I wonder how much more preaching Jesus could have done if this leper would have obeyed Him. **he went out and began to proclaim it freely, and to spread the matter, so that Jesus could no longer openly enter the city,** So the "temple" visit and "silence" were seemingly ignored in favor of **proclam**ation, and Jesus preached to less folks because He took the time to make an exception to preaching, and heal a leper. Often we think that we're helping matters by being lose with the instructions of Jesus, when really…we should have trusted the plain teachings of our Lord. **but was outside in deserted places; and they came to Him from every direction.** Luke 5 says "to hear [Jesus' preach or teach] and to be healed."

Chapter 2

2:1-2

And again He entered[38] **Capernaum after some days, and it was heard that He was in the house.** The same **house** he was in chapter 2: Simon's house; the house where Simon's mother in law stayed; the house where the whole town had gathered on the eve of 1:35. **2 Immediately many gathered together, so that there was no longer room to receive them, not even near the door. And He preached the word to them.** Once again, you will notice that the last time He was in town, they flocked to be healed and delivered. Now they are flocking and what is the Master's preference? **Preaching the Word to them**, rather than miracles. This, by the way, is properly translated as "He was speaking to them."[39] This implies that what was about to occur interrupted Jesus' preaching.

2:4

when they had broken through, they let down the bed on which the paralytic was lying. This is best understood as occurring on a type of home where the roof is flat and stairs are provided for warm nights to ascend to one's roof.

2:5

---

[38]Matthew is the odd man out here when he puts the healing of the demoniacs (two of them) before this episode. Mark and Luke put the healing of the leper before this which Matthew includes much more previous to this episode. Here again is the Synoptic Problem: 1. The three Gospels are so much alike that you would say there was a source among them (if one of them was not actually the source); 2. The three Gospels contain enough of a difference (in this case, Matthew's preceding story) that one would think there were no blind copying at all. So, which of the two orders (preceding episodes concerned) are correct (Matthew or Mark-Luke) again must be in some way tied to specific geography and time (as Matthew seems to do the most with his statements in 8:1 and 9:1). From the perspective of this author (me), then, Matthew will be treated as the chronological overlord.

[39]<u>New American Standard Bible: 1995 Update</u> (La Habra, CA: The Lockman Foundation, 1995), Mk 2:2.

When Jesus saw their faith, He didn't notice their gumption or their effort or their resourcing, etc… We know there were at least two among the five who had faith. We aren't sure the man who was being healed "had no faith." Furthermore, verse 12 tells us the man had faith. Otherwise, he would have never "arose" as Jesus commanded and would have, for all intensive purposes, kept his palsy: "I am not getting up. This is dumb. This guy can't forgive my sins or heal my palsy."

He said to the paralytic, "Son, your sins are forgiven you." Very strange: Why would Jesus connect this man's paralysis to his sins? I do not want you thinking for a minute that I think that every ache, pain, sickness, disease, or infirmity, is the result of sin. I don't.[40] But, I think we say the opposite so much that we never think there's a connection. So why is this obvious sick man having his spiritual state addressed? It's not like he asked for any help with his sickness, much less his sin. Is it because it was a result of sin?

Let's not lose the marvel that a man has just been absolved from His sins. This is no small thing. The only reason Christ would say this is given in the text: "He saw their faith." No prayer; no trip down the aisle; just…**faith.**

2:10-12

10 But that you may know get it. Jesus is about to heal a man and talks about doing so in order to convince him that He is **the Son of Man on earth** and **has the power** this is not that word dealing with "ability" but rather "authority" and is used previously in regards to His "teaching with authority" (1:22) and His casting out demons "with authority" (1:27). This, then, rounds out a pretty sound trinity of comprehensive authority: to teach truth; to exercise position of the spirit world; to absolve sin. **to forgive sin.** That is why Jesus did miracles. That is why the disciples were later told to do miracles.

---

[40]John 9, the disciple said, "Lord why is this man blind? Is it because of his sin or his parent's sin?" And Jesus said, "In that case, neither, but for the glory of God." So, it's not always a connection between what we do and how we feel. On the other hand, the book of John speaks of a man healed at Bethesda (chapter 5) who is told not to sin "unless something worse comes on you."

Mark 16:19 So then, after the Lord had spoken to them, He was received up into heaven, and sat down at the right hand of God. 20 And they went out and preached everywhere, the Lord working with them and **confirming the word through the accompanying signs.** *Amen.*

Why is Jesus, verse 2, "preaching the word unto them?" That was His mission (1:38). Why did He do miracles? To show that he had authority to preach the Word. Why did the disciples follow His pattern after He ascended to Heaven? To show they had authority to preach what they were preaching in Christ's wake.[41]

that the Son of Man How does this work with Mark 1:11 where God calls Jesus His Son? Is there a connection? Consider what the reader would have thought when he read this:

Psalm 80:14 Return, we beseech You, O God of hosts; Look down from heaven and see, And visit this vine 15 And the vineyard which Your right hand has planted, And the branch that You made strong for Yourself. 16 It is burned with fire, it is cut down; They perish at the rebuke of Your countenance. 17 Let Your hand be upon the man of Your right hand, **Upon the son of man whom You made strong for Yourself.** *18 Then we will not turn back from You; Revive us, and we will call upon Your name.*

---

[41] Why did Jesus tell the man to get up? So that you know that He has the power to forgive sin. Why did Jesus do those healings when He was here on earth? One answer, dear friends. So that you would know that He has the authority to forgive sins. We have 2,000 years of history proving that Jesus can forgive sin. Converted hearts. You should not expect regular works of healing in a supernatural, apostolic sense anymore. Why? Because they were for the purpose of proving to His listeners that He had the authority to forgive sins. And the apostles are also those ones sent by Jesus and their job was to do great works to validate what they were preaching. How many Testaments were there when Moses came preaching? Zero. And so he had to do miracles to validate what he was preaching. So here comes Jesus and some apostles. How many New Testaments were there when they started preaching? Zero. How many books were available when they started preaching, in the New Testament? Zero. So they had to validate their new message by doing miracles. Friends, we're not going to get another Testament of Jesus Christ. So there's no need for this, proving that Jesus has the power on Earth to forgive sins any longer.

19 Restore us, O LORD God of hosts; Cause Your face to shine, And we shall be saved!

There are a great many things in this passage that speak of God's rejection of Israel in the time of Jesus and yet, the biggest lesson in this passage is that the **Son of Man** is known as the God's "Right hand man." They "share an office." In other words, when Jesus said He was the **Son of Man,** He was claiming to share the place of prominence with the Almighty.[42]

Arise, take up thy bed, and go unto thine house. Jesus expects no easy thing. Notice here that the crowd that would have kept them out at ground level is now that which could keep him in at ground level. The crowd that would have kept him from getting close to Jesus is now keeping Him from obeying Jesus. There may be some who never wish to be healed because they know the implications of not having excuses anymore to serve Jesus. "If He takes away their groaning and palsy, what will be the things they talk about anymore?" What will be the excuse for why they don't lay around anymore? They will be expected to be productive parents and children and citizens and church members.

2:13-16[43]

When people would cross over the Sea of Galilee into Jewish land, they would come over into Capernaum and the IRS was already there. They were ready to collect duties and tariffs and taxes and excises. The wealthy Hebrews would bid out for the opportunities from the Romans to collect taxes. It so happens that the best tax collectors from the Jews were Jews. And so the Romans knew that and they figured that the best way to get this done would be to hire a Jew. A Jew that was religious enough that everyone would know he was a Jew, but godless enough that he didn't mind taking money from his countrymen.

And He said to him, "Follow Me." So he arose and followed Him. Were there others there to watch the booth? We're not told. What

---

[42] More is said on this in the author's commentary on Matthew.
[43] More is found on this passage in the author's commentaries on Matthew (9:9-13) and Luke (5:27-32).

prompted Matthew to follow this guy? We're not told. **15 Now it happened, as He was dining in Levi's house, that many tax collectors behold, many publicans.** Oh my goodness. There are empty tax offices all over the city. And entire guild of thieves is empty. Maybe it's after hours? Maybe there was a shift change? We're not told.

they said to His disciples, "How is it that He eats and drinks with tax collectors and sinners?" The answer is because they are Levi's friends, and Levi is fishing. Why is this included here? Because it is natural to bring your friends to Jesus after you are affected. As in the last text we find "getting your friends to Jesus," we find the wonderful opposite here of "getting Jesus to your friends."

It's not a bad question. Haggai 2:13, Proverbs 13:20, 1 Corinthians 15:34, 2 Corinthians 6:14-17 confirm that prolonged relationships with ungodly people are not good for you as a believer. I don't need to argue this point because the text doesn't require it. What you have is a man who is newly saved and has a set of friends who don't know the "new Levi" and so they quite naturally, on the evening of this meeting, gather to meet this man that shows up and tells Levi/Matthew to follow him. Let us not be under the allusion that Jesus was here to "hang out" and "network", or even to "approve of Matthew's friends." Jesus tells us the reason He is there among Matthew's friends in the next verse.

2:17

When Jesus heard it, He said to them, "Those who are well have no need of a physician, One thing is clear, Jesus was interested in being a physician. He was ready to heal, particularly, those who were "sin-sick." Every one of our churches should pray as Pastor Spurgeon "Great Physician walk this hospital. Come and look on each special case, and may there be a masterpiece of Thy heavenly surgery in the case of each one of us."[44]

"How do I know it is His desire to heal folks from sin?"

---

[44] C.H. Spurgeon *The Pastor in Prayer* (Carlisle, PA: Banner of Truth Trust, 2004), 138.

Because in the next phrase we have a reference to "sinners repenting."

Of what are they "repenting?"

Their sin.

"What is sin?"

It is our crimes against God that keep us from peace with the King of His kingdom. Jesus is calling people as a "preacher of the Gospel of the kingdom" (1:14-15; 1:39) to leave their rebellion against Heaven to embrace Heaven's king. Imagine going to Heaven and finding people who love Jesus...but love their sin more. Since there is no sin in Heaven, perhaps you should ask whether you can live with hating there what you love here?

Yet in the deepest of our soul, if you find a panting after that which is holy and a desperation to be saved from your sin, I might admonish you to rely on your Savior to save you from your sin, and to desire a greater desperation that He do the same.

but those who are sick. I did not come to call the righteous, but sinners, [4]to repentance." Perhaps you have a version of the Bible that does not have "to repentance" at the end of its verse. I will tell you that if you have a newer version (besides something from the KJV family), it does not have the last phrase. Basically, translation committees, when confronted with which reading to utilize have to decide whether it was added by people trying to be helpful,[45] or whether it was deleted out of doctrinal bias, or whether it was added or deleted out of carelessness.[46]

---

[4] NU omits *to repentance*

[45]In the original copy containing their "helpfulness," it could have been very clear that it was their commentary, thus preserving their conviction that the Scripture was inerrant. Perhaps copies of this early "help" was less and less "addition" and became part of the understood text by the copyists, and thus, the reader.

[46]Accidental duplication of a line above the current line being copied is a good example of careless addition while losing one's place and skipping a word or phrase is a good example of careless deletion.

So what? Well, I have made a choice that reflects that of the KJV, the NKJV for three reasons: 1. It seems more likely that the phrase belongs in there. Why? Because the prepositional phrase acts as a "direct object" or a "receiver of the action" (to what are sinners being called? They are being called to repentance).[47] 2. I have made a philosophical choice against "textual criticism." That is, I do not believe in the "buried bible." That is, I believe the reading the church most likely had the majority of the time is the correct reading out of deference to Matthew 4:4. So, if we continue to find "variant readings" through archaeology and other such disciplines that we deem authoritative in some manner, it assumes that the church did not have the Bible in its entirety. 3. I have made a philosophical choice against the majority of the German scholars from the 1800's, predominately represented by Constantine Tischendorf.[48] I do not deem his actions to be honorable in the final analysis.

There's nothing in the passage that tells us the Pharisees were in the house. How did they know what was going on? There's nothing in verses 15-16 that says, "And Jesus and His disciples sat down with Matthew, the publicans, the sinners and the Pharisees." No. Pharisees wouldn't be caught dead in the house but oh, how they love to spot those who are. What are they doing? Can you see them? Oh, how miserable they are!

Ok, so are you willing to say that it is people who know they are sinners in need of repentance with whom He is sitting? After all, He calls them sinners, and to the Pharisees He says, "These folks need Me because I'm a doctor and they're sick." And sick people are, well... **sinners**. So if you are willing to say Jesus hangs out with sinners, I will

---

[47] If you don't buy that, how about the mere fact that Jesus is "calling [them to Himself]" which supposes they are leaving something else: their sinfulness qualifying them for the title "publican" or "sinner."

If you don't buy that, how about the first chapter's flow of John baptizing unto "repentance" for "remission of sins." They seem related and seem furthermore to naturally carry on with their connection in Mark 2:17. Moreover, the "calling of five disciples" thus far notes a "leaving of nets and fishing" and "leaving a tax office [in order to] follow [Jesus]."

[48] Quite the article was written about this character in the Biblical Archeological Review, November/December 2007.

go with you that far, as long as you'll go with me when I tell you the reason He goes to eat with sinners is to get them to repent. Not to dilly-dally with them and build a relationship with them, no. We need sinners to become repentant sinners, and then they look like Matthew. They get up and leave everything.

"Well, we just need to be more like Jesus."

I agree. Let's call more sinners to repentance.

"Jesus wouldn't judge."

Really? Because He just called a house full of people **sinners.** Here's some judging happening there. Otherwise Jesus would not be having this conversation. He's not eating with the scribes and Pharisees because the truth is they see themselves as righteous. You can never be a repentant person because you've never repented, because you've never been a sinner. The real problem with the Pharisees is they can't be saved. No good Pharisee ever gets saved. No good scribe ever gets saved. You have to become a sinner or you have no Savior; you have no Physician.

2:18

The disciples of John John the Baptist. We have a third party of hostile questioners after the scribes (verse 3) and the Pharisees (verse 11).

"Maybe they're just inquisitive?"

We might go that they were neutral, but reading the other gospels can keep us from making wrong assumptions. And one of those assumptions would be, "Ah, this is just an emotionally neutral party of people that were wondering some things about Jesus and His disciples." In John's Gospel, chapter 3, the disciples of John were upset because people were no longer coming to them to be baptized. They're going to Jesus. And they said, "Master," talking to John the Baptist, "All men go to Him." And John the Baptist used language like this; he said, "I'm the best man. Do you think I'm going to get upset when people are going to the bridegroom?" So, his people are already frustrated.

and of the Pharisees were fasting. Then they came and said to Him, "Why do the disciples of John and of the Pharisees fast, but Your disciples do not fast?" Oh, the Pharisees love questions. In 2:16, they're asking questions with a different party. We don't know how they know how often the disciples of Jesus fasted. The text doesn't say. Let's talk about the Pharisees and their fasting. You've heard Luke 18

> *And He spake this parable, Jesus did, unto certain which trusted in themselves that they were righteous, and despised others: Two men went up into the temple to pray; the one a Pharisee, and the other a publican. The Pharisee stood and prayed thus [Here's what I do: I fast twice in the week.]*

2:19

And Jesus said to them, "Can the [5]friends of the bridegroom fast Now the question is, why is Jesus making a connection between the fasting that the disciples are not doing and the mourning that they're not doing? Seems like they were mourning. So why were the disciples of John the Baptist mourning? We have a clue: 1:14 shows how the arrest of John the Baptist seemed to steer Jesus' ministry in going to Galilee after His baptism and temptation in the wilderness.

And then in Mark 6:14, we find out that Herod believes Jesus is somehow John the Baptist risen from the dead. Well in order for him to be rising from the dead he must have already died. So, in prison in 1:14 and dead by 6:14. [49]John, then, is at least incarcerated and possibly dead by the time of this episode in 2:17-22. So why are they fasting? They are mourning. Why are they mourning? Their leader is at least in prison and possibly dead.

while the bridegroom is with them? As long as they have the bridegroom with them they cannot fast. For the 2nd time in this

---

[5]Lit. *sons of the bridechamber;* interaction with this rendering is found in the author's commentary on Matthew (14-17).

[49]One can only imagine, as they read Mark 6:14-29 the disgusting affect drunkenness and avarice can have in the moral intentions of a believer—much less a pagan, degenerate king like Herod.

chapter, Jesus basically claims to be God. In the episode of the paralytic He forgives sins after reading thoughts. So He is omniscient like God in knowing thoughts, omnipotent like God in forgiving sin, and now He seems to be alluding to a promise of Jehovah from a prophet some 750 years before Him. Two points about that: This is the 2nd time we have seen a connection with this prophet named Hosea in this chapter: He has relations with harlots as Jehovah does in Hosea 1, and now he claims to be a bridegroom for this people of God as Jehovah does in Hosea chapter 2.[50]

2:20

But the days will come when the bridegroom will be taken away from them, and then they will fast in those days. Has the bridegroom left us? Is He in heaven today? Well, it's expected then.[51]

2:21

No one sews a piece of unshrunk cloth on an old garment; or else the new piece pulls away from the old, and the tear is made worse. The hole reappears because the new cloth hasn't shrunk yet. The new cloth shrinks and the hole that you are trying to patch is worsened.

2:22

And no one puts new wine into old wineskins; or else the new wine bursts the wineskins, the wine is spilled, and the wineskins are ruined. But new wine must be put into new wineskins." Well, if you take an old skin that is already expanded and you put new wine into it that hasn't expanded, once it expands the bottle breaks because the skin is not going to stretch anymore.

    Jesus is saying, "Your old system is like an old garment with a new patch. It's like an old bottle with new wine. It's just not going to fit." What is the old system pictured by **old wineskins**? Moses' Old

---

    [50]See my commentary on the Minor Prophets (Hosea) for both these references.
    [51]Of course here He's probably speaking more specifically of His death.

Covenant, holy and righteous and Heaven-wrought…yet exaggerated, reinterpreted, and abused. In this context, it is a re-interpretation on God's views of fasting (2:18-22) and Sabbath keeping (2:23-3:5)—not things we typically struggle with these days. By itself, if I could use base English, the Old Covenant brings mourning. Jesus isn't interested in new religion smashed into the old one. He came to replace, not revamp.

2:23-24[52]

The point of the passage is not "thou shalt keep the Sabbath," but maybe you should do it. One note: If the Sabbath is simply Jewish, then ask whether God is a Jew since He was the first to keep it (Genesis 2:1).

2:25-26

Leviticus 24:5 (and following) tells us about this table of showbread. Somebody is working, says this passage, on the Sabbath day. Deuteronomy 23:24 speaks of a person being allowed to eat as they wander through a neighbor's field (so long as there are no gatherings), and doesn't outlaw it on the Sabbath day. John 7:14 and following speaks of the need to circumcise on the Sabbath if the Sabbath happens to be the 8th day. In other words, you keep the "righter right" when you have conflicting "rights."

    Jesus is not saying "Do everything David does" as much as He's saying "you wish for the 'Son of David' to come, and look what David did! He did far worse than the Son of David did in picking this corn."[c]

2:28

Jesus says "I was back there when the Sabbath was instituted…and I instituted it!"

---

    [52] Details salient to Matthew's version are covered in the author's commentary on Matthew (12:1-8)
    [c] 1 Sam. 21:6

Chapter 3

3:1-5[53]

3 And He entered the synagogue again, On the same day, He goes to the place where He was sure would be even more confrontation.

4 Then He said to them, "Is it lawful on the Sabbath to do good or to do evil, to save life or to kill?" Notice the first of two things about actions in the life of the believer (or anybody else): They are not morally neutral. **But they kept silent. 5 And when He had looked around at them with anger, being grieved by the hardness of their hearts,** Notice the second of two things about the actions of man: they do not make God emotionally neutral. **He said to the man, "Stretch out your hand." And he stretched it out, and his hand was restored as whole as the other.** Another great reference to Jesus being better than Moses who merely saw healing of leprosy from his own hand.

3:6-10

Then the Pharisees went out and immediately plotted with the Herodians against Him, how they might destroy Him. Just a reminder, they wanted to destroy Jesus because He was "doing good" and not "evil" on the Sabbath. **7 But Jesus withdrew with His disciples to the sea.** The very same Sea of Galilee seen in the book at every turn already. **And a great multitude from Galilee followed Him, and from Judea** from the Northern and Southern parts of the kingdom… **8 and Jerusalem and Idumea and beyond the Jordan; and those from Tyre and Sidon, a great multitude,** From the capitol, from the southeast, the east, the northwest…from everywhere! **when they heard how many things He was doing, came to Him. 9 So He told His disciples A**

---

[53]Covered in the author's commentary on Matthew (12:9-13); Also, I cannot improve upon this treatment of both the meaning of the Sabbath Day and the treatment of David's historical contribution to this passage: http://www.sermonaudio.com/sermoninfo.asp?SID=731111227391 [accessed 5/12/17].

disciple is "an adherent to the doctrine of another."[54] A disciple is one who takes diligent care to follow the teachings of the one to whom he has committed him or herself.[55]

that a small boat should be kept ready for Him Let us not think for a second that Jesus was not a planner, a real leader.[56]

10 For He healed many, so that as many as had afflictions pressed about Him to touch Him. Apparently news is traveling about His touching lepers and healing them (1:41) because now they wish to have that same contact.

3:11-12
And the unclean spirits, whenever they saw Him, fell down before Him and cried out, saying, "You are the Son of God." This is the 3rd time He encounters "unclean spirits" (1:27, 1:34) and this is the 2nd time they pronounce Jesus' identity (1:27)…as if they have seen one another in another world.

---

[54]Noah Webster. American Dictionary of The English Language (San Francisco: Foundation for American Christian Education, 2002), ___.

[55]Therefore, "discipleship" is the "act of making people who adhere to the teachings of another."

[56]If you are a "big picture-type of visionary", you will be quite glad that you have detail-oriented "managers" below you. They are your "reality checkers". They are your "duration experts" when you have deadlines. They are your human resource facilitators when you have personnel expectations. They know what kind of trees are in the forest you are trying to clear off of the "field". The leader says, "I know that field needs to move". The manager says, "Yes, sir/maam. These are 'hickory' wood which will require x-number of chain saws with x-type of blades and x-number of trucks, skidders, and axmen. They will be able to clear this type of forest in x-number of days/weeks".

The leader then decides between several possible courses of action: 1. Clear the forest under discussion because we must absolutely have that field. 2. Find another field to clear. 3. Do nothing, and table the matter.

It is possible, you understand, that this leader was a good manager in this trade at one time or another, but this may not be so. A person who is a leader provides vision with direction (that is usually nothing more than left and right boundaries).

The last time, incidentally, that anybody called Jesus the Son of God was when His Father God did so (1:11). Apparently, when both Heaven and Hell speak, they can't help but say the truth about Jesus.

12 But He sternly warned them that they should not make Him known. And this is the 2nd time He told them to "hush." Why? Matthew tells us more, but the bottom line is that it simply wasn't time for the Kingdom. We have, believe it or not, a kingdom that needs a risen King.

3:13-19

And He went up on the mountain and called to Him those He Himself wanted. How do you feel about a God Who does this whenever He wants? This is the 2nd time He's gone away to get away (1:38-39). It was to be alone with the Father first (1:35), and it's to be, according to Mark, with the disciples now. **And they came to Him. 14 Then He appointed twelve,[57]** for what? Yet, another clue that Jesus knows Who He is: He is either the Lord of all (being the Lord of the Sabbath, 2:28) or He is greatly deceived.

twelve Why is He picking twelve? As stated numerous times, we have the "mediator of the New Covenant" showing us the beginning of a new Israel. Both Moses and Jesus were miracle workers. Both spent 40 days fasting. Both came with a law. Both had a baptism.[58] Both worked with the heads of 12 tribes.[59]

> *Numbers 13:3 And Moses by the commandment of the LORD sent them from the wilderness of Paran: all those men were heads of the children of Israel. 4. And these were their names: of the tribe of Reuben, Shammua the son of Zaccur. 5 Of the tribe of* **Simeon***...25 they returned from searching of the land after forty*

---

[57] Luke 6:12-13 confirms that he called some to Himself and then, out of that crow, He chose some. *Now it came to pass in those days that He went out to the mountain to pray, and continued all night in prayer to God.* *[13] And when it was day, He called His disciples to Himself; and from them He chose twelve whom He also named apostles:*

[58] 1 Corinthians 10:1

[59] Matthew 19:28 speaks of these same men ruling the "12 tribes of Israel."

days. These are the spies, one from each tribe—12 in all, sent to spy out Canaan and they did it for forty days.

Both sent their "12" into the land to do a sort of survey...thus the next verse, and thus the probable purpose of this passage in the Gospel of Mark. We find that when the heat is on from the Herodians, you go on the offensive to give the persecutors more to do. Now, instead of keeping their eye on one man, they get to watch 13.[60] So in Jesus being the New Moses, we have the connection with the Christ's Gospel (Mark 14:23-25 shows that Christ, after gathering the "tribes" into the wilderness around Him in these verses, introduces them to His New Covenant), and in it being the twelve, we have the connection with Christ's afterlife as found in the church (Mark 16:15-20).

that they might be with Him He could have pre-programmed these disciples for their mission. This seems almost too easy, but "physical proximity" has much to do with how well people are discipled. Disciples, pupils, and learners do not treat their teacher and leader as nothing more than the captain of the bowling team whom they would like to see once or twice a week. This is a relationship to which both parties commit for a longer term. It is, after all, a changed lifestyle. One cannot expect to become an "adherent" to the teachings of someone else if they cannot have personal contact with them on a regular basis.[61]

He was in charge of demons, disease, and disparagers so far in this Gospel. He didn't need anybody. A trip to Psalm 50 would tell us "If I desired sacrifice, I wouldn't tell you." In Acts 17, Paul declares God doesn't need anybody.

and that He might send them this is the verb form of the noun "apostles" used elsewhere. Also, notice that Jesus chooses people for these two purposes: 1. Personal development, and 2. Purpose for life. Yes, contextually true, but true about the character of God. If He feels

---

[60]Incidentally, this is a sly reference to Jesus being the new High Priest of this New Covenant. Levi was the 13th tribe so to speak after the two sons of Joseph were each given an inheritance, and as the reader probably knows, the Levites were given no land grant in the promised land as the "priestly tribe."
[61]Merrill C. Tenney. The Zondervan Pictorial Encyclopedia of the Bible Volume 2 (Grand Rapids: Zondervan, 1976), 130.

close to the Lord, it is because you are being prepared for further service.

He is on a mission. There is no passivity in Jesus. Prayerfully awaiting the will of the Father, and then moving forward are His trademarks and I think they should be ours. Spending time with the Lord is fantastic, but if you love God, God draws us close to spend time with us only to send us out to be effective for Him.

Often people build relationships with God off of a desire to have a true husband (for the woman struggling to find purpose in relationship outside of marriage). Those with no father figure are drawn to God when the sense true fatherhood. They find it, and are glad. Some have never had a true friend, and they love to be close to the Son and find a "friend that sticks closer than a brother." BUT, after we have found all these things…we have found a King. And a King has subjects. And subjects do their Master's bidding.

That is, every leader in the Christian faith since the time of Christ, officially or non-officially, was at one time, a disciple. There are no good leaders who did not master "following".[62] But in a less legal sense, authority is something to which the true disciple and believer submits himself to all of his days upon this earth.

out to preach, Given our Master's emphasis on "preaching" in the Gospels, one would wonder, "Is everyone supposed to preach, or was that a particular command given to the disciples because they were apostles?" Is there a gift of preaching, and not just a general command for all believers to preach? If one believes they are sent ("apostle") by God, then they should see the need to do what is seen here (or at least consider it).[63]

---

[62]Furthermore, one cannot dishonor God's "stand-in" and still claim to honor God. "The powers that be are ordained of Him, after all" (Romans 13).

[63]On the other hand, if one is supposed to simply "preach because they're Christians," we have two dilemmas: 1. If "every Christian" is supposed to "preach" then where is the proof text saying so? 2. If "every Christian is supposed to preach" and the references to the apostles or disciples are to be taken wholesale, then what is the prooftext for seeing apostles and disciples as different parties within the text?

16 Simon, to whom He gave the name Peter; We are not told by Mark when this name was given to **Simon.** Peter's last mention was in chapter 1 (1:39) when He let the Lord know that those in Capernaum who had seen Him at his house the night before were looking for him again.

17 James the son of Zebedee and John We haven't seen these guys since they were called and since they escorted Jesus into Peter's house.

the brother of James Mark's way of distinguishing him from the other John (the Baptist) of which He had been speaking.

18 Andrew, we last saw him in chapter one when he was listed as a co-owner of Peter's (his) house.

Philip, Bartholomew, Matthew, Thomas, each of which mentioned only here in this Gospel (unless you believe that Levi is **Matthew**, in which case, even so, he is not mentioned again in this Gospel)[64]

James the son of Alphaeus, The first of perhaps three times he is mentioned in this Gospel.

Thaddaeus, Simon the Cananite; each mentioned only here.

19 and Judas Iscariot, who was also, "sent out to preach, and given authority to heal sicknesses and cast out demons."

who also betrayed Him. Mark is prepping the reader for what they will discover about this man. **And they went into a house.** This is an entirely different Greek word than that used to portray Peter's or Matthew's house and appears to have reference to a different "home" than was already mentioned in this Gospel.

3:20-21

Then the multitude came together again, again? In the house? So he gets away from the house to get with the Father to get away in 1:37-39

---

[64]Matthew seems to wish for us to make the connection in his own list (Matthew 10:3).

and he gets away from the multitude in 3:7 because some are seeking to kill Him, and here he goes into a house go get away…and **they could not so much as eat bread. 21 But when His** [q]**own** we are choosing this rendering over the KJV rendering of "his friends" because of the contextual flow picked up in verse 31. Also, His "friends" would have been newly commissioned as apostles in the previous episode. Their mere "friendship" would have been pretty shallow if they were already questioning the sense of their leader. **people heard about this, they went out to lay hold of Him,** [r]**for they said, "He is out of His mind."** So the idea is that his family is far enough away that they need to travel. They appear to get to Jesus in 3:31, thus requiring the episode which follows to take place in the meanwhile. Mary need not be singled out here, but merely a part of group of perhaps 6 or more which mostly believed Jesus was crazy. Also, Mark had no seeming discrepancies to "clear up" as he makes no attempts at Mary's inside information about Jesus' personhood. More notes in 3:31.

3:22

And the scribes who came down from Jerusalem said, "He has Beelzebub," "lord of the flies" or "lord of the dung" are the composition of the parts of this word in the original language.

"He has Beelzebub," When Heaven speaks: "Beloved Son" (1:11). When Hell speaks "Holy One of God" (1:24). In this context, the demons say He is the Son of God (1:11); the family says "He's crazy" (1:21); the enemy says "He's demon-possessed."

3:23-30[65]

So He called them to Himself and said to them in parables: "How can Satan cast out Satan? So here, the terms "Beelzebub" and **Satan** and "ruler of demons" are deemed synonymous by Jesus. Now, I don't want us to lose the wonder of Jesus appealing to the logic of these antagonizers. I find no clue in this passage or others that the Jesus spoke

---

[q]Mark 6:3
[r]John 7:5
[65]See also the appendix on suicide for more on these verses.

these logical checks for the benefit of the bystanders alone. No, Jesus called them over and engaged them.

He gives three logical fallacies: a divided house, a divided kingdom, a self-conflicting 'Satan'. This really is the cost of opposing Jesus: You become illogical. I'd like to remind you that you live in a world where two laws of thermodynamics exist, the first of which is "Energy can be neither created nor destroyed." Supposedly, there has never been less energy in the universe than there is now. The big bang began out of this same energy merely changing forms and if you've done any physics you know that F=MA. For energy to exist in the same quantity in the universe and for us to have expanding mass…every expanding mass, then acceleration must be decreasing…yet it is not. Rather, they are noticing that acceleration is increasing the further away from the point of this so-called explosion. Then those who say that acceleration is not increasing will say that it was infinitely fast before the big bang in order to allow for all pre-expansion mass to be in an area the size of a pinhead. So, to summarize, one of the best explanations, without a creator, for everything that now is... is that everything that now is existed in an area the size of a pinhead and was traveling at infinitely expanding speeds of acceleration until a bang occurred. We might ask, "when did the mass consolidate to an area this small to allow for the increase of acceleration at this rate?" When you disregard the Creator—or better, the Creator Who became flesh—you become illogical and of greater faith than any Christian could ever be!

Jesus is concerned for these men. He didn't have to engage them, yet the only alternative is that He is indeed the one Who bound the strong man. Jesus must be casting them out by the Spirit of God because there are less and less demonic fruits in their existing kingdom. For example, less blind and mute folks are living around there…so Jesus must be "binding Satan."

The implication, of course, is that Jesus did all by the power of the **Holy Spirit.** This sin seems to be summed up in the following statements:

1. Men and Women continually confess what they believe (Romans 10:9-10).

2. The Scribes were continually confessing that Christ's Works and Words were from Satan (see tense of 3:30).
3. This confession was speech against the real origin of His Works and Words: The Holy Spirit.
4. This confession against the Holy Spirit is called **blasphemy.**
5. So long as they confessed this, they indicated they had a heart that thought this.
6. So long as they had a heart that confessed this, they could not be forgiven…for they were rejecting what the Holy Spirit produced in the Person and Work of Jesus.
7. So long as anybody rejected the witness of Jesus Christ, as empowered by the Holy Spirit, they were unforgivable and were damned.
8. Believers, by definition, cannot commit this sin.

28 "Assuredly, I say to you, all sins will be forgiven the sons of men, and whatever blasphemies they may utter; It seems as though we should never get over the fact that not only is "forgiveness" man's greatest need,
but it is also God's most significant provision to us. This word for **forgive** is used previously of dropping nets (1:20), a fever departing (1:31), and of sins forgiven—oddly enough by this very selfsame "Son of Man" (2:5-7).

    Incidentally, 2:5-7 drives us to remember that this forgiveness was granted to the one and only person granted forgiveness of sin thus far by "faith," not prayer. Maybe we should just stand back and admire our Lord Jesus Who is actually offering forgiveness to these shameless men who accused Him of being demon possessed to begin with…and continually did so (see the imperfect tense of 3:30.

29 but he who blasphemes against the Holy Spirit never has forgiveness, but is subject to eternal condemnation"—30 because they [x]said, we are not free, then, to simply say "blasphemy of the Holy Spirit is merely resisting the Holy Spirit." **"He has an unclean spirit."** So, if Jesus is not filled with demons as the Pharisees said, and if He is not crazy like His family said, then He must be Who He says He is: "He

---

[x]John 7:20; 8:48, 52; 10:20

truly owns us," the disciple says. "He alone has power to forgive sin. He controls demons and disease." This changes everything: For if He controls the laws of nature in the storms and in the diseases and in the demons, then He controls the laws of morals and controls forgiveness and the judgment to come. Won't you seek forgiveness? It's only logical.

3:31-32

Then His brothers There have been a number of suggestions: 1. These are really Jesus' cousins and Mary remained a virgin (this seems unlikely because Mark has a term he uses for "cousins"/"kin" in chapter 6)[66]; 2. These were children born to Mary with Joseph after Jesus' birth; 3. These were children Joseph had before his marriage with Mary (previous wife had died or he had been divorced). **and His mother came,** Was Mary really questioning Jesus' sanity (3:20)? We have other places in John's Gospel where His brothers were rather antagonistic to Him, but the two Gospels with birth narratives (Matthew and Luke) leave no room for Mary to not be aware of Jesus' Personhood and mission (let alone His origin).[67] **and standing outside** of the house (3:19) in which the multitude found Him, keeping Him from eating (3:20) **they sent to Him,** Probably a Mark 2:1 scenario where they couldn't get in.[68]

3:33-35

But He answered them, saying, "Who is My mother, or My brothers?" Jesus did not sever identification from His brothers, and sister, and family. He is still known as one of the family members of Joseph and Mary (Mark 6:1-3).

Jesus did not drive the audience to believe they should dishonor their parents. As a matter of fact, Jesus takes great issue with people who were finding ways around the honoring of their parents (Mark 7:9-13).

---

[66] "G4773 - syggenēs - Strong's Greek Lexicon (KJV)." Blue Letter Bible. Web. 8 May, 2017. <https://www.blueletterbible.org//lang/lexicon/lexicon.cfm?Strongs=G4773&t=KJV>.
[67] More comments under 3:21.
[68] Luke 8:19 removes all doubt.

Jesus did not ignore his family outside the house. It is here where some have gone outside the text and said things like "Mary, who had nursed and dressed Jesus and love him all the way into his magnificent manhood, and now had come for him in loving concern, was crushed. His brothers were likewise shocked and perhaps angered."[69] The only problem, of course, is that the passage doesn't say that. As a matter of fact, the next time we see Jesus…in the very next verse, He's outside the house (Matthew's version confirms it was "the same day", 13:1). So, for all we know, Jesus got up to go outside to meet them and Mark is simply showing us that flesh and blood family doesn't get the final say on everything.

This is not the first or second time Jesus "distanced Himself" from His mother: 1. He did so at the age of 12 in the temple (Luke 2), and 2. He did so in John 2 with his response at a wedding. **34 And He looked around in a circle at those who sat about Him, and said, "Here are My mother and My brothers! 35 For whoever does the [z]will of God** which could be summarized as "fruit bearing" according to 4:8. **is My brother and My sister and mother."** This seems pretty saintly of the disciples until you think of who we're dealing with here, and "despite all their failures, Jesus acknowledged them as those who did God's will and therefore his true family."[70] Maybe we should remind ourselves that this, for conversation sake, includes Judas.

Jesus stressed "faith" over maternity: Jesus' salvation of Mary was no different than anybody else. Jesus gave His life for His mother (10:45). Imagine saying something like "Mary is no closer to Jesus than any who 'do the will of God'."[71] "Mary was more blessed in receiving the faith of Christ than in conceiving the flesh of Christ…Mary's

---

[69]R Kent Hughes *Preaching the Word (Mark): Jesus, Servant and Savior* (Wheaton: Crossway, 2015), 96.

[z]1 John 2:17

[70] James A. Brooks, *Mark*, vol. 23, The New American Commentary (Nashville: Broadman & Holman Publishers, 1991), 74.

[71]H.H. Halley *Halley's Bible Handbook, New Revised Version* (Grand Rapids: Zondervan, 1965), 439.

[bearing Jesus upon her bosom would have carried no benefit] for her salvation if she had not borne Christ in her heart" [Augustine].[72]

Jesus stressed his Heavenly Father over his earthly mother. "Every beat of Christ's heart was given to performing his Father's will."[73] Your precious children are given to you so that they can please the Heavenly Father. Let's not make it hard on them. "The truth is, many of the psychological problems in our families can be traced to parents whose affections bind rather than release and liberate."[74] The "mission field" seems like a great idea…as long as it's somebody else's family going.

Also, it cannot be overlooked that Jesus placed the faith family over flesh and blood. Surely you can see this man's frustration with "worship of flesh and blood:"

> *Many Christians and non-Christians alike have made the family [virtually] everything. Every moment of every day, every involvement, every commitment, every engagement is measured and judged by the question, how will this benefit my family? While this is generally commendable, it can degenerate into familial narcissism where the four walls of the home become a temple and only within and for those walls are any sacrifices made. Thus we commit domestic idolatry!*[75]

The spirit of this passage stresses the ideal of having your flesh and blood family in a right relationship with Christ. If we don't do this, priorities collide long-term, and we are not ready for them to think differently, and plan differently. It doesn't get easier later in Mark 10:28-30. So we know that we are interested in facing a day when we will indeed have to pick between families.

---

[72]Thomas C. Oden, ed. *Ancient Christian Commentary on Scripture, New Testament II –Mark* (Downers Grove, Ill: Intervarsity Press, 1998), 48.
[73]Hughes, 97.
[74]Ibid., 98.
[75]Ibid.

Chapter 4

4:1-2

And again Matthew says "the same day" as the previous exchange. **He began to teach by the sea. And a great multitude was gathered to Him, so that He got into a boat and sat in it on the sea;** seen first in 3:9 **and the whole multitude was on the land facing the sea. 2 Then He taught them many things by parables,** "earthly story with a heavenly meaning?" Sure, that will work for now.[76]

4:3-8

Signs of life do not equal fruit. We might see that those who show they are living are not "converted" or "forgiven" (verse 11). This speaks specifically of those who were dwindling from Jesus' crowd. They really loved what Jesus was saying….less and less. This definitely applies to Judas, yet it speaks even more definitively to those who claim to be close to Jesus in 3:31-35. In other words, "doing God's will" is something that happens naturally to seed sown in the life of one who is considered "good ground."

4:9-10

12 so that [f]"Seeing they may see and not perceive, And hearing they may hear and not understand; Lest they should turn, And their sins be forgiven them.' " God does not want everybody's sins forgiven—specifically, those guilty of the sin that is not to be forgiven from the last chapter. Why? They must kill Him. He does seem interested in how people hear (4:23), but apparently not the leadership that would kill Him.[77]

---

[76] I've always been taught that definition.

[f] Is. 6:9, 10; Rom. 11:8

[77] No matter how uncomfortable "sovereignty in salvation" talks make somebody, one has to admit that somebody is not going to be forgiven, and it's Jesus' fault.

One might notice that the point of parables is, in these cases, to conceal truth to the spiritually undiscerning. Yet, we might also notice that the Lord makes parables to make things even clearer to the one for whom they are intended (4:21-25).

4:13

And He said to them, "Do you not understand this parable? How then will you understand all the parables?" This is either the easiest or the most foundational of all the parables that Jesus gives concerning the kingdom (verse 11).

The Bible does not interpret everything it says. Perhaps, though, we should find other places the same language is used. Here, it is obvious and simple. It is very close (in the next verses). Listening is of vital (yes, critical) importance (verse 3, 9, 23).

all the parables? A select few parables or words of Jesus were given to us. Consider the plural of this verse and verse 33.

4:14-15

The sower sows the word…Jesus is obviously sowing the seed here so that we must see Him as the primary sower of the seed.[78] He does also work through those whom He has called (3:13-14).

the word He only has the Word to sow. Furthermore, we find that this passage does not tell us He controls the seed or the soil (4:26-29; that parable, although different, speaks of a sower and the life of the seed).

He furthermore controls nothing of the rate of growth (4:30-35). This parable, although different than the previous two, speaks of the kingdom growing as a whole, which supposes that it grows out of good ground (at the micro level; or better said "at the individual kingdom member level").

---

[78]Matthew 13:37 seems to confirm this in kingdom parables: the Son is the primary doer of the action.

We need, as good ground, to receive more Word (assuming we are good ground).[79] The seed brings fruit only on good ground, and it will bring fruit because it is in good ground. "Good ground" is listening ground. If we don't see some expectation from God from this text, then we can rightly question why the stress is placed upon the listener so often through these parables (4:23, for example).

We should not be surprised when many will eventually leave our congregation for other places. They are simply not good ground.

> *But let the time of testing come, when affliction or persecution arises for the Word's sake, immediately these people are offended. They turn back, and then they blame everything and everybody for their having turned back, when the truth of the matter is there was no heart work to begin with. It was just hollow, empty profession.*[80]

15 And these are the ones by the wayside where the word is sown. We are plainly told that the word is the seed; yet we are also told that **these** are referring to the listeners and in a way are the seed. How do we make sense of this? Well, the seed becomes a part of the ground. In this case, four types of ground. We therefore have 1 seed+4 different soil/seed combinations=4 different results. **When they hear, Satan comes immediately and takes away the word that was sown in their hearts.** Notice the universal influence of a non-omnipresent Satan. That is to say, He is seen as having many agents, or this could not be so. He is seen as but one of three frustrating influences to the lost-ness of mankind. He is not responsible, you'll notice in this parable, for the rocky or thorny peoples (4:17-18). If there is no Word, there is no faith. If there is no faith, there is no fruit. If there is no fruit, there is no conversion or forgiveness/salvation (4:9-10).

---

[83]Implication from the Old Testament exists that we may prepare ourselves, as active listeners, to be good ground: Hosea 10:12 speaks to the heart and pleads with the reader of Hosea's day to "break up the unplowed ground." Given the many connections with Hosea (see my commentary on the Minor Prophets), it seems this brings many windows of hope.

[80]Ervin W Wurz *The Gospel of Mark* (Grand Rapids: Diadem Productions, 1970), 52.

4:26-29

And He said, "The kingdom of God is

> *Sermons have been preached and books written on the kingdom of God; but Jesus, who knew all about it, contented himself by giving a few simple analogies which he knew men would understand. We would do well to try to imitate Jesus and thus avoid much waste of time, to say nothing of the flow of meaningless words which could be turned to more profitable channels. I am happy to drink in the simple words of Jesus, and I find myself exhausting my thought capacity as I attempt to sound the depths of his teaching.*[81]

So, then, it seems that the "**kingdom is** simply…"

as if a man if the man scattering seed is the same person here that it is in the preceding parable, it is Christ and then the 12 He called in chapter 3, and then those who should follow in their testimony. **should scatter seed on the ground,** We should assume that just as people are one of four types of seed in soil in the first parable (verse 15 calls them "hearts"), this is a microscopic view of "good ground." Why? This is good fruit that comes out of good ground.

We should remember, then, that this is, for literature's sake, 25% of the seed He scattered.

and should sleep by night We need not assume that this man's sleeping and rising means he is not emotional about the outcome of his seed ("but you would not"; Matthew 23). It must be the same with those of us scattering the Word of God into the good ground as well. We should assume that this man, the scatterer of seed, is sure of the end result: the crop will grow. The end result in the meaning of this parable is that the Gospel of Christ is scattered on the good ground, and the scatterer goes to sleep knowing that, one soul at a time, the kingdom of God will grow.

---

[81]John L. Hill *Outline Studies in Mark* (Nashville: Abingdon-Cokesbury Press, 1945), 55.

This is salient to our conversation because these disciples would have been tempted to wonder if there was in fact real results from their preaching this Gospel. After all, they are watching miracles upon miracles take place, yet very few people are following Christ out of a heart change. They are meeting their "felt needs" of food, fellowship, fun, and fascination…but their hearts, the country over, are not changing. Jesus reassures them by focusing on three realities:

1. <u>A sleeping man doesn't control the soil; he simply scatters the seed.</u>
2. <u>A sleeping man doesn't control the seed; he simply scatters the seed.</u> The issue is that we are tempted to change the seed. You know, "maybe the soil will react differently if we change the seed somewhat?"
   Since we know we're headed to the cross, we must admit that Mark wants us to look at the entirety of His Gospel with the deepest truth of the Gospel in mind (Mark 10:45 and Mark 15-16). It is the seed..the message of the cross.
3. <u>A sleeping man doesn't control the rate of growth; he simply scatters the seed.</u> If irrigation is as plentiful as one might expect, then God brings the seed to life in His time. If a man is sharp enough and resourced enough to irrigate, God—having provided the water—provides the seed in His time as well. In both cases, the rate of growth belongs to God. Many an uncertainty takes place in the darkness. "Is anything happening in that person's life?" God takes total responsibility for this person's growth.
   This is basically the point of 4:30-32 as well. The Kingdom will fill the earth and there will be "birds" (demons if we let the four soil interpretation of "birds" stand; or Satan himself) able to hide in and among this very mature kingdom that grows when God says so.

Some reflective questions:
I. <u>How should you listen?</u> Those without the Gospel are at a horrible point. They must follow the instructions of the previous parable to "listen well." Presumably, this is so they may become good ground and bring forth Kingdom fruit.
II. <u>How do our prayers matter?</u> Hosea 10:12 encourages people towards being good ground in the first place by responding to

God insomuch as they are able. **This is not Gospel salvation.** Gospel salvation, which is the overall view of Mark, is the seed, and the seed only brings fruit on "good ground" (verses 1-25). This parable is a microscopic view of the "good ground" from the last parable, and this seed brings fruit out of good ground automatically.

III. How does this affect the way we preach the Gospel? We recognize our limitations (soil, seed, rate of growth), and do what we can as we recognize good ground. "Scripture tells us to preach the Word! It doesn't tell us to make it grow."[82] Little by little, our seed lands on good ground and we see the blade poke through the ground (4:28), then, the head of the crop…

This movement doesn't make much noise. We who scatter seed on this soil…we hear very little by way of response, but God knows every movement on earth in its proper frequency and when a sinner repents, there's "joy in the presence of angels" (Luke 15:5).

IV. How does this affect the way I look at fruit in my own life? I anticipate magnificent secondary and tertiary fruit from the Gospel in my life. "The sacrifice of Jesus is that which makes the world bearable to a holy God…"[83] A hint of the full crop is seen though the ear and the blade. Let us be patient with what God is doing in our own lives.

V. How does apply to Christians training Christians? We admit that our parenting is caring for the fruit first wrought by the Gospel fruit in our young folks' lives, and we patiently and expectantly await even more fruit.

We sow and we go to bed…praying.

4:35-37

On the same day, which is the same day as his family's visit and the parables of the first part of this chapter (Matthew 13:1), **when evening had come, He said to them, "Let us cross over to the other side."**[84]

---

[82]Wurz, 56.

[83]C.H. Spurgeon *The Greatest Fight in the World; C.H. Spurgeon Classics* (Scotland: Christian Focus Publications, LTD., 2014), 23; in a forward by Tom Nettles.

[84]More can be found in my commentary on Matthew (8:23-27).

36 Now when they had left the multitude, they took Him along in the boat as He was. And other little boats were also with Him. See verse 41 for some thoughts on this. **37 And a great windstorm arose,** at 600+ feet below sea level and surrounded by mountains, falling, turbulent cool air through the tributaries of the "sea" would mix with the warm air incipient on the waters and storms could quickly rise.[85]

Why would a person go through a storm to travel 8 miles across the Sea of Galilee? To calm a storm in the soul of a man. He valued this man. Mark tells us it has been a full day of teaching in the house, sparing with the antagonizers all the way back to 3:20 and all the way forward to teaching from the sea (through 4:33). He is looking forward to a night of relative sleeplessness, discipleship with some doubters, restoration of a demon-possessed man with his family, being chased out of town, only to cross back over the sea in 5:21 and have several more engagements before he finally leaves town in 6:1.

4:38

But He was in the stern, the KJV says "the hinder part of the ship." The "bow" is the front. **asleep on a pillow.**[86] **And they awoke Him** Real sleep. Who dares to wake Him? Only those who are desperate.[87]

If Christ is a part of the "us" who needs saving from perishing, and the disciples are coming to Him saying, "Lord, wake up, or we, including You, are going to die," then they haven't been paying very good attention: Certainly the One who can heal people who are corrupted and cast out demons is "from God."[88] How about the fact He

---

[85] Hughes, 111.

[86] I have said (in my commentary on Matthew) that this is a comparison between Jesus and Jonah, but here in Mark, I'd like to appreciate the weariness of our Savior. He was really tired, and He was really asleep.

[87] Desperate in infertility like Hannah who asked the "LORD of Armies" to "take notice of [her] affliction", and "the LORD remembered her" (1 Samuel 1); Desperate in fields of battle where the foes outnumber, outskill, and outflank us as 2.5 tribes of Israel called out to God (1 Chronicles 5); Desperate in fetters and chains when taken into strange lands as Manassah (2 Chronicles 33); Desperate in fear of unknown when traveling in the perfect will of God as Ezra (Ezra 8).

[88] We're told the answer with Jesus' question concerning their faith. Here would be an alternative: Do they think the we who are perishing includes Jesus? If not,

claims to be the Son of Man—the "one from God's right hand?" That counts for something! Where have they been?

Storms do that to us. We say things we never would have dreamed we would have said. We do things we would never have dreamed we would do. Already, He has dealt with disease with a leper, delirium with the fevered, demons at every turn, and the spirit of the deceived within the scribes, Pharisees, Herodians and the disciples of John the Baptist, and He claims to be able to save a cripple from damnation resulting from His sin!

And Jesus' response, "I will get them into a storm when they are very tired so they can see how little faith is in the core of their thinking." I can really fake it well when I'm rested; when I have money and to spare; when I have lots of people pleased with my work…back in "comfortable Capernaum." But on the boat, in the middle of a storm…it's so different. I have very little control.

Jesus, on the other hand is asleep and full of faith. He trusts His Father. He knows He's been told of work that must be done, both in His soul and in the Scriptures…He's been told.

4:39-40

Then He arose and rebuked the wind, and said to the sea, "Peace, be still!" Psalm 65:7, Psalm 89:9, and Psalm 104:7 are clearly referenced here as the 2nd Psalm we can ascertain, and Mark is being supernaturally—cognitively or not is hard to say—used to show that Jesus is God, and the disciples are Israel (praying Psalm 44:23's sentiment in 4:38). This will show up later when He feeds them in the wilderness. This is the new Israel. Remember, they are 12 (as the tribes), and they have a new Moses, and have a new way to conquer the Promised Land (through preaching and spiritual warfare), and will

---

this is pretty irrational: If you stay with the One who is not in danger of perishing that would mean you yourself cannot perish. If He's not a part of the "we" then He is not in danger of perishing. And if they, in danger of perishing, are in the same boat with He that is not in danger of perishing, then indeed this is most irrational. So really, I suppose the answer is stay with the One who's not in danger.

receive a new covenant.[89] This really is the purpose of this passage from a Holy Spirit-inspired perspective, but the truths that prove to be 2ndary and tertiary in this passage have earth-shattering effects on us, the follower of Jesus.

And the wind ceased and there was a great calm. 40 But He said to them, "Why are you so fearful? How is it that you have no faith?"[90] **Great** is *megas*. The calm is not in proportion to their **no faith**.

What is confronting them in the ship is a great storm (5:37). The story ends with them experiencing a **great calm.** The only thing that is not **great** in this story is their faith. The calm that He brings to the storm is not in proportion to our faith. It's in proportion to the storm He sends us into. I'm going to say it again: The only thing small in this story is our faith. The storm: it's big, we don't want to be in it; it's displeasing. We're always waiting for the timing of the sleeping One in the boat. Jesus is not going to leave you alone in the storm. He leaves us in the storm long enough for us to take a look at our faith. And then He brings a calm in grand proportion to the storm He brought into our life. Do you want to experience **great calm**? I do too. Are you equally as willing to experience great storm? It appears from this story, this true account, that you cannot have one without the other.

4:41

 And they feared exceedingly, literally, "they feared fearfully." **and said to one another, "Who can this be, that even** quite the word here. In other words, after all they had seen with the "demons" running away from them, this was remarkably different…**the wind and the sea obey**

---

[89] What is even more striking than this, in my opinion, is the reality with which the poetry of the Psalmists are being fulfilled.

[90] Interesting difference here between no faith and "little faith" of Matthew 8:26. It seems as though the difference is easily settled in the order of things. He rebukes them for "little faith" before He calms the storm and then accuses them of no faith after calming the storm. This seems like an easy settlement of the issue.

On the other hand, our gut should tell us that the "then" of Matthew 8:26 is more of "approximate sameness of time" rather than exact order so our issue remains. The "no faith" of Mark is that quantity of faith which is lacking from their reasonably expected faith (after all they'd seen) leaving behind their "little faith" of Matthew.

Him!" This fearful fear is one of a realized, horrible underestimation that could have been disastrous in each of those individual's lives. "The only thing more terrifying than having a storm in the boat was having God in the boat."[91] Perhaps, this is why we don't see the "other little boats" of 4:36? Perhaps they are no more? Perhaps these disciples see how close they were to death? It makes us understand "who we're dealing with" a little better. Have you considered how disastrous it is to underestimate Jesus? Here is perhaps a better way of summarizing it:

> *They know who alone calms the sea. Their fear testifies to the inability of the old cloth and the old wineskin to contain what is happening among them (2:21-22). Mark's readers, however, are well-prepared by Mark's prologue (1:2-3) to answer the question "Who is this?" Jesus is not just a powerful teacher.*[92]

---

[91] John MacArthur, ed. *The MacArthur Study Bible* (Nashville: Thomas Nelson, 1997), 1467.
[92] D.A. Carson, ed., *NIV Zondervan Study Bible* (Grand Rapids: Zondervan, 2015), 2018.

Chapter 5

5:1-13

This passage was dealt in some detail in the appendix on suicide and in my commentary on Matthew (8:28-32). There has been much question about whether we have one men or two in this passage.[93] By the way, my research has turned up a belief that these "unclean spirits" are not those who fell with Satan but are rather the spirits/souls of the giants (the offspring of those in 2 Peter 2:4).

> In particular [we] see the Christian *Testament of Solomon* 5:3; 17:1. In 5:3 (within the section 5:1–11), the author reinterprets the demon Asmodeus—this is a deliberate reference to the Book of Tobit which follows the longer recension (cf. Codex Sinaiticus at 3:7–8, 17; 6:14–15, 17; 8:2–3; 12:15)—one born from a human mother and an angel. In the latter text (in the passage 17:1–5) the demonic power thwarted by Jesus (in an allusion to M[ar]k 5:3) is identified as one of the giants who died in the internecine conflicts.[94]

5:14-15

So those who fed the swine fled, only instance of pig farmers in the Bible (besides Luke 15 and the "prodigal son"). **and they told it in the city and in the country. And they went out to see what it was that had happened.**[95] **15 Then they came to Jesus, and saw the one who had been demon-possessed** He just returned from calming the storm and now, he's about to calm a man. The story is very simple. It's like this: Sometimes the Lord calms the storm and sometimes He calms me.

---

[93]"Only Matthew speaks of two demoniacs, but he does not thereby contradict Mark and Luke. Neither of the other Evangelists refers to "only" one. Perhaps one of the two dominated the conversation. But Matthew elsewhere includes two characters, where parallel accounts have one (9:27; 20:30)"; Craig Blomberg, Matthew, vol. 22, The New American Commentary (Nashville: Broadman & Holman Publishers, 1992), 151.

[94] Michael S. Heiser, <u>Reversing Hermon: Enoch, The Watchers & The Forgotten Mission of Jesus Christ</u> (Crane, MO: Defender, 2017), 33.

[95]More can be found in my commentary on Matthew (8:33-34).

That's not original; I got that from a song.[96] This man, watching the storm from his hillside cemetery little knows that the reason the clouds parted and the winds surrendered is because the Master of the Seas controls, yes, even the demons of hell, and He is coming to beach nearby. With this man, the great shaking wasn't on the sea, it was in his soul. That's the stuff that just crushes us. The stuff that we can't explain, we can't fix, and we can't make go away, we just have to sit and deal with it.

and had the legion, sitting and clothed and in his right mind. And they were afraid. Strange, this is the 2nd straight miracle where some were **afraid** (and it happens again in 5:33). **16 And those who saw it told them how it happened to him who had been demon-possessed, and about the swine. 17 Then they began to plead with Him to depart from their region.** Mark doesn't seem to be emphasizing the response of the man. He's not necessarily concentrating on the helpless world of therapy or treatment, although it says he broke whatever chains they employed.

    The town does, however, reject Jesus over their precious pigs. Humanly speaking, God was making a legitimate offer to a city on the east side of the Sea of Galilee and they would not have Him. He could have done more, as at other places, if the townspeople would have desired Him more than their precious pigs. Think about it: swine carcasses floating everywhere. A man breathing deeply, hugging his family for the first time. Jesus and His disciples talking among themselves. The sun is rising in the morning with the clouds in the sky. The disciples are still rubbing sleep out of their eyes from the nap right before the boat hit the beach. The fresh air is blowing in from the sea and a fishing vessel across the field, sitting on a beach.

    Now we see a group of people coming out of the city? They're not happy that a man that hasn't been home in years now has a prospect of a family that loves their husband and daddy who can now hold a job and be a responsible citizen. They're not happy a man that hasn't been able to hug his sons and daughters babies before bed is now able to do so. They're not happy that a man is having his first clear thought in

---

[96] https://www.youtube.com/watch?v=_yoN62hb--I [accessed 6/19/17].

years. They're not happy that he's able to sit calmly. Oh they'll say, "We're happy about that." But, they cared more for hogs than human souls and that often happens today.

18 And when He got into the boat, he who had been demon-possessed begged Him This is the 3rd time Jesus has been begged: He was **begged** to prolong the demons' time on the earth; he was **begged** to leave town after causing the stock market to crash; He was **begged** here to put one more person on the boat.

20 And he departed and began to proclaim in [5]Decapolis all that Jesus had done for him; and all marveled. This man had quite the fascination with his new Savior. Notice the change that Jesus makes when a man has been possessed: Seated (5:15) versus running around and uncontrollable; [97] clothed (5:15) versus minimally covered;[98] in his right Mind (5:15) versus a lack of concentration or focus; ready (5:18) to work for Jesus.

Along the lines of the man's readiness, we see here that this man wanted more of Jesus. More devotions. More missions trips. More adventures. He wanted to always feel what he was feeling now. Jesus had different plans. This man, in contrast to the leper of chapter 1 is not an Israelite and could therefore evangelize as it would not be a mob from Decapolis that should kill our Lord. Jesus makes this man the beachhead for his own world east of Decapolis. Jesus may have been the first one to offer himself to this civilization, but he wasn't the 2nd. This man was, and he was told to go to a people that had already rejected Jesus. Was he successful? The only other time in the book of Mark where Decapolis is

---

[5] Lit. *Ten Cities*

[97] What's the problem today? It could be demons…or it could be parenting. Do we not see the effect Jesus has in the life of a person? We're not talking about nervous, childhood energy being demon-possessed. What is clear is that Jesus on the scene makes a great deal of difference in how calm a person becomes in contrast to how uncontrollable one is.

[98] I wonder how naked he was? Do you suppose, as a side note, that if he put on a speedo or a pair of board shorts that he would have been considered "clothed?" Do you suppose, that if this was a woman, and she was healed of a demon—running around naked in the tombs—that if she put on a bikini somebody would have said, "My what a difference Jesus makes in a person's life!" He was naked, and now the writer Mark sees a very clear and distinct difference in appearance.

mentioned is in Mark 7:31? I can't be positive, but when we review the accounts between this passage and that, we are left with seeing this man as the biblically-sole reason Decapolis sought after this Jesus.

5:21-24[99]

Now when Jesus had crossed over again by boat to the other side, a great multitude gathered to Him; how did they know to gather to Him? It could be that the "little boats" of our previous episode had brought news of His return. **and He was by the sea.** So, reaching back to the middle of Mark 3, we find we are still on the same weekend (see 4:35 and its notes), and He cannot get away from the boat. First, let's remember that if we have two chapters and two days, we see how little of Jesus' life we really have. If His baptism occurs at age 30 in chapter 1, and He dies on the Passover in his 34th year, we have 16 chapters covering roughly 3.5 years. However, Palm Sunday is chapter 11 which means the last six chapters of the Gospel deal with the last week of Jesus' life leading up to His resurrection. So, two chapters covers two days and five chapters covers seven more days, that leaves 7 chapters of Mark for the other three years, 171 days of Jesus' earthly ministry. Or to say it better, perhaps, we have 7 chapters of Mark employed for 9 days of the 12,000+ days of Jesus' earthly life. We know precious little about this man; this God-man.

Why did He cross again? Arguably to reach Decapolis. Was he successful? Not really. He affected, according to Mark, one person.

22 And behold, one of the rulers of the synagogue one word in the Greek and used only in this account in Mark.[100] **came, Jairus by name. And when he saw Him, he fell at His feet** why is this perfectly healthy man falling down before Jesus? What is it about Jesus that allows a man to fall down in a posture of worship and yet we find nothing about which we can raise a hand or shout "Hallelujah" when He saves our never-dying souls again and again? **23 and begged Him earnestly, saying,**

---

[99] More can be found in my commentary on Matthew (9:18-19).
[100] "G752 - archisynagōgos - Strong's Greek Lexicon (KJV)." Blue Letter Bible. Web. 25 Jun, 2017.
<https://www.blueletterbible.org//lang/lexicon/lexicon.cfm?Strongs=G752&t=KJV>.

"My little daughter lies at the point of death. Come and lay Your hands on her, had he heard about the leper? Certainly the One Who can heal a leper can heal a little girl. **that she may be healed, and she will live." 24 So Jesus went with him,** Now that's strange. When you see that what should immediately enter your mind is, "What is He doing following anyone?" Hasn't He been telling people to follow Him this whole time? One thing is certain, this little girl cannot come to Jesus like the man in Mark 2:1-12; she isn't healthy enough to be brought to Jesus. Here we are told nothing of the faith of the little girl. So strange: In 2:1-12 we know the man has faith and so does his friends. In 5:1-20 we find a man with no exercise of faith whatsoever and yet finds deliverance from demons. Here, we are left to assume that the only faith to be found in this story is the faith of a parent.

and a great multitude followed Him and thronged Him. Imagine the relief this man feels when he says, "Jesus, come." And Jesus gets up and the man says, "Oh, good, good, good." What a stroke of relief! The star of the city is following this man! And they're walking quickly and here comes a woman who wants to be healed, and I can't help but think that if I was this man I would be irate with the woman. "I need Jesus to work right now and you are a hindrance!"

5:25-34

Now a certain woman had a flow of blood for twelve years,
According to Leviticus 15:19-31, she was unclean and deemed so. One could not come into contact with her or anything she touches is unclean. Furthermore, he or she nor the woman was allowed near the tabernacle while unclean. In other words, for 12 years, this woman was unable to live with her husband or see her children or be around their house of worship. It appears that this is a tumor in her uterus, perhaps. Remember, after she's purified she has to be separated a week at least. Well, she hasn't been purified in twelve years. So she's been living away from home for twelve years. A very lonely life. Even if she had family, and they wanted to visit her it had to be done from a distance so that husband and children could still attend worship. So everything that she has endured, she has endured alone. There's been very little family time. She hasn't heard her children laugh in her presence. They haven't played a board game in twelve years. They haven't been outside for

twelve years. Her husband and she have not been together in any way, intimately or not, for twelve years. Here's a family that hasn't had a wife or mother for twelve years and might I say, there's probably been a mother and a father that haven't seen their daughter in twelve years.

26 and had suffered many things from many physicians. She had spent all that she had This is not a slam on medical professionals any more than the previous story is a slam on psychologists. "Fetters" for the demon-possessed are the **physicians** for this woman. This is furthermore probably the biggest connection with the preceding story. This is just the unfortunate situation where a lady is broke because of her specific medical condition and had nothing after twelve years. She is first a "victim" of a religion and now a "victim" of a medical system. The odds are stacked against her, it seems. **and was no better, but rather grew worse.** Again, this isn't just summarized as "bad." She is doing what she thinks will work and some of it is at the advice of others. For some of us, it's "trying another church," and realizing that didn't fix the problem. For others it's "trying another woman," and that doesn't fix the problem. World religions leave people empty: fastings here and exercises there and no betterment.[101]

27 When she heard about Jesus, when Jesus is all that's left, we find out that's all we need. **she came behind Him in the crowd and touched His garment.** Mark 3:10 says this was normal. For some reason, they thought there was healing in touching Jesus' clothes, and we'll get a chance to look at this later in chapter 6. Let's just say that much is made of the "hem" of Jesus' garment in the Gospel of Matthew, but not here; so it shall not be the emphasis in Mark.[102]

28 For she said, "If only I may touch His clothes, I shall be made well." This is life and death: **well** is the idea of being "saved."[103] Jesus

---

[101] https://www.thenewamerican.com/world-news/item/12817-interpol-reportedly-hunting-saudi-christian-convert-who-fled-country [accessed 7/1/17].

[102] The Hebrew audience of Matthew would have been greatly interested in this perspective awash with O.T. significance (covered in my commentary on Matthew 9:20-22).

[103] "G4982 - sōzō - Strong's Greek Lexicon (KJV)." Blue Letter Bible. Web. 26 Jun, 2017. <https://www.blueletterbible.org//lang/lexicon/lexicon.cfm?Strongs=G4982&t=KJV>.

responds with this same word in verse 34, and in the context of a bleeding hemorrhage seems to be agreeing that Jesus is the last hope…just like the demon-possessed man. All the fetters and all the chains and all the doctors…no hope. "If Jesus doesn't work, I'm done." This isn't frivolity. The demon-possessed man wasn't wasting his money on fetters and chains and this woman wasn't wasting hers on medicine. These were just…occurrences of life.

30 And Jesus, immediately knowing in Himself that power had gone out of Him, The body in which resides the power of the sun felt power go out of Him? Does He really feel when He heals? Does it really cost Jesus when He ministers grace?

turned around in the crowd and said, "Who touched My clothes?" Mark 2:8 already told us that He can read minds so we must assume that Mark would just assume that his reader would just assume that Jesus knew which lady touched Him and where. This is the same Jesus who asked "Have you never read what David did?" in 2:25 and Who asked "Why are you so fearful?" in 4:41 and asked the demon possessed man "What is your name?" in 5:9. He asks, yet He seeks no enlightenment.

      On the other hand, this is the One from the right hand of the One Who came searching for Adam and asked "Adam, where are you?" He asks us things in our hearts in the creaking of the morning floors to get us to moan along with Him.

31 But His disciples said to Him, "You see the multitude thronging You, and You say, 'Who touched Me?' " 32 And He looked around to see her who had done this thing. "Jesus, why didn't You let her go unnoticed? Why didn't You just let her be healed and then just keep walking? What is it about You Jesus that turns around and makes people look at this woman that didn't want to be looked at? Certainly Jesus is not going to have such an ego that He wants to bring attention to this woman, is He?" Bringing attention to the woman He brings attention to Himself. Because if He did not heal her and the issue of blood did not dry up, there's nothing to talk about. But if He did heal her, and if she was healed that very hour, then there's much to talk about. And we find all of a sudden the reason that Jesus is pointing this woman out is so everyone can know something did happen.

33 But the woman, fearing In both of these episodes we find fear (verse 33 and 36). Fear pervades our lives, it seems. I wonder why?[104]

We've been told of disciples that were "fearful" (4:41), and townspeople who are fearful (5:15) and now we find two more people who are quite afraid and we see that in this Gospel of Mark our Savior wishes for His followers to be fearless.

and trembling,[105] why? She broke the law.

knowing what had happened to her, came and fell down before Him and told Him the whole truth. "Here's my story." What a comfort to find somebody that wants to hear your story. **34 And He said to her, "Daughter,** I think we can agree that Jesus is a man of about 32 years of age. He speaks to a woman who has been bleeding for 12 years. She is probably at least His age and He says **daughter.** So maybe we should remind all of us that when you find that pastoral figure in your life it changes your relationship. "No, Pastor Bill, I want a pastor that I can think of as my homeboy, and…"

5:35-43[106]

36 As soon as Jesus heard the word that was spoken, He said to the ruler of the synagogue, "Do not be afraid; only believe." Implying that the little girl would be healed.[107]

38 Then He came to the house of the ruler of the synagogue, and saw [7]a tumult and those who wept and wailed loudly. There is some talk

---

[104]One thing is certain: our habits are doing us no favors concerning our fears. McMaster University in Ontario, Canada conducted some research and found that "young adults who spend excessive time using the internet and social media are more likely to suffer from anxiety, inattention, depression, impulsiveness, and ADHD;" "Caught in the Web" *The American Legion Magazine, July 2017* ; Vol 183, No. 1, page 17.

[105]Used only here in Mark and used only in this account in Luke. Another textual reason for believing Mark was the original of the three Synoptic Gospels.

[106]More to be found in my commentary on Matthew (9:23-26).

[107]Confirmed in Luke.

[7]an uproar

that there were professional mourners to set the tone properly for the passing of life, but we'd have to take that on faith here as we're not told.[108]

40 And they ridiculed Him. But when He had put them all outside, Sometimes Jesus will just come sauntering on into our life and say, "I actually can take care of that for you. I don't need you to do that." "But, but, but Jesus! This is how I get my value! I feel valuable being here mourning." And Jesus says, "I'm not here to help you feel that way. I'm here to heal people and make them whole, and if that means that you have to find something else to do with your time besides mourning or farming pigs, then that's what it means."

You know, some folks just hope Jesus is something that gets added to some other things in our lives. In the story in the first half of this chapter it was "We don't wish to lose our pigs." In this story it's, "We don't wish to be underappreciated" (v. 40). Jesus once again shows that He is not interested in sharing the attention. The woman who was healed drew attention to Jesus through her healing and this young lady is going to have something done for her, in like manner, without everybody's help…except for Jesus. "If you try to put anything in the middle of the place that was originally made for God, it is going to be too small. It is going to rattle around in there."[109]

He took the father and the mother of the child, so much for the idea that the woman healed of the issue of blood was the **mother of the child.**

and those who were with Him, and entered where the child was lying. 41 Then He took the child by the hand, He never went to a funeral where the person actually got buried. This, by the way, is the second time He touches a lady's hand to heal her. Peter's mother-in-law being the first and this. **and said to her, "Talitha, cumi," which is translated, "Little girl, I say to you, arise."**

---

[108]Even if they were not wealthy enough for this "luxury" there may have been cultural expectation that some show up for their neighbor or friend to also set the adequate ambiance of grief.
[109]Timothy Keller *The Freedom of Self-Forgetfulness* (Farington, UK: Timothy Keller, 2012), 15.

Touching a corpse made Jesus ritually unclean, but this was of no consequence to him. Mark and the oral tradition before him valued and preserved the Aramaic words Jesus used on this momentous occasion. Four instances of this are in Mark (also 7:34; 14:36; 15:34), more than in any other Gospel and something that may indicate the primitiveness of Mark. Since the return from the Babylonian exile, Aramaic had been the language of the common people in Palestine. [110]

42 Immediately the girl arose and walked, for she was twelve years of age. There's something to this. Herein lies the only time Mark mentions the duration of one's suffering (verse 25) and the only time Mark mentions a person's age[111]…and they're the same. I'm just not sure what the significance is. Mark is, after all, the most frequent mentioner of the number 12 in the New Testament.[112] **And they were overcome with great amazement. 43 But He commanded them strictly that no one should know it, and said that something should be given her to eat.** Once again, back in the Promised Land, He commands them to hush.

---

[110] James A. Brooks, *Mark*, vol. 23, The New American Commentary (Nashville: Broadman & Holman Publishers, 1991), 95.
[111] Carson, 2019-2020.
[112] "G1427 - dōdeka - Strong's Greek Lexicon (KJV)." Blue Letter Bible. Web. 26 Jun, 2017.
<https://www.blueletterbible.org//lang/lexicon/lexicon.cfm?Strongs=G1427&t=KJV>.

Chapter 6

6:1

Then He went out from there and came to His own country, and His disciples followed Him. This seems completely unnecessary to say this. Why not just say "and His disciples went too?" **Follow**ing is a theme being continuing from 1:18, 2:14, and it need not be specific to **disciples**—although they are to be marked by both a patient Jesus Who allows them to be with Him, and a commitment to go to the places where the outcome is not sure or predictable.

6:2-4

And when the Sabbath had come, He began to teach in the synagogue. And many hearing Him were astonished, saying, "Where did this Man get these things? Contextually, the **things** that He has been teaching. **And what wisdom is this which is given to Him, that such mighty works are performed by His hands!** Notice here that **wisdom** is not merely the articulation of words. The fact that his is the only time this word is used drives us to rely on the immediate context and it seems that they are acknowledging that Jesus is way ahead of His age in doing **mighty works.** If Mark is indeed casting forth Jesus as the ultimate replacement for Moses, then Moses' 80 year old **hands** bringing forth miracles is nothing compared to one less than half His age.

3 Is this not the carpenter, the Son of Mary, This was the equivalent to calling Jesus the illegitimate son of a whore.[113] **and brother of James, Joses, Judas, and Simon?** Much could be said here about how two books from our New Testament come from this group of brothers who yet disbelieve in Him. The end of chapter 3 tells us how they thought He was crazy. **And are not His sisters here with us?"** At least some of His family were still living in Nazareth. **So they were offended at Him.** When you read the Gospel of Luke (specifically 4:23), you

---

[113]Hughes, 130.

come away a profound understanding of how little Mark says about these folks other than they "stumbled over Jesus" and their lack of faith. **4 But Jesus said to them, "A prophet is not without honor except in his own country…**[114]

6:5-6

Now He could do no mighty work This term is used here for the 2nd time in this passage and although it is two words in the English, it is one word in the Greek from which we get our term "dynamite." Now, Mark speaks of this situation pitting the Israel of the Old Testament against the Israel of the New Testament (This does seem, once again, to be the reason for this passage in this book). and we see there is precious little difference:

> *Psalm 78:40-42 How often they provoked Him in the wilderness, And **grieved Him** in the desert! 41 Yes, again and again they tempted God, **And limited the Holy One of Israel**. 42 They did not remember **His power**: The day when He redeemed them from the enemy,*

there, except that He laid His hands on a few sick people and healed them. One thing is certain: healing **a few sick people** was not what Mark had in mind when He described the **mighty work** that could have been done if these folks weren't so full of **unbelief. 6 And He marveled** This appears to be a much less emotional term than "astonished" or "shocked" in 6:2, but why is Jesus "wondering" or "marveling?" Maybe we should be shocked that Jesus is marveling? Maybe the fact that He knows all things and all possible outcomes of all things and yet He can be emotionally affected should…affect us.

What is it that causes the Very Son of Man to marvel? Is it the wickedness of the Nazarenes? Is it the lack of technological development or vocational laziness or zeal and pride in one's work

---

[114]Here's a word that has me wondering. It is used only in this passage, and only in this same passage in Matthew and Luke. So what is the likelihood that Jesus only used this word here? Not high, in my opinion. It must be that if Mark is the most original and earliest of the Gospels that he also got this information from another source. Again, what are the odds that Mark only uses the word in this passage and that the words are his original words? Not high in my estimation.

displayed in Nazareth? They don't have God's attention in this passage. **their unbelief.** We make Heaven rock back on their heels and tap their elbows, scratch their heads, and stroke their chins when we see the **mighty work**s of God done in other parts of His world and in other parts of history, and we continue, mysteriously in **unbelief.** What a terrible thing! What awful thing "to amaze God with one's unbelief!"[115]

Now, what does their **unbelief** have to do with Jesus' inability to **do mighty work**s? How did Capernaum exercise their faith that Jesus was the Son of Man or the Man sent from God? How did they show they believed that Jesus was a great prophet and able to do more of these miracles and **mighty work**s? They did so by bringing people to Him. Take another look at 1:33-37, 2:1-2, 3:7-8, 3:19b-20, 4:1-2, 5:21-24 for a reminder. So the only way we can show our belief and await **mighty work**s that Christ desires to do…would do…is when we bring them to Him.

Then He went about the villages in a circuit, teaching. Same **villages** as in the morning of Jesus' great prayer in 1:38.

6:7-11[116]

7 And He called the twelve to Himself, the **twelve** of 3:13-19 and we find out there that He "appointed them that they might be with Him and that He might send them." Well, all this time now they have been "with Him" and now it is time to "send them." There is always both a devotional and practical side to our walks with God. Maybe it would be better said this way…as it applies to our relationship with the Lord, there is always a lover's function, and a servant's function. As it relates to "feeling close to Jesus," we should be shocked when people are not getting around Him in the assembly studying the Word. The Scripture is the only offensive weapon (Ephesians 6:17), and folks want to be around it "only when necessary." **and began to send them out two by two,** At this point, we get a good idea of why verses 14-29 are even in the book of Mark. It must be that this is when Jesus is causing some real issues in

---

[115]Hughes, 132.
[116]Much more elaboration in my commentary on Matthew (10:6-42).

the palace of Herod in Galilee.[117] Really, verses 17-29 exist to explain verses 14-16. We know this was occurring while the disciples were sent out because in 6:30 they return and retreat in order to report to the Lord.

Again, Mark is stressing the difference between Moses and the children of Israel and Jehovah and Jesus with the disciples as the beginning of a New Covenant and New Israel. They conquer through preaching and demon destruction rather than through destroying cities and killing families: Holy Spirit power and a demand for repentance anticipating the arrival of the King.

and gave them power over unclean spirits. The implication is that He was sending them out to have power over **unclean spirits.** Both Matthew and Luke speak of His sending them out to preach, and verse 12 seems to indicate that we are to assume that here as well.

8 He commanded them to take nothing for the journey except a staff—no bag, no bread, no copper in their money belts—this is a rather humorous word earlier translated as "girdle" in 1:6. **9 but to wear sandals, and not to put on two tunics.** Maybe I am missing something of Old Testament significance here (all though I don't think so as will be seen in the work under verse 11), but we at least know how freeing it can be to be free from baggage, and how faith building it can be to depend on the Lord for extra clothing, and provisions. Hughes says it right: "The English Church of the 18th and 19th centuries was scandalized by fat country parsons who were authorities on hunting dogs and the vintages in their cellars. True Christianity, world-changing Christianity, is not comfortable."[118] By the way, there is a curious absence of Paul's tent-making perspective. This reflects a real urgency and lack of time for clientele building.

While we would say the overall inclusion of this body of writing is to show the Moses/Jesus comparison, we would say that this "I've been rejected now you shall be rejected" idea is why this account is included here.

---

[117]This is not Herod the great who sought to kill Jesus, but rather the Herod who tried Jesus in Luke and died of worms in Acts.
[118]Hughes, 134.

10 Also He said to them, "In whatever place you enter a house, stay there till you depart from that place. "be content, and don't jockey for a better place to stay." You're there for a reason and you don't need a reputation of getting sidetracked by better offers. You're about your Father's business. Don't get a reputation for 100 different things. Be known as disciple-makers and repentance preachers.

11 And whoever will not receive you nor hear you, when you depart from there, shake off the dust under your feet as a testimony against them. As if to say, none of me shall stay with you, and none of you shall stay with me. There is a clear separation that takes place when somebody stands against your Lord. We live consistent lives and show proportional pleadings to the benevolence of the prospective seeker, but when we have gone and returned from a Gospel witness…it is they who must make a decision, and that decision, verse 12, is to repent.

Assuredly,[2] I say to you, it will be more tolerable for Sodom and Gomorrah in the day of judgment than for that city!" You see the footnote from the NKJV after **assuredly.** I am disposed to believe that it belongs in the Scripture. However, the ESV, the ASV, the NASB (1995), the NRSV, the HCSB, the NET Bible, the ISV, and the RSV, the Darby, and the Douay-Rheims are all without it.

All of these same versions have agreement with the NKJV (and the KJV) on Matthew's version (10:14-15) and Luke's version (10:11-12) which contain this very phrase. Basically, the newer translations would say that Mark's copyist (since Mark is deemed the first Gospel by so many they must say it was added by a copyist some time after the writing) added it to be uniform with Matthew's and Luke's account.

Probably, the reason we believe it to be original[119] is because it provides a very natural contextual explanation for why two men went

---

[2]NU omits the rest of v. 11.

[119]It seems prudent here to understand that translations come, in part, from Greek Texts, which come from Greek manuscripts. Getting 25 different accounts of what occurred into a singular account (dropping weird variances) and then putting the singular account into legal language that is both acceptable and concise before the

into a singular home of a particular city—relying on that home for all levels of hospitality until the time when they would depart and leave it for eventual judgment:[120] Sodom of Genesis 19 endured quite the same issue. That is, two men came with nothing but the clothes on their backs and stayed in one home only to rescue some and leave with them, the city burning behind.

Perhaps, though, we should take into serious consideration the awfulness of the promise that **Sodom** would have it easier than these cities in Israel in the **Day of Judgment!** This **Sodom** of mob violence[121] that was incited to rape angels![122] An awful offense it is for anybody to be less than hospitable to anybody—yet more awful indeed it is for one to be less than hospitable to Christ or His extension, the apostles. What an awful **day** indeed to face the very God of Heaven in His glorified form when you see He was in your grasp. He knocked on your door. He offered reconciliation with God…but none was gained.

6:12-13

So they went out and preached that people should repent. Jesus was the first to preach this them (1:14-15),[123] and he is the first one to **preach** while "casting out devils" (1:39; 6:13). So at this point we want to stress how these disciples are not auxiliary (or extras) ministries to

---

judge is about what we're discussing here: Gather manuscripts; Drop the weirdities; Translate into language of choice.
    There are more at stake here than simple Greek manuscripts. There are ancient translations, lexicons, and early church fathers that also bear record as to whether a reading is original; William Grady *Final Authority* ( ), .

[120]In these cities' cases, it took place around A.D. 70. See my commentary on Matthew 10:23 for more on this.

[121]We do some awful things with a mob we would never do: http://www.cnn.com/2012/05/24/justice/famu-hazing-documents/index.html?hpt=hp_c2 [accessed July 16, 2017].

[122]This article is offensive to the soft-skinned, but I think it helps a lot of discussions continue: http://wouldjesusdiscriminate.org/biblical_evidence/sodom_and_gomorrah.html [accessed July 16, 2017]. Consider, for example, that there were women there in the mob, and that their lack of hospitality was a potential replay of the opening verses of Genesis 6.

[123]Yes, I am aware that John the Baptist preached it first, but this is not recorded in this Gospel.

Jesus; they're not even alternatives (or replacements) to Jesus. No, they are extensions of Jesus. He appointed them to be with Him, and then to send them. Jesus cannot be everywhere in the body, so He consecrates bodies of others for such a service. On the local church level your church has a shepherd over your own flock, and every ministry is therefore an extension of that shepherd and his pulpit.

13 And they cast out many demons, ᴾand anointed with oil many who were sick, and healed them. This is the word for our word "therapy." This is not as 6:5 or 16:18 as it contains the unusual detail of **anoint**ing **with oil.**

6:14-16

15 Others said, "It is Elijah." We discussed in chapter 1 (appendix 1) why John the Baptist and Jesus reminded some of **Elijah.**

And others said, "It is the Prophet, A certain reference to the expected prophet of Deuteronomy 18:18.

16 But when Herod heard, he said, "This is John, whom I beheaded; We don't know which news is more amazing: 1. That Jesus' ministry was so much like John's in His message of "repentance" (1:4; 1:14-15) as revealed in His disciples' ministry (6:12); 2. Or that John was so sublime in His conduct that He and Jesus were this similar! For example, I find it incredible that somebody who infuriated an adulteress so much had the favor of her shack-up—to the point where he protected him in his own prison (verse 19-20)! **he has been raised from the dead!"** and now what follows is an explanation of this. Incidentally, it would have been something if we had an ending to the story to give us hope that this troubling of the conscience caused him to repent. This account was so notable that somebody told Mark (or Mark's source). **Herod** is freakishly afraid of somebody coming back from the dead to haunt him, and we have no record of his repentance (nor do we have record of the five brethren of the rich man, Luke 16:19-31).[124] What a show of grace

---

ᴾJames 5:14

[124] As a matter of fact, Luke 23 tells us that he was the same man—a scorning, blaspheming, Christless man.

and mercy, though. There was time to repent even after his murder, it seems. **17 For Herod himself had sent and laid hold of John, and bound him in prison for the sake of Herodias, his brother Philip's wife;** as a matter of fact, it is said that he not only **married** his sister in law, but that she was already his niece.[125] **18 Because John had said to Herod, "It is not lawful for you to have your brother's wife."** He's right.

> *Leviticus 18:16 You shall not uncover **the nakedness of your brother's wife**; it is your brother's nakedness.*

> *Leviticus 20:21 If a man takes **his brother's wife**, it is an unclean thing. He has uncovered his brother's nakedness. They shall be childless.*

One has to really take note of a couple of things concerning this exchange:

1. <u>John the Baptist changed his message for nobody.</u> Perhaps John found an audience with Herod in his palace or 2nd hand through somebody else. Perhaps Herod came to take part in this national phenomenon called "John's baptism."
    Having known the possible cost of preaching such a message, he still preached the message. What indeed does it cost a man to tell someone God's demands upon their life? John yearned for a nation, ready for a king and His kingdom. It's not like loose living profited the nation. God was not interested in bringing His kingdom to a godless people so the angst in John is not just that the people are offending God, but that the godless people were suffering from their own devices. Rome was in charge because they were a stubborn people.
    On a very personal level with Herod, John is forced with staying true to his conscience. In other words, when he looked at a man with great influence and had the opportunity to tweak his message, he rather addressed the man as a mere member of the congregation to which he was assigned. Some have said that Joseph was a man who "lost his coat but kept his character" and I

---

[125] Hughes, 137.

would say that John was a man who "lost his head, but kept his conscience."
2. <u>John assumed Moses' law was morally binding on everyone</u>…even non Jews. Herod was not a Jew. At best, he was a half Jew. In other words, John was not sympathetic to the person who was always trying to talk their way out of obedience to God by specializing in what verses didn't apply to them—not because they sought the heart of God outside of legalism, but because they sought the pleasures of this condemned world through antinomianism.

19 Therefore Herodias held it against him and wanted to kill him, but she could not; 20 for Herod feared John, This is marvelous because it reminds us of how awful goodness really is: "truth that sets us free first makes us miserable."[126] **knowing that he was a just and holy man,** There is nothing quite as stellar as one who is guided by an authority higher than him or herself. Those who have accused the Christian of needing God as a crutch should consider whether one Who submits to a Sovereign is leaning on anything? Rather, I say He stands on everything.

and he protected him. And when he heard him, he did many things,[127] like what? Because he didn't actually repent and kick the old girl back to her real husband. So what **many things** did he do? Like instead of getting married to the woman he slept with he gave to the orphanage fund?

and heard him gladly. Everyone likes a short diet of "tell it like it is." This is not spiritual. Everybody likes a man who keeps from profanity while eloquently making a case for a cause. This is not spiritual. Everybody likes a polished statesman or a sideshow loon or a congenial opponent or a diplomatic and friendly foe…but that doesn't mean anything has changed. I would say that there are a good many people who leave preaching services, and do not change. They love feeling stirred, but they don't ever repent.

---

[126]Hughes, 138-139.
[127]The NIV has an unfortunate translation here of "greatly puzzled."

22 And when Herodias' daughter herself came in and danced, and pleased Herod and those who sat with him, Let's talk about what we don't <u>know</u>: 1. We don't <u>know</u> that this scenario was planned by the wicked **Herodias;** 2. We don't <u>know</u> how old this stepdaughter of Herod's is; 3. We don't <u>know</u> the type of **dance** she was dancing; 4. We don't <u>know</u> that there was anything sexual in the so called "pleasure" in the **king and those who sat with him** (this word is used sparingly, but it is used in many common ways in the New Testament and no time is the context demanding a sensual understanding; it could have been an acrobatic dance or something—the point is that the possible perversion is not the point of the passage or it would be obvious).

However, we should be suspect that the king's stepdaughter is dancing for the evening's entertainment. We should not suspect that a bunch of drunks merely admired her feminine qualities. Oh, no. A godless man who would bed his own niece would probably have no issues falling for a stepdaughter. And so I ask…who is supposed to teach your daughter to act feminine? Who is supposed to teach your daughter what a godly young lady does?

Where did this girl learn to be so god-awful immoral—enough to entice her stepfather and his drunken friends; enough to ask for the head of a preacher on a platter (it was, after all, not mama's idea to put it on the platter; 6:24-25). Was it with her friends or was it from her mother or was it from her palace life?

6:30-31[128]

31 And He said to them,[129] **"Come aside by yourselves to a deserted place and rest a while." For there were many coming and going, and they did not even have time to eat.** This is the second time we find this said of Jesus and His disciples (3:20).

---

[128]Specifically near Passover (John 6:4), the 2nd of 3 obvious Passovers in the life of Jesus, and the 3rd of perhaps four mentioned by John (3 of them being explicitly referenced). This would of necessity (given the instructions of Moses), require that the greater body of these folks were men; or less, that very few of these men brought their women and children.
[129]We find out that it was news of Herod's quaking that caused Jesus to depart like this; see my commentary on Matthew (14:13-21).

6:32

So they departed to a deserted place in the boat by themselves. So I believe there's a big deal here with the baskets to be found at the end of this episode. For who? Well, if it's for the multitude, Jesus failed in every way, because he consistently avoids the multitude in this book of Mark. If this was to influence them more towards following Him, then He failed them in every way as He fled them at each turn.

I believe the message was for the disciples, and here's why: 1. This passage begins with exhausted disciples; 2. The problem and its resolution continues with the disciples; 3. The next episode begins with the disciples; 4. The Everything in the book of Mark, it seems, is done for the disciples (Mark 2:15; 2:23; 3:7-9; 4:33-36; 6:1).

Having said all of that, it seems that this miracle has something to do with the baskets primarily, and secondarily it has something to do with the disciples.

6:33-37

But the multitudes saw them departing, and many knew Him it looked like His boat? **and ran there on foot from all the cities.** These are the cities no doubt referenced (at least, in part) in 1:38.

34…they were like sheep not having a shepherd. This is found often in the Old Testament[130] as a figure of speech for a flock without direction (or in this context of a coming kingdom…"a nation without a king") and carries forth Jesus' greatest concern: His people need a kingdom but they will receive no Heavenly King.[131] Given the Numbers 27:17 connection, it should be obvious to the reader that Jesus is again superior to this Moses—ensuring he remained sinless and thus arranged for His continued ministry after resurrection…multiplied by His disciples, enabled by His Spirit.

---

[130] Num. 27:17; 1 Kin. 22:17; 2 Chr. 18:16; Zech. 10:2
[131] John's version of this episode makes it clear they would have one of their own making.

37 But He answered and said to them, "You give them something to eat." In verse 37 He gives them an absolutely impossible task. You think Jesus needed to count the people? The One who spoke the world into existence is about to speak fish and bread into existence. He didn't need anyone's help counting the people and He also didn't need anyone to count the money in the purse. So if that's true, why is He giving the disciples something they can't do? The lesson must be for them. We find out later that 5000 men are counted. What if only twice that number were in the crowd (with the women and children mentioned in Matthew)? Why would He give them a command that they cannot do, so that 10,000 people can learn? No. They wouldn't have known what was being said up there.

And they[132] said to Him, "Shall we go and buy two hundred denarii worth of bread and give them something to eat?" This is incredibly like "Moses and the prophets"[133] in that whatever they have may not be enough to feed their respective flocks. Jesus is here and now demonstrating that He can, by Himself, access the treasuries of creation. Is Judas the bag carrier (John 6)? Is this 200 days' wage (Matthew 20:1-14)? The average family income for Hickory, NC in 2015 is just above $52,000. This means, by today's standard, the disciples were saying "$35,000 is not enough to feed all these folks in the nearby villages (verse 36)."[134] If this isn't what they had in the bag after counting (or asking Judas), then it seems pretty arbitrary.

6:38-40

But He said to them, "How many loaves do you have? Go and see." And when they John's Gospel says it's Andrew.

40 So they sat down in ranks, in hundreds and in fifties. Let's say they sat down in groups of fifty within the groups of hundred, and let's

---

[132]Specifically, Philip (John 6:5).
[133]Num. 11:13, 22; 2 Kin. 4:43; the desert place certainly reminds us of the wilderness and the manna of Moses' day. John confirms this was the real interpretation of this miracle from a gospel-harmony perspective.
[134]http://www.deptofnumbers.com/income/north-carolina/hickory/ [accessed 7/24/17].

say there really were just 10,000 people in attendance, how many groups of 100 is that? 100. Don't you think it was an extra bit of work to collect up all the scraps? They didn't have to do that. What's the point of doing that?

"To prove that we shouldn't waste our food!"

Nonsense.

6:41-43

43 And they took up twelve baskets full of fragments and of the fish. Here is a hint that this is for the disciples as there are twelve baskets remaining and there are twelve disciples. So, perhaps this is why He uses what they have. So that He can share the reward of His feeding the multitude.

Jesus has a basket for every one of them and He provided them the fish and the bread to start it off with. You see, they have five loaves and two fish. He gives disciples the wherewithal to find the fish and bread, and then asks for it back, to bring them an ultimate reward. Let me say that again. God is the ultimate broker. A normal broker will take things that you provide, and try to get something back for you, and get a fee. God is much better than that. He gives you the wherewithal to find precious little. It seems like a letdown. And then He lets you down again and tells you to do something impossible with what you barely found. And He asks for it anyway. And then He says, "Here's your basket." If this were a "here and now" sort of promise, then the next episode is a complete let down…

6:45-46

Immediately He made His disciples get into the boat and go before Him to the other side, to Bethsaida, while He sent the multitude away. How many disciples were there? 12. How many baskets? 12. Do you suppose that every one of them took their basket and got into the ship? They are about to see a crazy storm in the following verses. Now are you trying to tell me that they went through all that trouble to take their baskets into a ship so it could get rained on? And they got fish and soggy bread in twelve baskets on a ship? Probably not. This is a lesson of the ultimate broker broadcasting for us that each one of us, with our meager investments into the lives of others, will get a wonderfully equal share with our community of workers in Christ's kingdom.

Let's respect, though, the fact that Mark is in the middle of an argument about this New Moses being so much better than what we have seen so far. When the reader thought of Moses they thought of powerless living under the law and when they thought of Christ they thought of "new wine" (Mark 2) living under the law of Christ. The reality is that this New Moses is interested in reminding us that if we're not careful, we'll follow Jesus because we like His boat and His tricks and His food and His show, but at the end of it all…we're still hungry if we don't follow the Shepherd.

Immediately as is Mark's custom, he lets us see the efficiency of Jesus. The baskets are barely counted before **He made His disciples get into the boat** What would they have preferred to do? They never got their retreat. They could have had one now, and the reason we know this is because Jesus finds time alone in the next verse to retreat for prayer. So the reason **He made** them get into the boat is because they must go, and they would not go of their own choice. May I just stop here and say that although we are talking about the disciples, we should find what Jesus is doing as an overflow of the character of His Father, yes, but of the Holy Spirit Who drove Him into the wilderness in 1:12. After baptism (one of the Baptist church ordinances), and after the Lord's Supper preview here (the other Baptist church ordinance)—both of which are foretastes of glory and the quintessential experience of Heaven on earth—Heavenly influence presses the participant into times of both Satanic (chapter 1) and natural (here) conflict.

So, their getting into the boat is Jesus' idea, and their finding the storm is a result of their obedience. All of the discomfort they are going to experience is primarily because of their obedience…and secondarily because of their hard hearts (verse 52). They simply would have not known the state of their hearts if they would have felt close to Jesus the entire time. He was, after all, moved with compassion just a few hours earlier (6:34). Did they know they looked nothing like Jesus? Everything is easy and cliché and Christianese…until we're made to get into the boat.

46 And when He had sent them away, He departed to the mountain to pray. This is another similarity to chapter 1. There, he is overcome with the multitude and gets up before dawn while here **He sent the multitude away** to get His time with the Father.

6:47-48

Now when evening came, Mark 13:35 shows the reader that **evening** is the first of the night watches. We know it is relatively late because the previous passage says that the time of day is why they fed the multitude to begin with. We also know that if it ended at around 9pm and that Jesus came walking in the "fourth watch" (verse 48), then Jesus "saw them" (verse 48) **in the middle of the sea;** for hours before He left **the land. 48 Then He saw them straining at rowing,** So just as the Lord Jesus lovingly stacked the deck against them in 6:37 with less-than-necessary resources, He "puts more on them than they can bear" in the storm.[135]

for the wind was against them. Now about the fourth watch of the night Just like the man in his 11th hour (Matthew 20:1-14), and the family of Lazarus (John 11), these disciples realized Jesus is never late.

walking on the sea, and would have passed them by. In typical Jesus form (Luke 24:28). What is this about Jesus? He acts as though He doesn't see you? Well what's clear is that Jesus did in fact see them **straining at rowing.** He always sees us straining.

He saw them straining at rowing, We become great appreciators of all of God's character through Jesus. Perhaps this is why we love Jesus (aside from His death on the cross): He shows us exactly what God is like. Perhaps this is why we are confused about Jesus: He shows us the God we weren't expecting:

---

[135] See more on this in my commentary on the Minor Prophets (Hosea 13).

It seems that we are dealing with "a Jesus" (and therefore, "a God") who doesn't do anything, except watch us. Truly, He does "watch" us (Proverbs 15:3). And if this is all He does, well, we understand the disillusionment in popular culture.

Perhaps another aspect of God that is shown to us is **His waiting.** We pointed out that He waited from "evening" until **the fourth watch.** Indeed, He does wait, and He is waiting now (1 Peter 3:20). And if all He does is w**atch** and wait, we understand the frustration the disciples may have faced wondering where the storm whisperer had gone!

Perhaps we suppose this God is still distantly waiting and watching and sometimes wandering about. He does, in fact, make His rounds (2 Chronicles 16:9; Jeremiah 23:23-24), and it can seem as though He is otherwise distracted and not so much able.

We may suspect that He simply whispers through His Word. These are anecdotal and wonderful and sometimes they are comforting…if we only forget that often He makes so many promises that we don't seem to see fulfilled from this very same Word of God. We know He "guides our steps" in His Word (Psalm 119:133), and we know that He provides instruction (2 Timothy 3:16), and yet we are painfully aware that we either have a God that is "uninterested" or "unable."

So…what is He doing with all of His time? John 5:17 says God has been working since Genesis 2:1. God is working. This *(ergozomai)* is the word we get for our modern English word "ergonomics".[136] Presumably, we are still on God's Seventh Day[137] and God's still working on His Sabbath. It must mean, then, that Jesus sees that as a prooftext for His Own work on the Sabbath.[138]

---

[136] "G2038 - ergazomai - Strong's Greek Lexicon (KJV)." Blue Letter Bible. Web. 15 Aug, 2017. <https://www.blueletterbible.org//lang/lexicon/lexicon.cfm?Strongs=G2038&t=KJV>.

[137] There must then be a Sabbath work that is Holy and not anti-Mosaic (Mark 2:23-27) as God would not transgress His Own Law. Rather, His Law is an outgrowth of His character.

[138] Genesis 2:1 gives no ending that parallels that of the first six days ("evening and morning") and so it seems reasonable that the 7th day has not ended.

Philippians 1:6-27 gives us the noun form of this verb when it says that God promises to complete the work He started. If we perform work, It is God's working! What is the work He completes? Gospel work! When we have Gospel influence in our lives it is the rulership and the redemption of God in our behavior (Philippians 1:27), and it is God who is working that in us.

It is therefore no marvel to us that God in Christ Who brings us news of a kingdom and a suffering Savior is using a methodology in their lives. Hey! Listen…if Jesus controls the winds from the boat! He controls the winds from mountain!

> *Romans 8:28-29 All things work together for good to them that love God; to them who are the called according to His purpose. For Whom He did foreknow, He also did predestinate to be conformed* ***to the image of His Son.***

The word for "worked" is the word where we get our word "synergy"[139] or "working together." Since it is God as the "He" in verse 29, it is God behind the "synergizing" of "all things" in verse 28. He started it, He finishes it. What is God doing? He is taking the hospital bed you're lying in, the loved one Who has cancer, or the aging parent who is declining, or a traumatic experience or accident and He is moving it in a way that it makes somebody more complete in Gospel holiness and Christ likeness. He is not watching it take place. He is not aloof. He is not wandering about. He is not simply whispering niceties. He is not whimpering about His inability. He is not simply waiting for a turn. No! He is working. The one who calmed the storm from the boat could have done it from the mountain, you know?

---

[139] "G4903 - synergeō - Strong's Greek Lexicon (KJV)." Blue Letter Bible. Web. 15 Aug, 2017.
<https://www.blueletterbible.org//lang/lexicon/lexicon.cfm?Strongs=G4903&t=KJV>.

6:49-51

And when they saw Him walking on the sea, they supposed it was a ghost, Why? Because they weren't expecting Jesus to show up like He did when the winds were calm and something as "simple" as creating thousands of fish was needed [This, by the way, hasn't been done since creation week, and provides for us the second reference to day 5 of that week in first identifying the "heavens" He spreads in Mark 4 (Job 9:6), and then also showing us the first (and most recent) creation of fish to fill the seas]. And this is exactly what is meant when it speaks of their "hard hearts" and undiscerning of the presence of God (verse 52 speaks of the One Who masters the seas in filling them also masters the seas in controlling them).[140] **and cried out;** Now that's a lot of fear. (verse 50). Exactly how loud was He speaking to be heard above the winds.

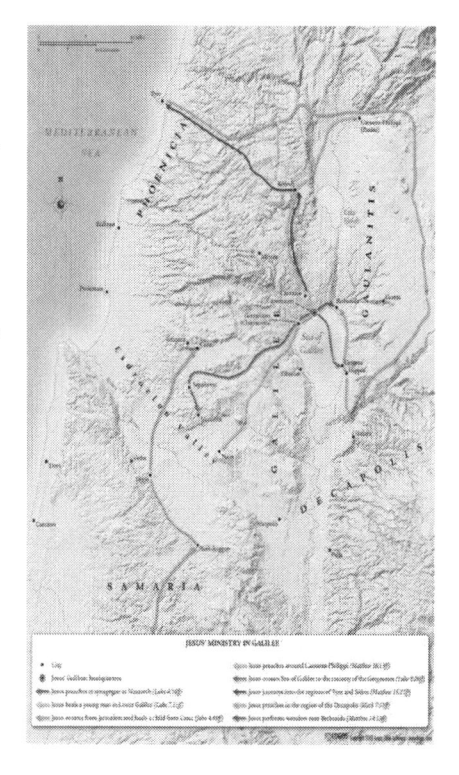

51 Then He went up into the boat to them, and the wind ceased. Interesting that this is only the 2nd time in the book that this word for **ceased** is used and it was when the **wind** last **ceased** (Mark 4:39).

It is at this point that we realize that the Holy Spirit gave us the episode at the end of chapter 4 and this very same episode as helpers to identify this Jesus as the One Who appeared to Job out of the whirlwind (Job 9:6; 38:1). This is, perhaps, even more greatly accentuated when we realize that neither the miracle of suddenly landing on the shore (as in John's version) or the walking on the water (as in Matthew's version) are the focus at all. If they were the focus, all of these versions of this

---

[140]Hughes, 155.

great miracle would have been myopic. Instead, they're synoptic and provide only enough similarity to tell us that it is not Peter's faith or nautical anomaly that are ever life's lesson, but the Christ of God is Who He says He is—the Jehovah and All-Powerful God of the Old Testament; our Creator and Our Sustainer and Our Life and Our Absolute Truth, and that anything short of an all-consuming fascination of this Man and an all-embracing assimilation of His character, and an all-investing reliance upon His redemptive work—resulting a wild-eyed worship and a death-defying, soul-wrenching quest to make His Name known among the nations—is horribly and utterly and devastatingly…disappointing.

This story also proves to be a cross section of human frailty. That is, it really did occur in the lives of these disciples, but it also occurs all the time and has always occurred—most specifically with the children of Israel (Psalm 107:27-30). Two seeming constants: man's weakness, and God's strength (as displayed in Christ; Isaiah 40:22-30)

And they were greatly amazed in themselves This may not seem like a major statement, but we should point out that this is the same word used by those accusing Jesus of being "crazy." They were, using the same word, "beside themselves." He didn't even speak to the wind and waves at this point. **beyond measure,**

6:53-56

the land of Gennesaret[141] and anchored there. See my commentary on Matthew (4:21-22) for coverage of these verses.

---

[141]There is also a plain of "Gennesaret" in which a second Bethsaida is found (John 12:21). Luke 9:10 gives the first Bethsaida in which the feeding of the 5000 occurred. There is no contradiction. Matthew 11:21 puts the "Bethsaida of Galilee" (John 12:21) in concert with towns which are clearly in Galilee. In other words, they went from Bethsaida (Luke 9:10) to Bethsaida of Galilee (Mark 6:45; John 12:21).

Chapter 7

We are now in the last year of Jesus' life. We know this because there are explicitely three Passovers in Jesus' public ministry (John 2, 6, and 18). He dies on the fourth one. John 5 may be another. In any case, if he was 30 when He began His public ministry (says Luke 3), and if the feeding of the 5000 found in the previous chapter comes after the 3rd of 4 Passovers (see John 6 and John's version of the feeding miracle), then we are in the last year of Jesus' life. This helps us see that out of Jesus' 33 years, we have 10 of Mark's 16 chapters covering the last 33rd of Jesus' life. Or, to say it this way, the last 60% of Mark's Gospel covers the last 3% of Jesus' life.

7:1[142]

Then the Pharisees and some of the scribes came together to Him, having come from Jerusalem. Jerusalem is nowhere around the Sea of Galilee. Its' about forty miles. It's forty miles of mountain. That's a lot of effort to harass Jesus. Forty miles the scribes and Pharisees which were of Jerusalem came.

7:2-5 (the complaint of the Pharisees & scribes)

4 ...And there are many other things which they have received and hold, like the washing of cups, pitchers, copper vessels, and couches. The later *Mishnah* included 35 pages on such things as these.[143] **5 Then the Pharisees and scribes asked Him, "Why do Your disciples not walk according to the tradition of the elders,** Perhaps these started out as simple safeguards, but at some point a zeal for the law led to building "hedges" or fences around the law.[144] If there were no law, it is doubtful that there would be any traditions.

7:6-13 (Jesus addresses the Pharisees & scribes)

---

[142]Matthew 15 has a version about this and is dealt more in my commentary on Matthew.
[143]Hughes, 160.
[144]Hughes, 159; here Hughes relays the hazard of spitting on any dirt on the Sabbath for fear you might scuff your sandal and be thus guilty of cultivating soil on the Sabbath.

He answered and said to them, "Well did Isaiah prophesy of you hypocrites, This is a very strange word in the Greek language. It means "stage player." They wanted to look like they were worshipping and they had a sort of kit ready for that. It was traditions. It was the way that they perceived, or they were perceived to others, as being right with God. How? Well, they couldn't obey God's law, or rather they didn't wish to do so, and so what did they do? They made laws they could perform that others could not. And so they started feeling very spiritual.

The scribes and Pharisees would never have said they didn't believe Moses. They would have never said, "We don't believe the prophets" (perhaps the Sadducees would have). It was the only Bible they had. The scribes and Pharisees never would they have said, "We don't believe the Bible." No. They would have said, "We make our living believing the Bible, copying the Bible, interpreting the Bible, writing the Bible in notebooks and giving them to you. We make our living with the Bible. How dare you tell us we don't believe the Bible." And yet, Jesus said that was just a mask. They only looked like they believed the Bible.

Apparently there was a lot of people in this day that said, "I believe the Bible." But when they were confronted with explicits in the Bible, they couldn't be found playing that part.

10 For Moses Interesting that Matthew records Jesus saying that "God commanded." Certainly He did as the one being quoted, but here Jesus said the Moses was the source. Which is it? God said it, and Moses wrote it down. This does, by the way confirm the general notion that Moses wrote Exodus.
said, 'Honor your father and your mother'; from Exodus 20 **and, 'He who curses father or mother, let him be put to death.'** from Exodus 21 & Leviticus 20:9.

11 But you say, 'If a man says to his father or mother, "Whatever profit you might have received from me is Corban"—' (that is, a gift to God), "I can't give it to you. Because it's a gift." That was another of their traditions.[145] They had this little racket worked out where if you didn't want your parents to be leeches on you in their older days, you would gift your property to the priest at the temple. And after your parents died, you and the priest would split it.[146] That's quite the arrangement.

12 then you no longer let him do anything for his father or his mother, 13 making the word of God of no effect "You've made it empty and vain." How? **through your tradition**. And then, and then somehow, somehow, here's how we know when a tradition has gone wrong: when it gets elevated to the point of the word of God and all of a sudden now the word of God is not being obeyed.

which you have handed down. And many such things you do." Jesus seems to be saying "your tradition would be bad enough if it weren't sanctioning the sloppy dismissing of God's commands.

7:14-16 (Jesus addresses the crowd)

When He had called all the multitude to Himself, This is the first time He's done this in the Gospel. Up until now, He has been only interested in calling the disciples while the mob simply found Him (and then He'd send them away). **He said to them, "Hear Me, everyone, and understand:** So much for confidentiality and "keeping things hush, hush." **15 There is nothing that enters a man from outside which can defile him;** Again, we're not talking about defilement like, "Oh you didn't wash your hands. Now you're going to get a virus." We're talking about ceremonial and traditional defilement. **16 If[6] anyone has ears to hear, let him hear!"** This statement, along with verse 18, leads me to believe that Jesus usually meant something deeper than simple surface meaning. Also, a good Jew would be confused here that perhaps Jesus is affirming one part of the law (defilement by bodily secretions) while denying the other parts (food and consumption)—both of which are found in Leviticus. Of course, Jesus is not only not denying the dietary

---

[145] Explained by Mark because his readers didn't know Hebrew.
[146] That last part is an assumption of mine. I don't know why they would have tried to protect their assets from their parents through this method.
[6] NU omits v. 16; as well as the hinder part of verse 8.

laws (but rather ceremonial washings), but He is also not speaking of bodily secretions as will be seen next.

7:17-23 (Jesus addresses the disciples)

When He had entered a house It seems that this could be the house that He had always stayed in given the time He had to go through the region and wind up in Capernaum (6:52-54). **away from the crowd,** Why were they so easy to leave? Perhaps we are in a little window here where they knew Jesus was far more interested in conveying truth than doing miracles. **His disciples asked Him concerning the parable. 18 So He said to them, "Are you thus without understanding also?** "You still don't get this." Now, what we're about to read is not as salient to the scribes and Pharisees (since Jesus didn't bother to talk about defilement at all with them). It's not even as intended for the "crowd" as it is for the disciples (otherwise He would have clarified it even more for the crowd, or at least entertained their confused questions so they could get further understanding).

19 because it does not enter his heart but his stomach, and is eliminated, [7]thus purifying all foods?" 20 And He said, "What comes out of a man, that defiles a man. 21 For from within, out of the heart of men, I said previously that Jesus wanted His disciples to get the crux of the matter. This doesn't mean that nobody but them had heart problems, for it was the heart of the accusers (7:1-6) that was the issue (7:6). Rather, He knew that only those who were His could find a heart issue treated…and it needed to be treated (4:15).

23 All these evil things come from within and defile a man." So, we see that all of the sins of mankind begin in the heart, and this is seen in Numbers 13:33-14:1 and echoed in Hebrews 3-4 as the "evil heart of unbelief."

So this passage is not a slam on religion more than a religion void of authority above the religion itself, nor is it a slam on tradition more than tradition that displaces the Bible. Paul gives a list in Romans

---

[7] NU sets off the final phrase as Mark's comment that Jesus has declared all foods clean.

3, and 1 Corinthians 6 and Galatians 5 and Ephesians 5 and 2 Timothy 2 that almost mirror Jesus' words here and—we might say—were greatly influenced by Jesus' words. The problem is the heart and has always been the heart (Jeremiah 17:9).

What cure, though, does Jesus give His audience? What cure does Mark relay for us? After all, in 6:52, the disciples hearts are hardened. In 8:17, the heart is still hardened. What indeed is the cure? To further complicate matters, Mark 12:30-33 says we must love God with this same hard heart, but how can we do this when we have hard hearts, particularly since we must do so to be in the kingdom (12:34)?

It is here where grace enters and we see that we must have a new heart and that we must die with our old heart to be raised with a new one which finds disgust with the blights of our sins which start in the heart and work their way out. Perhaps best said by Eric Geiger: "transformation is not about trying; it is about dying."[147] This required death is reflected in Mark 8:37.

7:24-25

From there He arose and went to the region of Tyre and Sidon.[148] And He entered a house and wanted no one to know it, but He could not The second of only two times in the Gospel of Mark where Jesus is seen to have inadequate power to accomplish something.[149] The first was when He **could not** do but a few mighty works (Mark 6:1-4). **be hidden.** This is an active verb.[150] He **could not** "hide."

We are saying that the Christ Who had been endued with power at His baptism **could not be hidden.**

We are saying that the Jesus Who resisted the temptation of Satan for 40 days **could not be hidden.**

---

[147]Ben Trueblood *Student Ministry that Matters, 3 Elements of a Healthy Student Ministry* (Nashville: B&H Publishing Group, 2016), xv.

[148]More can be found in my commentary on Matthew (15:21-28).

[149]Behind the "could" is the word we get our word for "dynamite."

[150] "Mark 7:1 (KJV) - Then came together unto him." Blue Letter Bible. Web. 29 Aug, 2017. <https://www.blueletterbible.org/kjv/mar/7/1/t_conc_964024>.

We're saying that the One Who came from God's Own Right Hand, the Son of Man, **could not be hidden.**

We're saying that the well-pleasing servant of Isaiah, the "well-pleasing Son" **could not be hidden.**

The One Who **could** cast out devils **could not be hidden.**

Jesus Who **could** heal leprosy **could not be hidden** (chapter 1).

He Who **could** heal the fever **could not be hidden** (chapter 1).

He **could** heal the palsy and **could not be hidden** (chapter 2).

He **could** invent the Sabbath Day and **could not** hide in a house in a city (chapter 2).

He **could** control the weather (chapters 4 and 6), and **could not** hide in a house.

He **could** control 2000 demons (chapter 5), and **could not** hide.

He **could** raise a dead girl (chapter 5), but **could not** hide.

He **could** stop a hemorrhage (chapter 5), but **could not** hide.

He **could** feed thousands—creating fish and bread on the spot (chapter 6), but **could not** hide.

Could not go unnoticed; **could not,** if He wanted to (which He did), remain secluded. As a more modern reading rightly says…"He could not escape notice."[151] While Luke has Jesus avoiding folks (Luke 4) and Jesus avoids kingship in John (John 6), Mark wants us to see something a little deeper. He cannot do what He does and still be able to hide. He can **not.**

---

[151] <u>New American Standard Bible: 1995 Update</u> (La Habra, CA: The Lockman Foundation, 1995), Mk 7:24.

He was unable to escape notice. He did not have the power to avoid being noticed. Jesus will be noticed. He will be noticed when He enters a town: streets, corners, houses, suburbs. It's not that He is actively seeking to not be ignored in this story. No, to the contrary…though He is actively seeking to "hide," He is passively being noticed. He put no effort into being noticed. It simply happened. It's His character; His virtue; His Spirit that will be noticed.

Humanly speaking, Jesus had his mind on a house in this region where He could find some rest. Think about it, He had to travel more than 40 miles to find this place on the Mediterranean coast to find reprieve from the multitude. **25 For a woman whose young daughter had an unclean spirit heard about Him,** who told her this man was in town? I don't know, but verse 32 tells us it happens at the next place as well, and all we're told is that people "recognized Him" (6:54).

7:26

The woman was a [9]Greek, a [1]Syro-Phoenician only time this is found in the New Testament **by birth,** It isn't plan B. God has always pursued Gentiles (widow of Zeraphath, from this same location; Job; Namaan; Ninevites).

and she kept [2]asking Him to cast the demon out of her daughter. The second d**aughter** brought to Jesus by a parent. The first was in chapter 5 (Jairus' daughter). This is, however, the first of two children inhabited by a d**emon** (the second being a boy with the fire and water in chapter 9).

7:27-28

But Jesus said to her, "Let the children be filled first, for it is not good to take the children's bread and throw it to the little dogs." This is not the same "dogs" which are banished from the New

---

[9] Gentile
[1] A Syrian of Phoenicia
[2] begging

Jerusalem; this is a different word and we don't know with what tone Jesus said it. Rather, this woman had a place in the house, but it was under the table, and all blessings that fall to her should be first offered to the children.

28 And she answered and said to Him, "Yes, Lord, She agrees with Jesus. Jesus does not argue and she will not argue with Him. Rather, she states further **yet even the little dogs under the table eat from the children's crumbs."** If she doesn't get fed directly because she is not the correct ethnicity or status or target, then she supposes she can at least get what the **children** refuse or mishandle.

7:29-30

30 And when she had come to her house, she found the demon gone out, and her daughter lying on the bed. Mark doesn't tell us anything about how we make these theological issues work. No talk about predestination or election or anything. Deal with it. Somebody who did not belong…now belongs.

7:31

Again, departing from the region of Tyre and Sidon, He came through the midst of the region of Decapolis to the Sea of Galilee. He skirted around the Sea to go through a particular region from which He was expelled two chapters earlier. What Jesus is about to experience from the "they" who bring the "deaf and dumb" man to Him and His succeeding fame with them is seemingly a direct result of the man with the Legion's work in chapter 5.

7:32-34

Then they brought to Him one this is the only Gospel that covers this episode. **who was deaf and had an impediment in his speech, and they begged Him to put His hand on him.** Why would they have thought this did anything? It's not like Jesus did this for the man in chapter 5. It seems like this was a sort of universal gesture for anybody that was respected as a religious leader who had the ability to bless (Mark 10:13). **33 And He took him aside from the multitude,** why did

Jesus do this? It's the only time He does so in this Gospel. Perhaps, in the spiritual sense (which we will prove later), this shows that a person must have an individual relationship with Jesus. Having one because the crowd does will not do. **and put His fingers in his ears,** This is really specific when all they asked was for Jesus to "place His hand on Him." **and He spat and touched his tongue.** Did Jesus spit on His fingers or on the man's face? This is a reasonable question since later Jesus spits on a man's eyes (8:23). **34 Then, looking up to heaven,** just like he did in the last chapter as He blessed the bread and fish. Do you suppose this is biblical? Why do we have "heads bowed" and "eyes closed?" Is there anybody who "bows his head" when He prays? Yes, a man ashamed of his weighty guilt did in Ezra 9:6, and a man ashamed in his unworthiness did in Luke 18:13-18. **He sighed,** Why is Jesus doing this? Is He angry or sad or disappointed or tired? It's the only time Jesus does this in the Gospels. It's a sort of groan. **and said to him, "Ephphatha," that is, "Be opened."** Once again, Mark is interpreting this for his Greek-speaking readers. Jesus was speaking Aramaic[152] and not Greek. This means, then, that there was an audience outside of the geography wherein this language was spoken.

7:35-37

Immediately his ears were opened, Just like Isaiah 35:5-6 said would happen. **and the impediment of his tongue was loosed,** Does this mean that his impediment wasn't related to his deafness but was rather an unrelated malady? **and he spoke plainly. 36 Then He commanded them that they should tell no one; but the more He commanded them, the more widely they proclaimed it.** Why? If this is the same location where he told the man with "Legion" to tell everybody? **37 And they were astonished beyond measure,** This happens nowhere else in this Gospel. **saying, "He has done all things well.** How do they know? What was it about the way Jesus handled this episode that led the multitude to believe He did everything **well?** How had Jesus proven Himself trustworthy in all matters of life.

---

[152] "G2188 - ephphatha - Strong's Greek Lexicon (KJV)." Blue Letter Bible. Web. 4 Sep, 2017.
<https://www.blueletterbible.org//lang/lexicon/lexicon.cfm?Strongs=G2188&t=KJV>.

1. Even if we have all these questions answered, it doesn't answer why this passage is here.
2. Even if we know all the passages from the Old Testament and how they contribute to this passage, it doesn't answer why this passage is here.
3. Even if we know how this relates to other New Testament passages, it doesn't tell us the author's intent for this passage.
4. Even if we have life lessons in this passage, it does not tell us the reason this passage is in here.

What is glaring is that we have three places up to this point that have mentioned one's ears (Mark 4:9; 4:23; 7:14-16). And then once after this passage we have one very sad castigation of these disciples (Mark 8:14-18).

In the mind of Jesus, then, there was little more frustrating or heartbreaking than having ears to hear, but not hearing. Clearly, in these four passages we are getting a foundation for this only other time we find "ears" that cannot hear. How sad to have the obvious potential to hear, but not being able to do so! How heartbreaking it was for Jesus to see those who were equipped to receive His Word, but not able to do so! How consternating it was to see ears on the heads of His hearers, but not seeing that they were taking it in or hearing in their subsequent conversations that they had learned a blasted thing!

We see, then, that we have a license…more than that…an expectation to see this miracle as teaching a spiritual principle rather than just displaying for us a literal miracle…although it was that. Here is a man who cannot hear and because he cannot hear…he cannot speak clearly. His life is publically shameful, and he is usually deemed demon-possessed (no doubt) and the Lord Jesus gives the man His undivided time. Why? To show us something magnificent…We don't have a nagging Jesus Who finds displeasure in people who don't meet the standard. Rather, we have a super mentor; a super coach; a hands-on teacher; a sympathetic Savior. More than that, gladly, He is God's Hand.

Does God have a standard that doesn't break and doesn't bend?

Yes.

Does God expect people to listen carefully and bend their ears to their Creator?

Yes.

Does mankind typically listen to their Creator like obedient children who know that He knows best and to do the opposite is s sure way to heartache at best, and damnation at worse?

No

But does God open ears to some so that they may hear?

Yes…He interferes with a stalwart resistance to listen. He intervenes with hearing enablement. He interrupts our stiff-necked intents. So, some notes about this man:

1. **Not every deaf man was healed.** There were many deaf people in other parts of the country this day who were not healed and this man was healed. We cannot come away from this story and say "We know from this miracle that God wants all men everywhere to hear." But we can say those who find themselves in His path today can find sublime enablement to hear His Words and to find new life.
2. **This deaf man was healed, humanly speaking, because somebody brought Him to Jesus and had a conversation with Him on behalf of their friend.** This man had no way to know what Jesus was saying or what Jesus could do without somebody guiding him. Somebody had to have pity on him. Somebody had to care that he was an outcast. Deaf people don't get all the inside jokes. Deaf people don't get all the information. Deaf people, even if they know sign language, have to communicate a little slower than the average rate of speech of those who communicate normally. The reality is that somebody had to get Him to Jesus.
3. **We hear because Jesus speaks and touches.** Everything that happens in life of any value is because Jesus speaks. When Jesus speaks, it contains power. All power is given to Him and when

He speaks, God speaks. A man hears because God speaks his hearing into existence. Often we talk about God "turning on the lights" or "opening our eyes", but here, the metaphor is that He speaks through our deafness and vibrates our spiritual eardrums. Think of it…all of the sudden, eternity pierces us because God wills it. He is involved. He touches us and we turn to Him in faith both individually (taking us apart from the crowd as He did this man) and strangely (as He spits on this man's tongue).

4. **Hearing men and women have loose tongues.** God gives those who know His Son a tongue to say so (Matthew 10:32-33; Romans 10:9-11; 1 Corinthians 12:3). Even though the man had his tongue loosed as a separate action from his restored hearing, he would have not been able speak clearly if he could not hear. When God speaks and we hear, we are able to speak so everyone else hears (Psalm 40:3; Psalm 51:13).

5. **The way He allows some to hear assures us He "does all things well."** If Jesus can handle something as gigantic as healing the ears of a deaf man—much less the spiritual ears and hard hearts of unsaved men—He can do all things, mundane to extreme, extremely well.

Chapter 8

8:1-3[153]

2 "I have compassion on the multitude, because they have now continued with Me three days and have nothing to eat. 3 And if I send them away hungry to their own houses, they will faint on the way; for some of them have come from afar." He didn't browbeat these poor planners like I might have done. In other words, He doesn't seize the opportunity to tell them why they're in the mess they're in. Jesus knew there would be a food shortage. He's not an idiot. Furthermore, we find out that He allowed them to follow Him through mountain paths for **three days** and backtracking, at this point, would not have helped. They would actually **faint** or die of exhaustion if they attempt to do so. Jesus, therefore, led people to the point where they had nothing. He could have produced more food on day one or two, but they must first consume their own meals. Jesus waited so they would have no food. At this point, there is no way anybody can steal God's glory. Jesus has achieved His maximum potential…giving God a chance to receive even more "glory".

"I have followed Jesus for what seems to be days and days….." Good…our first two days of resources need to pass. American Christianity has been incredibly resourced, and sometimes we think God is worthy of us so long as we can have our tax deduction and our political party…and really what we need is a few less resources. God will not do His work while we're stealing His glory.

8:4

Then His disciples answered Him, "How can one satisfy these people with bread here in the wilderness?"
Where will they get the resources to feed 4000? I would almost think Mark was making this up to teach us a lesson, but in 16:7-11 Jesus

---

[153]This is dealt with in more detail in my commentary on Matthew (15:32-38).

references both these miracles (the 4000 and the 5000). Somehow…it seems as though God blinded them.

8:5

He asked them, "How many loaves do you have?" Jesus answers a question with a question…again.

8:6-10

So He commanded the multitude to sit down on the ground. And He took the seven loaves and gave thanks, Once again showing us how to pray by giving us a "when" as in verse 7. **8 So they ate and were filled, and they took up seven large baskets and they took up seven large baskets** in the first miracle it was "coffins" but in this one, we are dealing with much larger baskets and so called **large baskets.** There are apparently large enough for a man to fit in (Acts 9:25).[154]

9 Now those who had eaten were about four thousand. Matthew says this is "besides women and children." Maybe Mark is trying to get the reader to identify with both Moses (who fed with both quail and manna) or Elisha (the woman with the son for one last meal, 2 Kings 4 and the school of prophets). In both feedings, we have well resourced disciples around those who planned poorly and asked stupid questions.

And He sent them away, 10 immediately got into the boat with His disciples, Here again, unless we know of a particular mission on His mind (which may be inconsequential to the point I'm about to make) He seems to have needed to get on the boat to be alone with His followers. **and came to the region of Dalmanutha.** Matthew says it was "the region of Magdala." Maybe so: 1. Maybe there was a change in the label between Mark's and Matthew's writing (least likely); 2. Maybe there were two names for it all along for all who knew about it; 3. Maybe there were two names for it all along for two different groups (the

---

[154]"G4711 - spyris - Strong's Greek Lexicon (KJV)." Blue Letter Bible. Web. 11 Sep, 2017.
<https://www.blueletterbible.org//lang/lexicon/lexicon.cfm?Strongs=G4711&t=KJV>.

Romans versus the Jews, perhaps—thus catering to their respective audiences).

8:11-13[155]

Then the Pharisees came out and began to dispute with Him, seeking from Him a sign from heaven, Interesting. In view of Matthew 24:31 one might wonder if that was Jesus' answer for their request of a sign from heaven, but then why didn't Mark make the connection (not calling it a "sign", 13:26). On the other hand, the fact that Matthew gives an exception clause—identifying the "sign of Jonah" as the **sign** for that "generation"—give good reason why He, in fact, calls the coming of the son of Man a "sign." **testing Him. 12 But He sighed deeply in His spirit,** This is a slightly different reaction than in healing of the deaf man—although the bottom line may be the same. **and said, "Why does this generation seek a sign? Assuredly, I say to you, no sign shall be given to this generation." 13 And He left them, and getting into the boat again, departed to the other side.** This is the second time He boards a boat in four verses and seemingly crosses again.

8:14

Now the disciples had forgotten to take bread, and they did not have more than one loaf with them in the boat. How did they do this? There were seven baskets full when they left the other side! I don't get it! This is ridiculous! I would have had a fit with these knuckleheads.

8:15

Then He charged them, saying, "Take heed, beware of the leaven This is yeast and it doesn't take much yeast to affect an entire loaf (or lump of dough). **of the Pharisees and the leaven of Herod."** Lest the commentator get too creative, Matthew says the **leaven** was the "doctrine of the Scribes and Pharisees."[156] I should point out that Penny,

---

[155]More information in my commentary on Matthew (16:1-4).

[156]Should we assume, comparing Matthew to Mark, that the Scribes and "Herod" are the same folks? Probably not. Probably, they both shorthanded the whole crew of 3 by selecting two of the three.

a dear congregant, said (while attempting to quote me) that this was the "rising up" (yeast action) of the enemies of Jesus in view of 8:31: their part in "rising up to kill Jesus." My goodness. I think I like that explanation even better! The Pharisees and scribes and Sadducees and Herodians and Chief Priests teach and teach while their teaching takes on an aggressive and tangible form until it finally permeates the nation who "rise up" to kill Jesus.

8:17-19

But Jesus, being aware of it, said to them, "Why do you reason because you have no bread? Do you not yet perceive nor understand? How can we be this silly? **Is your heart still hardened?** Mark 6:52 has this same frustrating question answered. Mark makes no doubt that this is absolutely what is going on here, and it is a theme carried on through Jesus' private discussion with them in 7:17-21.

18 Having eyes, do you not see? And having ears, do you not hear? And do you not remember? Psalm 115:4-8, of course, reminds us of how the Pharisees became like the false gods they had concocted. This is actually almost a direct quote.

19 When I broke the five loaves Jesus is about to connect the feeding miracles He performs with the teaching of the Pharisees. That means, that just as "leaven" is a picture of their teaching, the multiplying of bread by Jesus is a picture of His own teaching influence.

Didn't Jesus have fish at both miracles?

Yes. Yet, He doesn't reference it here because it was not the picture-making component for the miracles.

8:21

So He said to them, "How is it you do not understand?" This is the same thing He asked in 7:18. It seems as though Jesus is saying, "didn't you see me propagate or multiply bread?"

They would nod and say "well, yes."

"Then, what does that make me?" This seems to be the issue because Jesus asks them and finally receives a worthy response in 8:27-30.

"It seems as though it makes you the Son of God and the Messiah."

"What is the **leaven** of the Pharisees?"

"Jesus, it's their teaching."

"What is the bread I multiplied, then?"

"It must at least be your teaching and maybe your kingdom influence that will spread to untold thousands—thousands of image bearers redeemed by God."

"Then as obvious as my multiplication is…the false teaching of the Pharisees is just as covert and unobvious. It creeps through the body of dough—almost undetected."

8:22

Then He came to Bethsaida; This appears to be the **Bethsaida** on the northeast side of the sea of Galilee since they have crossed back over (8:10-13). In other words, they could have walked here. **and they brought a blind man to Him,** I find this fascinating. Here is another healing episode not found in Matthew (in addition to the deaf man of the last chapter). What is key here is that it seems as though—just like the deaf man, this blind man's healing was recorded by Mark not to show us that Jesus could heal blind men, but rather to show us that Jesus could open blinded eyes to truth:

1. Both are apparently only for the disciples (they are the only ones who were at both miracles).
2. Mark 8:17-18 is between them both as a spiritual barometer.
3. Both are brought to Jesus by a begging multitude.
4. Jesus touches both men.
5. Jesus takes both men away from the crowd.
6. Jesus spits on both men.

7. Both are commanded to tell nobody.

Perhaps the most striking thing about this is that in the following episode where I would have placed some grand statement about how "Peter now sees" as Matthew did (Matthew 16:17), we have to see that He is being made to see by implication. In other words, just as Matthew doesn't contain this miracle, Mark doesn't contain Matthew's record of Jesus' explanation to why Peter now knows who Jesus is (8:29). Jesus doubts His vision and then Jesus apparently teaches Peter that He needs to see as much as He needs to hear—through this miracle (a miracle not in Matthew)!

But more than that, it takes a giving of sight, that's true, but after that we need the Master to give us even clearer vision. Now, as a preacher, I have always disliked hearing sermons where simple miracles were not allowed to just be "simple miracles." However, Jesus made this miracle an issue of the heart earlier in this chapter when He coupled it with seeing and hearing. It is Jesus Who is to blame for showing us that this is a picture of the hearts that needs a healing touch and that Peter, only saw with "men like trees" vision. Or, Peter sees very well in 8:30; but not well enough in 8:33.

8:27[157]

...on the road He asked His disciples, saying to them, "Who do men say that I am?" Jesus has been reading minds for the entire book. Whatever the reason for this question, it isn't for His own information.

8:33

But when He had turned around and looked at His disciples, He rebuked Peter, saying, "Get behind Me, Satan!" He is either being heavily influenced by Satan (which is not outside the realm of possibility in Luke 22's reference to a discussion between Jesus and Satan about Peter) or **Peter** looks like Satan in his conduct. In any case, to deny the necessity of Jesus' redemptive work is Satanic.

---

[157]Please do see the additional detail in my commentary on Matthew (beginning with 16:13).

For you are not mindful of the things of God, but the things of men." What a charge! Who then thinks about **the things of God** if it's not an apostle who is consistently employed in the work of the Lord?

8:34-36[158]

When He had called the people to *Himself,* with His disciples also, He said to them, "Whoever desires to come after Me, let him deny himself, and take up his cross, and follow Me. "Come die with me." That is the invitation of Jesus. We don't "spend our lives." We give them. We are to seek for a life's work for which and in which we may die.

8:38
This will be dealt with under 9:1.

---

[158]Dealt with in some detail in the appendix on suicide.

Chapter 9

9:1[159]
And He said to them, "Assuredly, I say to you that there are some standing here who will not taste death till they see the kingdom of God present with power." There is good reason to believe this is primarily fulfilled in the following verses (the episode of the Mount of Transfiguration):

1. All three Synoptic Gospels place the Mount of Transfiguration after this promise. No variation of the order or proximity of these two episodes.
2. We do think Peter makes no equivocation that the Mount of Transfiguration was the Coming of Christ (2 Peter 1:16-18).

Now, I said "primarily", and the next few verses are simply one of two or more fulfillments concerning Jesus' promise (Mark 13:26-30[160] and 14:62 should be very easy to track repeats of the time-related dilemma of thinking it's only the Mount of Transfiguration or it's a far-off 2nd coming fulfillment). We will, however, use Mark 13:26-30 here as a reason why the next scene would be a clue that these three guys (listed in 9:2) are seeing this same event—but in preview form.

9:2-6

Now after six days after the location and discussion described beginning in 8:27. **Jesus took Peter, James, and John,** this special group of three is "the best of Jesus' best" as seen in Peter's home (1:29), Jarius' home (5:37), and later in the Garden of Gethsemane (14:33) **and led them up on a high mountain** None of the three accounts or the mentioning of the account by Peter give us the specific location. It is at this point we must decide whether it was because all four authors thought it wasn't important or whether it was because all four authors

---

[159] These verses are better examined in my Matthew commentary (16:27-28).
[160] The very reasons why dual fulfillment would be acceptable to see an immediate and distant fulfillment of Mark 8:38-9:1 would be why we could expect a dual fulfillment of this passage.

thought that their readers already knew the location from some other form of recorded tradition. It seems rather far-fetched that the Hebrews (Matthew), the Romans (?) (Mark), Theophilus (Luke) and the "strangers" of 1 Peter 1:1 all knew it was—if the tradition is correct—Mount Hermon. It rather seems that it was inconsequential to the account, and therefore, to Mark's message.[161]

apart by themselves; and He was transfigured "change of form" is the idea **before them. 3 His clothes became shining,** but not just His **clothes** or Mark would not have first described Jesus.

4 And Elijah appeared to them with Moses, Now if both of them were "glorified in their bodies," that would mean that Moses had been resurrected as well (which would give us some reflection on the drama behind Jude 9).[162]

---

[161] Or Matthew's, or Luke's, or Peter's.

[162] They could have both been "in the spirit" or without their bodies. The reader might be thinking "well, we know Elijah didn't die." 2 Kings 2:11 says Elijah was "caught away into Heaven." The Hebrew text reads "the Heavens." Take a look and you'll notice a few translations get this right (Young's, Darby, etc...). So we know "Elijah was caught into the Heavens." This has a significantly different demand on our attention. So what?

First, 2 Chronicles 21:12 says Elijah was writing letters or prophecies...after he left (yes, there are some out there that say he wrote it before he left). Elijah is apparently delivering mail from "Heaven" if he already left for there. When looking at the parallel timeframe in 2 Kings 8:17 and one realizes this takes place a full 6 chapters after Elijah is carried into "the heavens," we have some thinking to do.

Second, John 3:13 is pretty clear. At the time of John's writing, nobody except Jesus had gone to Heaven in the body ("ascended"). Either John forgot about Elijah....or Elijah didn't go to Heaven (as in the abode of God)...he rather was whisked away into the Heavens temporarily.

Some head scratching continues: "How high was Elijah to be whisked away into 'the Heavens?'" Apparently low enough that the birds could fly at that level (Genesis 1:20).

"Where did he go after he was 'taken into the Heavens'" (in 2 Kings 2:11)? I don't know. And that was the "rub" for another prophet in 1 Kings 18 (Obadiah) who feared Ahab's temper in the case that Obadiah tells Ahab of Elijah's whereabouts and find "as soon as I am gone from you, that the Spirit of the LORD will carry you to a place I do not know; so when I go and tell Ahab, and he cannot find you, he will kill me" (1 Kings 18:12).

Apparently, Elijah and his fiery chariots were an ordinary enough thing that other prophets (like Obadiah) knew about it. Elijah, then, was carried by the Holy

Now, if this is a foretaste of the Second coming, why are **Elijah and Moses** here? They have nothing to do with the Second Coming…unless they represent something. What do we know about Moses? He died in a remote place (Deuteronomy 34). What do we know about Elijah? He was caught away to the Heavens (2 Kings 2). 1 Thessalonians 4:13-18 tells us this represents the two types of believers: "the dead in Christ" and "we who are alive and remain."

6 because he did not know what to say, for they were greatly afraid. We are some weird ones, aren't we? Not sure what to say, so we say whatever seems appropriate in our shaken states. Peter's mistake was thinking that Moses and Elijah and Jesus all carried the same weight. They did not: Moses and Elijah were foundational to a true appreciation of Jesus.

9:7-8

And a cloud came and overshadowed them; and a voice came out of the cloud, saying, "This is My beloved Son. For the second time in this Gospel, by a second set of witnesses, we have a voice from Heaven identifying Jesus as God's **Son**. He is the **Son** that pleased the Father—unlike the **Son** of the Old Testament who was obstinate (Exodus 4; Deuteronomy 6-7). Hosea 11:1 calls this **Son** Israel while Matthew takes this text and applies it to Jesus. Hence, we are confronted with Galatians 3:13-29 that "Abraham's seed" is Christ and those who are "in Him" by faith (Galatians 3:7) are recipients of the promises to Christ through Abraham. Furthermore, this is a "new creation" and all those in Christ are the "Israel of God" (Galatians 6:15-16). We can therefore understand why the Old Testament **Son** passages are a little unclear to the Jew while the obvious Christiocentric passages are more thought of as the "suffering Israel" passages by the orthodox Jew.

Hear Him!" The second time this occurs.

Spirit somewhere and we're not told anything about his post-chariot life other than he was occasionally involved (as in 2 Chronicles 21) by way of written correspondence. He's not the only one about whom we're told nothing concerning their end of life (consider Melchizedek).

Incidentally, Moses was the one to **Hear** when God last spoke from a cloud from Heaven (Exodus 19-20). No longer. Moses and Elijah are the two main divisions of the Old Testament and they were but witnesses of the coming Christ while they yet lived. Ultimately, we only need to see **Jesus; Jesus only.** So, when Heaven has a chance to speak, what does it say?

I. Heaven speaks to Earth:
    a. As it applies to nature, it speaks of Christ through the stars. This is evident enough in that Job is a prequel to Jesus (Luke 24:44) and speaks so often of stars, but this is also evident in Psalm 19, and in the story of the wise men (Matthew 2).
    b. As it applies to the Scriptures, when one looks at the first book of Genesis and finishes in the last book of Revelation, they have no problem noticing God's emphasis: Jesus, the seed of the woman, will crush the seed of sin (Genesis 3:15; Revelation 20:10).
    c. As it applies to the crescendo of God's prophets, there is no "last word" like God's last word: the "Word made flesh" (John 1:14), and God's declaration of what is on His mind (Hebrews 1:1).
    d. The rare times in Scripture when Heaven opens up, or Heaven's king speaks, He speaks of the Son of God (as at Jesus' baptism and now here). This informs us as to what is always on God's mind. His Son is always on His mind.

II. Resulting Earthly Priority:
    a. An epitaph to be remembered for anybody: "a Son who pleased me well"
    b. A reputation to be heeded for anybody: "this man is worth listening to"

9:9-10

Now as they came down from the mountain, When you come down from the mountain… **He commanded them that they should tell no one the things they had seen,** this seems in keeping with every other aftermath of every other miraculous display (other than the maniac of chapter 5). **till the Son of Man had risen from the dead. 10 So they kept this word to themselves, questioning what the rising from the dead meant.** At least they're learning not to "rebuke" Jesus' talk of death (like they had done in the previous chapter, Peter specifically). If this is true, and if this is a picture of the coming of Christ with His kingdom:

1. We should expect all Messianic hope from the Old Testament to be fulfilled. Moses and Elijah are here symbols of the Old Testament (Luke 16:29-31) and we find in the coming of Christ the events of all the hopes of centuries past fulfilled.
2. We should be sure we're on the right side of the coming (8:38). Whether living or dead, we should make sure we are "not ashamed" (1 John 3:18).
3. We should anticipate a grand reunion (9:4). Nobody had to make introductions.
4. We should think about having our speech prepared (9:5). Not much left to say than "It's good to be here."
5. We should be prepared for Jesus to be the center of attention (9:7-8). It's the Father's idea. Moses and the Prophets are not the center of attention now so we should not expect Old Testament ideas to be a big concern in the Kingdom.[163]

9:11

And they asked Him, saying, "Why do the scribes say This really keeps me from having to preach a sermon on Malachi because the three men do not even mention the prophet. **that Elijah must come first?"** This **first** points to the answer of the previous passage. The Mount of Transfiguration is a preview of the coming of Jesus, and there is coming a time when **Elijah must come first,** before the Second coming.

9:12-13

Then He answered and told them, "Indeed, Elijah is coming first So, there is a **coming** of **Elijah** anticipated by Jesus **and restores all things.**

---

[163] And if the kingdom comes with Him (2 Timothy 4:1), we should really take "literal offerings" and such (Ezekiel) with a great deal of poetic levity.

And how is it written concerning the Son of Man, that He must suffer many things and be treated with contempt? Daniel 7-9 seems to be the only place in Scripture where this reality exists (although the suffering Savior is seen with other titles throughout—particularly Psalm 22 and Isaiah 52-53).

13 But I say to you that Elijah has also Is this **also** pointing to: 1. Another coming of **Elijah**; 2. Or is it speaking of what occurred to **Elijah** in addition to the "suffering" of "the Son of Man" (verse 12)? **come,** Jesus not only affirms the words of the scribes (verse 11), but he speaks of one that was **Elijah** who had **come.** While we could see if the other Gospels identify who this **Elijah** was,[164] it would be helpful to know that when Jesus was thought to be **Elijah** (8:28), He was also thought by others to be "John the Baptist." In other words, they all three (as seen in the first chapter) resembled one another in some manner.

In other words, just as the Mount of Transfiguration was a preview of the second coming, "John the Baptist" was a preview of **Elijah** "who must come first" (9:11).

and they did to him whatever they wished, as it is written of him." Probably best understood with the first **him** being John and the second **him** being **Elijah.** This must be speaking of the portion of Elijah's life where he, like John, was pursued by the wicked wife of a wicked king.

9:14-16

And when He came to the disciples, He saw a great multitude around them, and scribes disputing with them. While this episode is discussed in the appendix on suicide, it seems fitting to include some commentary here because of its continuing context through at least 10:16. You'll notice that this episode is about a child (*paidion*) in 9:24, and that there is a seeming sermonette in 9:33-41 comparing real leadership with children and another sermonette in 10:13-16 comparing a kingdom partaker with a child. The last time this word is found in chapter 7 and the next time it is found is another book.

---

[164]Matthew tells us this was John the Baptist (Matthew 17:13).

Another real clue that this is one context is that Matthew and Mark jumble up the exact order of some of these things with one another. Matthew packages the two discourses concerning children slightly different than Mark does, and so these were seen as one large package of two conversations (earlier called sermonettes).

9:20-22

Dealt with in the appendix on suicide.

9:24

See under 9:14-16.

9:28-29

And when He had come into the house, His disciples asked Him privately, "Why could we not cast it out?" They seem puzzled as to why their normal methods did not work. Jesus added to their light in verse 29.

9:30-32

These verses were handled primarily in my commentary on the minor prophets (Hosea 6:1-3).[165] **30 Then they departed from there and passed through Galilee,** Here is our change of location, now—setting us up for the next phase.

32 But they did not understand this saying, and were afraid to ask Him. The last time they said anything about this, Peter was called "Satan." This is a small improvement here.

9:33-41[166]

36 Then He took a little child He would not have taught this lesson if He was against "greatness." He would have said, "Don't be such a mis-

---

[165]More can be found in Matthew commentary (17:22-23).
[166]More can be found in Matthew 18-19 (in my commentary on Matthew).

manager of time! Don't seek greatness!" **and set him** This one that would believe the Gospel (9:31; 9:42).

37 "Whoever receives one of these little children in My name receives Me; and whoever receives Me, receives not Me but Him who sent Me." Praying in Jesus' name has nothing to do with saying "it." It is "praying as Jesus would pray" just as here "receiving one in His Name" means to "receive one as He would."

38 Now John answered Him, saying, "Teacher, we saw someone who does not follow us casting out demons in Your name, Here again seems to be the tie with the previous episode: Jesus speaks to those who struggle to receive "little children in [His] Name" (verse 37) but seem enamored with the power to **cast out demons** and who should be doing it. Jesus is not deterred when He speaks of the efforts of "little ones" in bringing refreshment to one's soul (verse 41).

40 For he who is not against us is on our side. This removes the notion that one can be "on the fence." There is no "fence."

9:42-48

"But whoever causes one of these little ones who believe in Me "receiving" (verse 37) and **believ**ing in Christ are what is necessary to be saved. What must they **believe?** 8:31 and 10:45 tell us!

to stumble, it would be better for him if a millstone were hung around his neck, and he were thrown into the sea. This sounds a lot like the end of 2 Peter 2. Basically, we don't want anybody stumbling on their way to be saved. 1 Corinthians 8-10, like the Gospel of 1 Corinthians 15:1-4 are both Paul-like and Jesus-like, as seen here.

43 If your hand causes you to sin, to **offend** one of these little ones is to **sin** against yourself. In other words, we're going to see in these verses that whatever causes you to cause others to be kept from believing is keeping you yourself from believing and puts you in a very uncomfortable place of damnation. Perhaps we should see that there are no promises of life to those who "used to be a believer," and that a willful causing of one to sin is actually a sure way to be sure you do not end life as one who believes this Gospel of which we have heard so much concerning.

Jesus pays temple tax He doesn't need to pay in Matthew 17 (took it out of a fish's mouth), not because He owes it, but because people—little ones—are watching. In other words, sometimes we do things we don't have to do because **little ones** are watching.

"I don't care what anybody thinks!" is not in keeping with the Spirit of Christ here demonstrated. Some of us have hard choices to make and we should be asking "what would Jesus think of this and what would the world see?"

It is better for you to enter into life maimed, rather than having two hands, to go to hell, into the fire This is one of three Greek words[2] which is typically translated with this word. **fire.**

45 And if your foot causes you to sin, perhaps this could have been written earlier, but maybe this is also Jesus turning to the "little ones" who may later blame the adults around them or the important folks in their lives for why they won't believe the Gospel. Jesus doesn't let them off the hook here.

It is better for you to enter life lame, This supposes some really strange reality, and would probably better be rendered "if there were a chance you would go to the Kingdom with one foot, fine! It's better to do that than to go to the fire with two!"

48 where 'Their worm does not die And the fire is not quenched.' So even if this refrain doesn't belong in 44, some of 45 and all of 46, it belongs here and its previous omission doesn't change the passage's message (for the obvious reason that it is here repeated word for word).

By the way, this Scripture that Jesus is quoting is in the last phrases of the book of Isaiah (66:24) and should instruct the reader that the "carcass" there mentioned should not lead the reader there nor here to an automatic stance in the "conscious, un-ending torment" affirmed

---

[2] Gr. *Gehenna*

by so many. Since the desirable "maiming" or "lameness" or "blindness" in the kingdom is figurative, maybe the **worm** only figuratively lives on and maybe the **fire** only figuratively burns on unquenched.[167]

49 "For These next two verses are, because of this word, related to the previous thought. Just how they are related is beyond me. Much greater men have felt the same way:

> *A difficult verse, on which much has been written—some of it to little purpose.*[168]

It really seems others should've table their own treatments of this verse:

> *The only connection between vv. 48 and 49 is the catchword "fire." The two verses must be interpreted independently. Here is a rare case where consideration of the context hinders rather than helps the interpretation.*[169]

everyone will be seasoned with fire, ʳ**and** ⁷**every sacrifice will be seasoned with salt.** On the one hand, if the variant is truly correct and the last part of the verse doesn't belong there, then we still have the problem of making sense of: 1. What does Jesus mean when He says **everyone will be seasoned with fire?** 2. Why this sudden change of topics from **season**ing **with fire** to the **good**ness of **salt** in verse 50?[170]

However, it must be quickly admitted that having the phrase at the end of this verse gives us the conundrum of having something in the first phrase of verse 49 that seems awful and doomful and adding to it

---

[167] Jeremiah 7:20 does leave the door open for this. God is not speaking literally there about unending, unquenchable fire.

[168] Robert Jamieson, A. R. Fausset, and David Brown, *Commentary Critical and Explanatory on the Whole Bible*, vol. 2 (Oak Harbor, WA: Logos Research Systems, Inc., 1997), 81.

[169] James A. Brooks, *Mark*, vol. 23, The New American Commentary (Nashville: Broadman & Holman Publishers, 1991), 154.

ʳ Lev. 2:13; Ezek. 43:24

⁷ NU omits the rest of v. 49.

[170] We've already discussed how *paidion* requires a continuing context so we are not at liberty to assume verse 50 is the beginning to a new train of thinking.

something incredibly opposite in its sense (or feel, if that word is better).[171]

---

[171] How do I know it feels better? Jesus tells the reader to "have salt". So while we don't want to be peppered with fire, it seems as though we are desiring to be peppered with salt. Again, if this is so, why the change from something awful to something good in a verse where they seem to be equally evident.

Chapter 10

10:1[172]

Then He arose from there and came to the region of Judea by the other side of the Jordan. He is now east of the Jordan River opposite the southern 3rd of the Promised Land. There has been a lot of geographical movement in recent episodes (9:30; 9:33).

10:2

The Pharisees came and asked Him, "Is it lawful for a man to divorce his wife?" testing Him. They were not seeking information. They were like many who ask questions to either 1. Catch you in a bad answer, or to 2. Provide an opportunity for them to tell you what they think.

10:4

They said, "Moses permitted a man to write a certificate of divorce, and to dismiss her." It's true. He did (Deuteronomy 24:1), but we find out that the reason this allowance was made was because men's hearts were hard. By the way, when you read my comments concerning "the exception clause" in my commentary on Matthew (chapter 19), you will see that I don't think Mark intended on his readers knowing Deuteronomy 24 as much as he wanted them to know that Jesus believed **Moses** did indeed allow it.

In that culture a woman could not divorce a man and so a hard-hearted man would make marriage miserable for a woman and there was no pleasing him. The word "but" at the beginning of 10:6 contrasts what one is allowed to do with what God's intention has been all along.

10:5-6

---

[172]More can be found in my commentary on Matthew (19:1-12).

And Jesus answered and said to them, "Because of the hardness of your heart the principles that we find at Calvary in Christ's Gospel (our economy of grace) are not those being found in the **heart** of the person pursuing divorce. The **heart** is continually on the mind of the writer throughout the Gospel so far. **he wrote you this precept. 6 But from the beginning of the creation, God 'made them male and female.'** We were **made** this way, and Jesus is not confused about the nature of creation or gender identity. Jesus is quoting from Genesis 1.

10:7-8

8 and the two shall become one flesh'; so then they are no longer two, but one flesh. Quoting Genesis 1:27 in verse 6 and Genesis 2:24 here. Furthermore, Jesus believes the Old Testament is authoritative for He gives a "bottom line" in the next verse. This **one flesh** idea is nothing more than sexual intercourse (1 Corinthians 6:16). This is seen in the context of Genesis 2:24 with both the "naked and unashamed description" shortly after and the command to "multiply and fill the earth" in the first chapter.

10:9

Therefore what God has joined together, God created the **togetherness**, and He did it through the sexual union.[173] One might notice, then, that two people must be able to do the Adam-Eve sexual union in order to marry by biblical definition. Two men, therefore, cannot be married. A review, then: the two becoming **one flesh** is the sex act and that is when God joins them **together.** Why do we then get licenses? Titus 3:1 says to "obey every ordinance of man." Why do we have marriage ceremonies? As a testimony before God's people for accountability's sake.

10:10-12

In the house His disciples also asked Him again about the same matter. What exactly did they ask Him and why? Perhaps it was the

---

[173]Not just the command to procreate (Genesis 1:27) or the nakedness (2:25), but also the definition of the sexual union as defined by Paul (1 Cor 6:16) make it clear.

exact nature of what would qualify as a "biblical reason" to divorce a wife? Jesus explains **11 So He said to them, "Whoever divorces his wife and marries another commits adultery against her.** This is probably a singular act. That is, one divorces a woman "in order to marry another." **12 And if a woman divorces her husband and marries another, she commits adultery."** Two things are pretty certain here: 1. Divorce is the result of a hard heart (10:5).[174] 2. The willful divorce from a spouse to do some shopping around for something more or better or for the intent of being with somebody else is **adultery.**

In the grand context reaching back through 9:42 and up through 10:16, it should be evident that 3. The biggest losers with divorce are the children: it causes them to stumble, and makes them grow up way too fast.

10:13-16

Then they brought "into the house" of 10:11.

Here is another opportunity to thank the Gospel writers for keeping us from making mistakes. If we didn't have Luke 18:15, I would have made the mistake of thinking these children had a desire in coming to Jesus based on verse 14, but this is a word Luke uses six of the eight times it is used in the New Testament and is nearly indisputably "infant."[175] In other words, these children were to be "allowed to come to Jesus in the arms of their parents." **little children to Him,[176] that He might touch them; but the disciples rebuked those who brought them.** who brought them? If it were the parents, then maybe we should remind the reader that you cannot be accused of bringing your children to Jesus if you don't even bring them to church.

---

[174]The sad thing is that with all the talk in Mark 7 and the "defiled heart," it should be evident to the reader that New Testament believers are to be completely baffled that anybody naming the name of Christ would have a hard heart.

[175]It's probably prudent to admit that these children do "come" (verse 14) and do "receive" (verse 15). So this may mean that there is some flexibility in this word in the original languages.

[176]It seems secondary to the point of the passage, but the Roman reader would have been struck with the tenderness of the Hebrew culture toward children; Hughes, 243.

Moreover, it is primarily the parents who are the primary religious educators (see Deuteronomy 6 for more on this).

but the disciples rebuked them. It seems like anybody would be happy about children coming to Jesus, it would be **the disciples.** The **disciples** are angry with the parents for bringing them to Jesus.

14 But when Jesus saw it, He was greatly displeased why? They weren't listening! He just told them about causing these to "stumble" (9:42)! **and said to them, "Let the little children come to Me [in the arms of their parents], and do not forbid them; for of such is the kingdom of God. Little children** don't have time to do all the grand works that these "important" people do or have done. They can't do these things—particularly since they "were brought to Him." By the way, 9:42 says these "little" ones are saved through believing.

15 Assuredly, I say to you, whoever does not receive the kingdom of God as a little child Well, what does this look like? We will now see an example of a man who found it impossible to do that. It's a good thing, because a child could never claim to be what this man was. The reoccurrence of "enter(ing) the Kingdom of God" in 10:23-25 removes the doubt one might have that this is one context. **will by no means enter it."** How do children do enter? They believe (9:42) the Gospel (9:31). A **child** served as an object lesson. One had to be **like a little child** in order to enter the kingdom.

16 And He took them up in His arms, laid His hands on them, and blessed them. quite meaningful for a Rabbi to put His hands like Aaron (Numbers 4) and Jacob (Genesis 49) and Simeon (Luke 2).

10:17

Now as He was going out on the road, one some have said Barnabas as a "son of consolation" (Acts 4) or "son of the 2nd chance" while I speak in my Matthew commentary about my opinion that it is the Apostle Paul. **came running,** Here now is one who needs to become like a child.

knelt before Him, he's made a trip down the aisle and he runs and kneels and prays with a proper salutation and asks for eternal life. Is he saved? Of course not. **and asked Him, "Good Teacher, what shall I do that I may inherit eternal life?"** He joins the Lawyer (Luke 10), Nicodemus (John 3:4), and the Philippian Jailer (Acts 16:30) who ask this question in some form or another.

10:18-19

So Jesus said to him, "Why do you call Me good? With the next phrase of Jesus' one might wonder if Jesus was attempting to get this man to admit His divinity. In other words, "Jesus, you are as **good** as God; so tell me how I can be with you one day."

No one *is* good but One, *that is,* God. You must, therefore, be as good as **God,** and that is why we find it "impossible"—other than through **God**—to "enter the kingdom" (verse 27). This **good**ness of God is seen in His Law, as will be seen. He is **good** because there is no impurity in Him—as described in His law.

10:21

Then Jesus, looking at him, loved him, The only person in Matthew, Mark, or Luke that is described as one that Jesus loves (although the Gospel of John records four others)[177] **and said to him,** Here is one might expect **Jesus** to argue with the man about whether he has really "kept these from [his] youth." Why doesn't he? Because Jesus is showing how critical it is for one to maintain child-like simplicity to "enter the kingdom." How do I know? 10:23-25 repeat what 10:15 introduces. Since we are adding more light to the aforementioned passage on children, it seems like Jesus is letting loose of the argumentation that doesn't actually matter. It's not that this man obeyed all the commandments that Jesus listed; it's that he is not obeying the commands that Jesus did not list. Of the Ten Commandments listed in Exodus 20, 4 of them deal primarily with God and man (vertical) while 6 of them deal with man and man (horizontal). Jesus lists 5 of the six leaving out only the command regarding covetousness.

---

[177]Lazarus, Mary, Martha, John the Apostle

"One thing you lack: Of the remaining Commandment, Jesus takes a litmus test of sorts: "I'll show this man He is a covetous man by showing him that he only 'wants' things that are here." It seems the greatest thing that keeps our little ones from coming to Christ is a love for stuff. Verse 22 tells us why this man couldn't find it within himself to **follow** Jesus.

Go your way, sell whatever you have and give to the poor,[178] **and you will have ⁱtreasure in heaven; and come, ʳtake up the cross, and follow Me."** Incidentally, notice how Jesus doesn't distinguish between those who "inherit eternal life" (10:17), those who "enter the kingdom" (10:23-25), those who need to be saved (10:26), and those who **follow** Jesus. We see that the issue of believing the Gospel (8:31; 10:45) is still the issue here when we find out this man's greatest problem was that he "trusted His riches" (verse 24).[179] How sad that some Bibles have decided to leave that out with little more than "some manuscripts include…"[180]

10:22

But he was sad at this word, and went away sorrowful, This is where we get on to Jesus because He is allowing the man to leave! "Go after him, Jesus! Make it easier to understand for him!" **for he had great possessions.** In reality, the young man knew exactly what Jesus was saying, and it was proper for him to leave.

10:23-25

24 And the disciples were astonished at His words. But Jesus answered again and said to them, "Children, how hard it is ²for

---

[178]The Rich Man was sort of guilty of this same thing, it seems (Luke 16:19-26). It is a tale told on his covetous heart.
ⁱMatt. 6:19, 20
ʳMark 8:34
[179]Rather than in Christ Himself (9:42) Who gave His life as our ransom (10:45).
[180] *The Holy Bible: English Standard Version* (Wheaton: Standard Bible Society, 2016), Mk 10:24–26.
² NU omits *for those who trust in riches*

those who trust See this is an issue of **trust.** Just as a little child is full of faith and ceases to struggle when placed in the hands of Christ, so anybody desiring entrance to the kingdom will find it impossible unless they simply **trust.**

25 It is easier for a camel to go through the eye of a needle if we fanaticize this as some sort of folklore—as though there really is a place in a wall where short people walk in middle eastern cities called **the eye of a needle,** we are missing the twofold point of Jesus: a **rich man** must become a child and can no longer seek to **enter the kingdom** as a **rich man;** 2. It really is "impossible to be saved." Not merely "hard" (verse 23), but "impossible" (verse 27).

10:26-27

27 But Jesus looked at them and said, "With men *it is* **impossible,** "hard" has been upgraded to **impossible.**

but not with God; for with God all things are possible." This is not a catch-all, theological statement as much as it is declarative within this context.

10:28-31

Peter finds an easy comparison.

began to say to him, "See, we have left everything Jesus doesn't argue with him. Not only that, if Peter was as well off as it appears (father having a fishing business), this was no small thing. However, what is also clear is that coveting need not be confined to only the rich. It seems as though the verses that follow (10:35-44) that the disciples were all too ready to covet, and they needed to be mindful they had not really **left everything.** Rather, their desire for precedence in the kingdom showed they merely swapped their **everything.** They were actually attempting that which was "impossible" (verse 27) and attain the kingdom through their hearty commitment.

10:32-34

Now they were on the road, going up to Jerusalem, and Jesus was going before them; and they were amazed. And as they followed they were afraid. It is as this point where the Greek texts vary as to whether it is the twelve disciples that were **follow**ing **afraid,** or whether it was a separate group.[181] One should take special note that the old commentators (like Henry) knew nothing of the textual variant.[182] This is instructive since we are assuming that the "buried Bible"[183] had not yet been discovered that should thereafter "correct" the misled faith of believers who for centuries were represented in the extant manuscripts. That is to say, besides the Byzantine texts (of basically any era),[184] every Greek text prior to the development of textual criticism in the 1800's had the KJV/NKJV reading—to include, among others, the 1550 Stephens,[185] the 1598 Beza,[186] and the 1624 Elzevir[187] texts.

This commentary, then, assumes it is the disciples who are both **amazed and afraid.** Jesus had already handled the fear dilemma with them.

> *Mark 4:41 And **they feared exceedingly**, and said to one another, "Who can this be, that even the wind and the sea obey Him!"*

---

[181] Finding those who pick a team is not difficult in these matters. Finding a commentator or exegete that explains why they pick a perspective beyond the snobbish "oldest manuscripts don't contain"-type comments is an entirely different exploration; "Mark 10:32 (KJV) - And they were in the." Blue Letter Bible. Web. 30 Oct, 2017. <https://www.blueletterbible.org/kjv/mar/10/32/t_conc_967032>.

[182] Matthew Henry, *Matthew Henry's Commentary on the Whole Bible: Complete and Unabridged in One Volume* (Peabody: Hendrickson, 1994), 1801.

[183] A reference to the Bible supposedly restored through archaeology.

[184] *The New Testament in the Original Greek: Byzantine Textform 2005, with Morphology.* (Bellingham, WA: Logos Bible Software, 2006), Mk 10:32.

[185] *Stephen's 1550 Textus Receptus: With Morphology* (Bellingham, WA: Logos Bible Software, 2002), Mk 10:32.

[186] *Scrivener's Textus Receptus (1894): With Morphology* (Bellingham, WA: Logos Bible Software, 2002), Mk 10:32.

[187] Maurice Robinson, *Elzevir Textus Receptus (1624): With Morphology* (Bellingham, WA: Logos Bible Software, 2002), Mk 10:32.

> *Mark 6:50 for they all saw Him and were troubled. But immediately He talked with them and said to them, "Be of good cheer! It is I; **do not be afraid**."*

Are we to find any application since this phrase does not say we should galvanize (or take solace in) our fears. Moses required fearful soldiers who might speak of their fear to go home (Deuteronomy 20:3). It was better to be one soldier short than to have the virus of fear recognized or discussed.

This phrase does not say we should romanticize or galvanize our immature fears as Christians—almost adorning them with admiration when the Apostle Paul said we are to be "anxious for nothing" (Philippians 4:6). We are to no more provide shelter to fears than we are to drunkenness or adultery.

This phrase does not say that we should minimize our fears as though they are nothing in comparison to other lesser sins. For Revelation 21:8 places "fear" beside the sin of sorcery as those things that belong in the lake of fire.

So what do we do when we realize that fear is not antithetical or mutually exclusive to belief? Do we sit about, immobile, because we lack adequate courage? Do we await a better time when perhaps we will have the spiritual maturity to stiffen our jaws and to move forward? We may be **afraid,** but we **follow.**

Somehow, these were **afraid** who were watching Jesus, in conference with Jesus, thankful for promises of eternal blessing (10:30), able to express months of miracle-working power, and yet they were **afraid.**

Why do we **follow?** Why did they follow? Their motives were skewed and misdirected and misinformed. All the more reason for us to know what we are **follow**ing. So what do we offer the believer today who chooses to **follow** even if it's **afraid and follow**ing? We offer nothing more than what Jesus offered: a cross and a 3rd day resurrection. Continued faith that He does all things well (7:37), and He does all things that only He can do (10:27).

Then He took the twelve aside again from the crowd later referenced in 10:46.

33 "Behold, we are going up to Jerusalem, Why did Jesus take them out of the way? Well, there were lots of people with them because they were in one of the four Passovers recorded in the Gospels (John 2, John 5, John 6 and Mark 14[188]). You understand that all male Jews were required to make a pilgrimage to Jerusalem[189] at the feast of trumpets in the fall, Pentecost and Passover in the spring. So most of Jesus' ministry since chapter 7 or 8[190] has been in a mob of people coming from northern Israel down through Perea on the east side of the Jordan River all the way across the Jordan Valley up to Mount Zion. So when it says that he "took them aside," there is a good reason. He was with a huge crowd of people and he wanted to discuss things with his disciples.

34 and they will mock Him, there is precious little that hurts me more than being made fun of. **and ⁵scourge Him, and spit on Him, and kill Him.** Now, this matters, because they were "afraid" (10:32) and yet they didn't know why, it seems. Not even the disciples seemed to have gotten the concept because it is after this that they sought supremacy in the kingdom as if Jesus said nothing about a death (10:33-44).

And the third day He will rise again." This was mentioned in 8:31 (Caesarea Philippi) and 9:31 (Capernaum).[191] There is no hint whatsoever as to how Jesus is going to die in those references. So if you were in that audience what are you going to think? "How is that going to happen?" How would the Jews kill people? They'd stone him, perhaps.

---

[188]Matthew 26.

[189]Jerusalem used to be called Jebus, according to Judges 19. It is the old part of Jerusalem. In the book of Joshua, it was ruled, as part of the tribe of Judah's real estate. Joshua says the Jebusites took it back over somehow. Then we find that it was reconquered by the tribe of Judah (under the command of Joab). David reigned there as king for 33 years of his 40 year reign and then Solomon reigned there 40 years and actually had the tabernacle resting there and built the temple there on Mount Zion.

[190]Matthew 14 or 15.

⁵ flog Him with a Roman scourge

[191]Matthew 16 and 17.

Now he tells them a third time, "I'm going to die," but he tells them how it's going to happen. They still don't know how to take it. He says he's going to be delivered to the Gentiles (verse 33). Well, who are the only Gentiles ruling and reigning there in Jerusalem? The Romans. And how did the Romans execute people? Crucifixion. They crucify him and on the third day he will rise again. Now for the first time he indirectly mentions crucifixion and then Mark 8:34[192] starts to make sense. "We're going to have to take up our cross to follow Jesus."

By the way, it's important for us to remember that Jesus is not a victim. One glance at Mark 10:45 tells us that. So it is not a marvel that we are likewise told to take up our crosses.

"Are you going to be murdered or are you going to commit suicide? I mean, this doesn't seem right. What are you talking about?" Can you understand the dilemma the disciples were facing? This isn't how it's supposed to work out. How are you going to both reign on your father, David's throne, and die? This is ridiculous." Again, the following verses should make it clear they are not, at all, following Jesus' logic.

10:45

See appendix on suicide.

10:46-47

Now they came to Jericho. The last stop on the way to Jerusalem, 18 miles to the southwest. **Jericho** is called the "City of Palms" in 2 Chronicles 28:15. I think it would be a little far-fetched to assume that those with branches in the next episode had carried them twenty miles to this processional.

As He went out of Jericho with His disciples and a great multitude, blind There is but one other **blind** man in this Gospel and it is found in 8:22-23, and we proved there that although this is a physical malady it is being included there to picture the condition of the heart. It seems reasonable, then, that this too is about the heart and mind of the person

---

[192]Or Matthew 10.

who has not yet been healed. If this is true, then, we should see this story is a picture of the conversion of a man or woman, and is applicable to the believer insomuch as this conversion story reflects the timeless character of God for all men and women—saved and unsaved: 1. Jesus hears the persistent prayers of unsaved/blind souls; 2. The prayer itself does nothing to save, but merely arrests the attention of one Who may stop and impart healing.

Bartimaeus, the son of Timaeus, "Aramaic name like Bartholomew, βαρ [*bar*] meaning son like Hebrew *ben* [*bēn*; בֵּן]. So Mark explains the name meaning 'the son of Timaeus'"[193] It seems this man's name was given for the clarity of the reader who would know him (just as "Alexander" and "Rufus" in chapter 15). Perhaps they were all known by the Roman audience of Mark? Probably, we could say that it is the Roman believers of the mid-late 50's A.D. who would know these men (particularly when you realize there is a "Rufus" in that church (Romans 16:13).

At any rate, the fact that Luke's version contains only one person and leaves him unnamed adds more credence to this view. In other words, although the temptation may arouse the preacher to make much of "a son who made much of his dad," he should resist the temptation.

sat by the road begging. Hughes provides us with a table setting for this man's plight:

> The day began like any other day…Waking up, he shook the straw from his shabby, torn garments, stretched, got to his feet, and began tapping his way along the familiar turns that led to the main gate in stops along the way. Arriving at the gate he took his regular place with the other beggars, where he drew his greasy cloak tight around him because, thought it was spring, it took the sun to dispel the chill.
> As he sat there, just like so many days before, he listened to the city come to life—first a donkey loaded with melons for market, after that several women chatting as they bore pitchers

---

[193] A.T. Robertson, *Word Pictures in the New Testament* (Nashville, TN: Broadman Press, 1933), Mk 10:46.

toward the well, then the clomp of camels' hooves and the aroma of fish borne along to market. Soon Jericho was humming, and the blind man was intoning his beggar's cry.[194]

blind later you will see that I believe this man could see at one time. Here's some reflection on that possibility.

Vincent says that diseases of the eye are very common in the East. He quotes Thomson on Ramleh: "The ash-heaps are extremely mischievous; on the occurrence of the slightest wind, the air is filled with a fine pungent dust which is very injurious to the eyes. I once walked the streets counting all that were either blind or had defective eyes, and it amounted to about one-half of the male population. The women I could not count, for they are rigidly veiled."[195]

47 And when he heard that it was Jesus of Nazareth, he began to cry out and say, "Jesus, Son of David, what does this man know about **Jesus** being **the Son of David?** He knows enough, apparently, because it was the title **Jesus of Nazareth** that prompted this man to call out to **Jesus.** What was it about **Nazareth** and **Jesus** that made this man connect both to **David?** This is, after all, the first time we see this title in Mark's Gospel. Are we to assume that Mark was merely recording the monologue of this man or did Mark expect the reader to know Jesus' lineage? There are many things like this (such as the title "king of the Jews" from chapter 15 and an accusation concerning the temple at his trial (also, chapter 15). See the annex on Psalm 86 and David's opening of that Psalm to see what may have been driving this man's words.

have mercy on me!" There were apparently enough things circulating about Jesus from previous years: He was said to be **Jesus of Nazareth, Son of David,** and one who could **have mercy on** Bartimaeus. What did Bartimaeus mean by **mercy?** A restoration of his sight (verse 51).

---

[194] Hughes, 256.
[195] Kenneth S. Wuest, *Wuest's Word Studies from the Greek New Testament: For the English Reader* (Grand Rapids: Eerdmans, 1997), Mk 10:42–46.

I cannot just flippantly use my English-dependent definition and say "**Mercy** is God withholding from us what we do deserve" even though that may be true in some contexts. This word is used three times in Mark and the time used outside this passage is easily rendered "compassion."[196]

10:48

Then many warned him to be quiet; Those who could see were a little irritated by those who could not. When responding to the blind man in the story, do we seek the cause of his blindness (as the disciples do in John 9)? After all, if this is an allegory of salvation we should perhaps admit that our deafness and another's lameness is analogous to this man's blindness.

Rather, maybe we pontificate the overall shame of universal sin and the sin problem and discuss how this is not God's idea and theologize the theodicy in this story? Do we sort of have a distant "that's what our sin did to God's creation" and move on?

Or, maybe we sympathize with a man who is in a condition and hates it. Do we desire the mercy for him that we do for us?

Let us rather allow the spirit of grace to bring Gospel reflection into the relationships we have with blind people—physically maladied or spiritually indifferent to the colorful Christ in all of His splendid, Heaven-sent glory?

10:49

So Jesus stood still Doesn't this mean that He was content to walk on? Like with the woman sick twelve years (Mark 5) or the Canaanite woman (Mark 7)? How about the poor disciples whose boat Jesus "nearly missed" (Mark 6:48)?[197] Why does He do this? Why does **Jesus**

---

[196] "G1653 - eleeō - Strong's Greek Lexicon (KJV)." Blue Letter Bible. Web. 8 Nov, 2017.
<https://www.blueletterbible.org//lang/lexicon/lexicon.cfm?Strongs=G1653&t=KJV>.

[197] This says nothing about the two on the road to Emmaus that Jesus was "making as though He was going on."

do this? Is it to drive the crowd to reveal their own hearts? Is it to drive the man to a desperate cry?

and commanded him to be called. Jesus didn't even hush the crowd and call out to the man. Presumably this has something to do with the size of the crowd and the labor intensive work of getting the call to him. This becomes marvelous when we see they most certainly part for the man to come to Jesus (verse 50).

Then they called the blind man, saying to him, "Be of good cheer. Why was this needed? If I was about to receive news that I was being beckoned you would most certainly not need to tell me to **be of good cheer**…unless I was still crying out for mercy and couldn't hear Jesus call for me and I needed to be calmed down with almost the same intensity with which I was crying out—almost as if **they** needed to work hard to calm me.

10:50

And throwing aside these two words come from one Greek word used only twice in the New Testament.

his garment, in this, our conversion story, we have a man who prior to healing was willing to **throw** off the tokens of his lostness. These were the garments of a beggar. Genesis 38 speaks of Tamar and her **garment**s of widowhood and **garment**s of prostitution.

he rose and came to Jesus. These probably illustrates the act of "faith" Jesus mentions in verse 52. If he was still blind, he would not have been able to find this **garment,** and if he was healed he would not have needed it. This should remind the reader of the "woman at the well" (John 4) who left her bucket at the well and Jesus who left behind His grave clothes (John 20). None of these three needed these items because there was a drastic difference of who they were with who they had been.

10:51

So Jesus answered and said to him, "What do you want Me to do for you?" What a ridiculous story! Who is this **Jesus?** It's bad enough that

Jesus knows what people are thinking this whole Gospel long and never asks questions to ascertain information, but anyone can look at a blind man who has been howling for mercy and figure out what he wants!

The blind man said to Him, [6]"Rabboni, that I may receive my sight." By the way, what's he wanting sight for? He must not have been born blind. What good would **sight** be if he had no idea what it was? I guess John 9 proves this. The man "born blind" is not recorded as asking for his **sight.**

10:52

Then Jesus said to him, "Go your way; your faith what was the token of this **faith?** How do we know he had **faith?** He cried out until he was heard. He named his need. He expressed his desperate trust in Jesus.

has made you well." The translation **made you well** could easily be "saved you." Mark 10:45 is the author's attempt to show the reader the object of faith: the One Who provided the Ransom. It is, however, very slight, and that is disheartening.[198]

And immediately he received his sight and followed Jesus on the road. Why did **Jesus** allow this man to **follow** Him when He told Him to **go** his **way?** Jesus appears to at least allow, if not encourage, disobedience for those all Gospel long that He told to "hush" and "tell

---

[6] Lit. *My Great One*

[198] It is at this time that I must admit a frustration with which I cannot ascertain the cause among two choices: 1. My own misunderstanding that one must believe the Gospel—making this "parable"/allegory difficult to Gospel-ize (even though Mark gives us no choice); or 2. Mark's lack of soteriological coherence with Paul who seems to say salvation is by believing the Gospel (Romans 3:23-25; 1 Corinthians 15:1-4). This merely compounds the salvation-related issue. I guess this moves me to, with great discomfort, admit that the Gospel they had to believe was the Christ they knew. What makes me even more uncomfortable with this is that it opens the doors to discussions about the heathen "who sincerely trust the God they know." Are they saved? It seems like they are in this "Old Testament saint" context.

Luke likewise aggravates me in my current disposition in these thoughts as not one time does he go further than "believing in Jesus" or "trusting Jesus" in his book of Acts. I would rather He become Pauline. See appendix on Apostolic Sermons and their components in my commentary on Acts.

nobody." Moreover, he tells the man in chapter 5 to "go home" and he does.

Chapter 11

John 12's version of this story places a figure, it says that "six days before the Passover" in the house of Lazarus in Bethany. Later in that chapter is says, "On the next day," and it tells this story. Well, with Passover on the Friday; six days before: that's a Saturday; the next day would be Sunday. That's how we get to a Palm Sunday.

11:1-3[199]

Now when they drew near Jerusalem, Of course this began in 10:33. Same massive group that required Bartimeus to scream for notice.

2 and He said to them, "Go into the village opposite you; "Go do something totally irrational. Go into a city and you're going to find two animals. Just assume that you can use them. And once someone comes and asks just assume that they're going to believe you when you say, 'My boss needs them.' He'll be cool with that."

11:8-10

And many spread their clothes on the road, This was pretty common among Jewish kings particularly (2 Kings 9:13).

10 Blessed *is* the kingdom of our father David That comes in the name of the Lord! Hosanna in the highest!" So, in other words, save us from our enemies who are the Romans. "This is David's Son Jesus who is going to come and save us from our Romans, our oppressors." This is the King. He is about to enter the city gates. In four days Jesus will have His last supper with some disciples who don't yet understand the gospel.

11:11

---

[199]There is some additional information discussed in my commentary on Matthew (21:1-10) and Luke (19:28-44).

And Jesus went into Jerusalem and into the temple. So when He had looked around at all things, as the hour was already late, maybe it was one day since 10:32? That's a lot of traveling and they were tired.

He went out to Bethany with the twelve. As I reflected on Mark, it donned on me that I had done much of my work of reflection on Matthew as a theologian, and therefore sought all the levels of Old Testament nuance. It definitely passed the "what the audience heard/saw" test, but did not obviously reflect "what the author intended" or "what the reader ascertained." Many of these backdrops, furthermore, passed the "what would preach" and "what would make interesting discussion" tests:

> **I.** I see Jesus passing through gates here (11:11) and I am reminded of how He will pass through the gates as King of Kings and Lord of Lords—through, perhaps, these same gates (Ezekiel 44:1-3) when He returns with His kingdom (Psalm 102:16-17; 2 Timothy 4:2). I am reminded of how Jesus came riding through the gates of Hell (Matthew 16:18) and how He ascended through the gates of Heaven at His ascension (Psalm 24; Hebrews 1:5-7). Yet, I have to admit, I don't know the Holy Spirit intended these thoughts through the pen of Mark.
> **II.** Then, I think of all the life lessons:
>> **A.** "doing what Jesus says" (11:2), and finding ourselves surrendering to His strangest of requirements. However, I must admit that this doesn't give any consideration to the overall theme of Mark. It may speak to the Mark-wide themes of Jesus' strange requirements, but you have to admit, there is far more in this episode of "Palm Sunday" than teaching us to go borrow people's convertibles for a grand caravan into town.
>> **B.** Returning stuff that belongs to people (11:3). Again, this seems as though it is outside the writer's intent.
>> **C.** Planning ahead (in case the donkey wasn't a token of Jesus' foreknowledge & omniscience but was rather just the product of good planning.
>> **D.** The virtues of being a donkey for Jesus (Matthew 21:2; Mark 5:5). Being meek and full of life for the King of the Jews, the Son of David; not being self-seeking, but

rather to seek the glory of the Son of God, and to keep our heads down and our steps steady so that we might showcase Jesus like this donkey. Indeed, that is a beautiful object lesson, but it was certainly not the intent of Mark.

III. How about a lesson of Jesus' omniscience? Jesus knew the location of this man's donkey at most. At least He had to be right that there was at least one animal upon which He would be allowed to ride. Matthew 17:27 speaks of Jesus knowing just where the coin us—which fish and where it could be caught.

IV. Fulfilled Prophecy

    A. These dear people are quoting Psalm 118 when they address Jesus in 11:10. Is the author trying to get us to acknowledge that they were doing so and then expecting us to have an exegetical understanding of Psalm 118 in order to fully understand the ramifications of this passage? Probably not. For one thing, Mark's audience isn't told at all—barring the one time Mark quotes Jesus as doing so (13:14)—that a prophet is being fulfilled. Matthew on the other hand makes reference to prophetic fulfillment 13 times, assuring us that one of his missions was to prove to His audience that Jesus was here to fulfill prophecy.[200]

    B. Of course, Ezekiel 23 has the glory of God departing from the temple, then the city, then is last seen on Mount of Olives whereas Ezekiel 43 seems to say the exact opposite. As a matter of fact, it is stated explicitly that the "glory of God" will return and set His "throne" among the people. This has an almost parallel understanding in Revelation 21:3 where one finds that "God Himself will be with them, and will be their God."

    C. We see that this riding on the young donkey was impressive and both Genesis 49:11 and Zechariah 9:9 speak of His riding this colt of a donkey. Yet, we must

---

[200] "KJV Search Results for "prophet"." Blue Letter Bible. Web. 13 Nov, 2017. <https://www.blueletterbible.org//search/search.cfm?Criteria=prophet&t=KJV#s=s_primary_0_1>.

ask whether Mark expected his reader to know Genesis or Zechariah?

V. We could discuss the necessity of being sanctified and set apart in our service to God: This was a donkey upon which nobody had sat (11:2). It is set somewhere between a birth from a womb out of which not child had been born and being laid in a tomb in which no man had been buried (neither of which are mentioned in the Gospel of Mark so it was either, again, assumed by Mark or not intended at all).

VI. Others have made massive amounts of ministerial punch in both sermon and song on the fickleness of man: Christian composers and comedians; professors and preachers have said much about how this crowd crying "Hosanna" later in the week cries out "crucify" Him (15:8-11). The problem is that with the statistic of well over a million Jews in and around Jerusalem (by first century historian Josephus) during holidays as this; combined with the four-five days that transpire; combined with the relative restriction of Pilate's court; it seems inconclusive at best that anybody who screamed for His destruction was in the crowd on Palm Sunday.

VII. Then, perhaps Mark's point is instructional; maybe Mark needed to share this to complete his portrait of Jesus. It is instructional, for example, that Jesus sent them after a young donkey (11:2). He has been walking for 20 miles (if it's the same day as 10:33), and so He was able to finish this journey on His feet (as the others would do, 11:9). Get that, the others had walked with Him the entire way and now they were escorting Him into Jerusalem with others that would join their crowd. Perhaps others had poured out of the city from the news that "the Lord was approaching" (11:3-6).

> **A.** There seems to be a certain building narrative here: He dies with an accusation nailed over Him: He's a King (15:26). Mark wants you to see the royal procession: A king is treated with a hero's welcome: "His car shouldn't even have to touch the highway and his body shouldn't have to touch the seat. No, here is our King. He heals all sick, raises all dead, feeds all hungry. Our army would be undefeated." Here's the problem…Kings on Stallions don't give their lives "a ransom for many" (10:45). He is

rather, a sharp contrast to what the Roman world would have called a victor: riding a young donkey. He is unimpressive and seeking to show that He is not there to lead captives back to the capitol, but rather mourners to His death.[201] Consider Mark 14:6-9 as the pre-Calvary step and the closing of the book as the climax: He sits enthroned (Mark 16:19-20).

B. We are seeing that God previews us the final second coming where our Lord returns on a white horse (Revelation 19).

C. We see a preview of how our Lord rules with a rod of iron and will tread the nations of the earth rather than garments and branches (Revelation 14).

D. We see a preview of how those around Him will not pray for deliverance from Rome, but will rather rejoice in His conquering of the beast and the false prophet (Revelation 19).

…but, are these the point of Mark?

11:12-14

Now the next day, It is now Monday if we hold to a Good Friday death (see note just below chapter heading above).

13 And seeing from afar a fig tree having leaves, In other words, it looked like it had life…**He went to see if perhaps He would find something on it.** Is it not marvelous that Jesus, the "Son of Man" (Psalm 80:17; Daniel 7) was **hungry?** He **went to** a tree **to find something on it.** Because, for a lesson He was about to teach, it looked like it had life.

14 In response Jesus said to it, "Let no one eat fruit from you ever again." This is either a tantrum for the ages or Jesus is teaching something. As if it was not a marvel enough that Jesus was "hungry," we find out that He is using His hunger to teach a lesson. This seems confusing, does it not? Jesus knows enough agriculture. He goes to it out of **season,** looking for **fruit** on it, only to act disappointed and even

---

[201] Lloyd J. Ogilvie *The Communicator's Commentary: Mark* (Waco: Word Books, 1982), 226.

vengeful against a poor tree. Just as we think of the drowning pigs of chapter 5 as being "poor" (even though we would have considered them rightly used as pork sausage), many a bleeding heart would find it difficult that a "poor tree" (otherwise used for good building materials or firewood) would be so judged and sentenced to cursing—particularly since the same Jesus that used His power to curse the tree to fruitlessness could have pushed fruit through this same "poor tree"[202]...unless He was trying to teach something. And in teaching a lesson to the foundation of the New Testament church (the apostles), He was not mis-stewarding the tree (any more than drowning the pigs to save a demoniac was a misuse of the pigs).

Some have thought about **the fig tree** as being ethnic Israel.[203] If this were merely Israel, Jeremiah 33:25-26 and Romans 11 would make no sense for Israel would n**ever grow fruit again.** So, this cannot be merely Israel, for they indeed do grow **fruit again,** and the nations do indeed eat (Isaiah 66).[204] Luke 21:29 further complicates the notion that this would be Israel for it would mean that all other nations would make comebacks if the **fig tree** is always "ethnic" or "national Israel."

And His disciples heard it. But what did they hear? They should have seen what happened next, and then did the math when they experienced verse 20. See those notes.

11:15-17

So they came to Jerusalem. Then Jesus went into the temple Now when we see the word temple in our passage we are probably thinking about the building, but that was a place that very, very few could go. Most of the time when we see the word "temple" in our Bible we are

---

[202]Hughes, 271; I do reflect, though, about those "vessels of mercy" and "vessels of wrath" deemed so and created by such in the All Powerful God as proposed by Paul.
[203]For good reason. Ethnic Israel is often seen as a fig tree (Jeremiah 8:13; 29:17; Hosea 9:10, 16). I think sometimes commentators and Bible teachers mistake all of "ethnic Israel" for the evils of Israel's leadership which is what is really being discarded here—their house of worship and its system.
[204]Jeremiah 51:57 does use "never" poetically in a sense that does not obviously mean "never ever."

seeing the great complex. You will find from John chapter two that took 46 years to build it, probably because they had to make the top of a mountain flat. And they did that only virtually because they actually built a platform.

and began to drive out those who bought and sold in the temple, this area which would equate to three football fields.

and overturned the tables of the money changers and the seats of those who sold doves. And that, that was going to make them pretty upset. Of course none of us would imagine setting up a craft booth in the middle of preaching or prayer time, but I have met one or two in our crowd that are willing to start going to a particular service or a Sunday School class, or even a church, because they they have something to sell and they have the latest magazine to give. Or, they found fresh clientele for their practice or their business or their sales base. Please tell me the difference.

      People would be buying and selling. They wanted the best place at the entrance of the temple and so they would pay top price, and then don't forget, you want to sell the animals, and we find in John 5 that there was a sheep market outside the northern part of the temple. They would sell the sheep and only sheep bought at the temple would strangely pass the test of being able to be offered to the priests. And so if you brought a sheep from out of town and you were a foreigner, well then that probably wouldn't pass the blemish test that the priests would give. And really, if you want the kind that are guaranteed to pass the test you could buy one here at the market. Oh, but before you do that you need the right kind of money. So you come on in here and you find the right currency and there's temple currency. We only have currency that can be used in the temple, and only currency that can be used in the temple can be used in the temple. And so you get ripped off swapping currency, and then you get ripped off buying your sheep with your new currency. So you lose in the exchange and you go out here and lose in the purchase. And then don't forget when it's time to leave you can't give the temple currency back, and so on your way out of town you find someone like Matthew that's ready to tax you for your temple currency. And Jesus says, "You've made this place a market. I can't even get the nations in here to pray. There's no room to pray. There's too much rubbish in the temple!"

17 Then He taught, saying to them, "Is it not written, Again we find ourselves quoting Isaiah (56:7) just as we refer to Isaiah in Mark 16:15 with "each creature."

'My house shall be called a house of prayer for all nations'? But you have made it a [k]**"den of thieves.'** " This is the second time Jesus cleanses the temple.[205] The first time is at the beginning of his ministry in John two. He comes into the temple and throws the money changers out. Why? Because he is purifying the Levites (Malachi 3:3). He is making the priesthood clean. Who is he talking about? The Levites, the people who were chosen by God to work the temple. "This is supposed to be house of prayer and look what you have done. You are supposed to watching after God's house and you have made it a place where cheaters and liars and thieves can be comfortable."

See **prayer** is a big part of meeting with God. Of all the things Jesus could have said in verse 17, He did not say, "It is written My house shall be called a house of preaching." Out of all the things Jesus could have called His Father's house, it is called **a house of prayer**. And so distracting someone from worship makes God very angry. Distracting someone from prayerful worship makes God very angry. Angry enough where you're ok with being mistaken as an angry man. And Jesus could have easily been thought of as an angry man in this passage. "Boy, He's just so… Man, what a temper! I wish He'd be more Christian! I just don't think you should ever get upset." You are quite the moralist. You're even better than Jesus.

11:18-19

And the scribes and chief priests heard it and sought how they might destroy Him; How ridiculous that they think they could after all

---

[k] Jer. 7:11

[205] It's a little unnatural to assume two purgings since Matthew's version and Mark's version read virtually identical except this difference of Mark 11:11. See my commentary on Matthew (chapter 21) for more discussion on this episode.

He had done to demonstrate His power. This is nothing short of the discovery of the "wrath of the Lamb" (Revelation 6:16),[206] in part, and to "stand in that day" (Malachi 3:2) would have proven impossible.

11:20-21

Now in the morning, Tuesday with the "Good Friday" scenario. **as they passed by, they saw the fig tree dried up from the roots. 21 And Peter, remembering, said to Him, "Rabbi, look! The fig tree which You cursed has withered away."** They should have remembered the day before: 1. Jesus cursing the fig tree; 2. Jesus confronting the beautiful and fruitless system portrayed by the beautiful and fruitless temple.

11:22-24

23 For assuredly, I say to you, whoever says to this mountain, is Mount of Olives. Matthew 6 is the prayer that will bring the Zechariah 14 fulfillment of this very literal, end-times prayer.

'Be removed and be cast into the sea,' and does not doubt in his heart, but believes that those things he says the Scripture of Zechariah 14, that is. You have no business claiming this promise if you don't have a Scripture promise upon which to base your prayers.

11:27-28[207]

Then they came again to Jerusalem. If we hold to a "Palm Sunday" scenario (which is also a death of Jesus on Good Friday scenario), then this is still, since verse 20, Tuesday (which continues through chapter 13). **And as He was walking in the temple, the chief priests, the scribes, and the elders came** Both this and the first time **came** is used show, in the originals, that it is a hostile meeting at the entrance of the

---

[206]Hughes, 274-5.
[207]Matthew's version provides some of his light (see my commentary on Matthew 21).

city: "As Jesus and his disciples came into the city and temple, the fellas who worked their came to meet Him."[208]

28 And they said to Him, "By what authority are You doing these things? The first of four hostile questionings: the issue of authority and origin.

11:29-30

But Jesus answered and said to them, "I also will ask you one question; Often we can say that Jesus asks questions seeking the honesty of those being examined, but here "Jesus' use of a counterquestion was not an evasion but a means of establishing the source of his own authority and all authority in the spiritual realm."[209] On the other hand, this party's unwillingness or inability to answer Jesus' question rendered them "irrelevant" as teachers of the law (Rabbis).

11:31-33

And they reasoned among themselves, saying, "If we say, and here is when we realize that our words have consequences. One of the best things a person can do for us is to ask us a question without innumerable possibilities. We ask questions that have obvious choices.

Jesus asks a question that doesn't have a "false dichotomy." He apparently knew they would affirm that there were only two options. They had, after all, said there were "demons" only in contrast to God (Mark 3:22). It seems, then, that to put a person in place where they must pick between the options they must agree with you about the options.

---

[208]Perschbacher, 173.

[209] James A. Brooks, *Mark*, vol. 23, The New American Commentary (Nashville: Broadman & Holman Publishers, 1991), 187.

Chapter 12

12:1-8[210]

Then on the basis of the closing verses and Jesus' summary of their response (or lack thereof), He tells this parable. This discourse continues through the departure of the "chief priests, scribes and elders" (21:12) and the arrival of "Pharisees and Herodians" (12:13), the arrival of the Sadducees (12:18), the arrival of a particular scribe (12:28), and finally Jesus' address to the entire crowd (12:35)—all of which takes place in the "temple" (11:27 & 12:35 compared with His departure from the "temple" in 13:1).

He began to speak to them in parables: "A man probably somebody who owns everything but not the Son of God (verse 7). **planted a vineyard and set a hedge around** *it,* **dug** *a place for* **the wine vat and built a tower. And he leased it to** [1]**vinedressers** This makes the contextual antagonists those who are left to oversee the **vineyard.** They agreed (verse 12).

and went into a far country. I shudder to think this must mean that God was once here as a man (as do the Brigham Young-ites). Not every point of every parable is to be doctrinal or instructive.

8 So they in the context of the conversation of this passage, it is the "chief priests, the scribes, and the elders"—those having legitimate places of authority in that system. **took him and killed** *him* **and cast** *him* **out of the vineyard.** This is contextually, just as He threw the merchants out of the temple. In other words, what Jesus did in the temple was a foretaste of what the Father will one day do to their religion.

9 "Therefore what will the owner of the vineyard do? He will come and destroy the vinedressers, and give the vineyard to others. Matthew reports that these words were the reply of those to whom Jesus gave this question at the beginning of this verse. **Give the vineyard to**

---

[210]See more on 12:1-12 in the appendix on Bibliology.
[1]tenant farmers

others at least means that the responsibility of bringing forth fruit will be given to leaders who have not yet led—specifically the unqualified disciples who will be the foundation of the church (Ephesians 2:20). By application, this at least means that God will gain the fruit through varying means as it pleases Him.

12:10-12

Have you not even read this Scripture: Of all the things that He probably shouldn't have asked them, that was it. They spent their time making dollars because they knew the Scriptures, or at least said they did.

'The stone which the builders rejected *Has become the chief cornerstone.* Everything that is right is measured off of Christ. Everything. This passage is also quoted in Acts 4 during the ministry of Peter, as well as in his own first letter (chapter 2).

11 *This was the LORD's doing, And it is marvelous in our eyes'?"* Jesus quotes out of Psalm 118. Psalm 118:17 gives a glimpse at the promise of resurrection. Psalm 118 was heavily upon the mind of Jesus as it is the main thrust behind a great deal of what happened on what we typically call "Palm Sunday."

12:13-15

Then they sent to Him some of the Pharisees and the Herodians, These Herodians: they're strange folks. These are people that are a small group of Jews loyal to the various members of Herod's family. They had made their peace with the occupying Romans and they saw taxes as an appropriate way to fulfill the responsibility as good citizens. These are offspring of Esau. These Herodians, they're Idumeans and that is the New Testament equivalent to the Edomites. They were not necessarily Jews unless they married into that ethnicity.

But here they are now and they are being sent out by the Pharisees, an absolutely opposing group. The Herodians embrace the occupiers and the Pharisees hated the occupiers. Here, both the Pharisees and the Herodians dislike Jesus a great deal. But they also disliked each other, until now.

14 When they had come, they said to Him, "Teacher, we know that You are true, and care about no one; for You do not regard the person of men, but teach the way of God in truth. Is it lawful Now then, what law do you think the Herodians were referencing? If you're talking about Roman law, of course it was legal. Of course it was lawful to pay tribute to Caesar. It was required, which made it lawful. So what law do you suppose the Pharisees were inquiring about through these friends of theirs, the Herodians? Mosaic Law. "Is it ok with Moses if we pay taxes to Caesar?" And you know Jesus couldn't win here because if He says, "No, you shouldn't pay taxes to Caesar," the Herodians would get Him. If Jesus says, "Yes, you should pay taxes to Caesar," the Pharisees would get Him. There is no winning here and that's precisely what they wanted. Whichever side He chooses, He loses.

15 Shall we pay, or shall we not pay?" But He, knowing their hypocrisy, The opposite of hypocrite in the Greek is "sincerity." It was a trade term, and it has the idea of a person who makes vessels of clay. And at times they would be mishandled and cracked, and a person would daub it and fill the cracks with wax. And the only time you could tell that the pot was a good vessel was when the heat was applied, and if the wax melted off the pot you knew that you had a hypocritical vase. You didn't have a sincere one. You didn't have one that was without wax. Jesus is here saying, "I can see right through the cracks. I can see right through you. I know what you're thinking." When it said "He knew their hypocrisy," it also says "He knew they were not sincere."

12:16

So they brought it. And He said to them, "Whose image and inscription is this?" They said to Him, "Caesar's." And superscription is typically now today a math term dealing with that exponent. Here it's "Whose picture and writing over this picture is this on the image?"

they said unto Him (these Pharisees & Herodians said), **Caesar's.** So He's holding up a coin. It says "Caesar: God and High Priest." He says, "Whose coin is this?" They said, "It's **Caesar's.**"

12:17

And Jesus answered and said to them, "Render to Caesar the things that are Caesar's, and to God the things that are God's." And they marveled at Him. So He didn't say, "Yeah, pay the tax." That would have gotten Him in trouble with the Pharisees. He says, "This is **Caesar's**. You ought to give it to him."

and unto God the things that are God's. This would have been a good time for the Lord to fix the economy or to talk about land ownership or about the evils of the occupation. Now would have been a good time for the Lord Jesus to talk about the illegitimate Roman government in God's promised land.

Could Jesus have done that? Certainly. He could have said, "Let's talk about this form of government. It's ridiculous. Who in the world made a senate?" He could have said, "Who made him God?" He could have talked about the constitutionality of certain things. Jesus could have at this point said, "Before you give Caesar what is his, you should fix this place. You should demand to be heard." He could have said, "No, before you pay this to Caesar you make sure they're not funding abortion. Before you give this to Caesar you make sure that they're not paying for Medicaid and Medicare for people of various lifestyles that have a high, high, high probability of dying before they're 50 years old."

The Lord is not talking about tithing here. If the Lord holds up a coin and proves that you should be paying taxes by showing you someone's image and blasphemous title on a coin, what would Jesus be holding up in His other hand if He were saying, "Give to God the things that are God's?" A coin. If He were teaching on tithing He'd be holding up a coin with the image of God engraved on it: a transgression of the second commandment (Exodus 20).

So there's a deeper truth here. He is telling those Herodians something that is very deep. This 2nd question is about ownership, and it was way deeper than they wanted to go. Just as the first group didn't intend on the first question being centered around their lack of authority in speaking on things that concern Heaven, so this question centers on their lack of willingness to serve God alone. These groups had questions, and Jesus had answers. Be careful when you come with your questions. These are tastes of the end of time when you think you'll stagger on up to the judgment and demand that God tells you this and that. "The coin: it has Caesar's name on it. If you don't want to pay taxes, quit playing with his currency. But then there is something else that has the image of God on it and it belongs to God and you give it to God." So He establishes the duty to pay tribute to Caesar because Caesar's image is on the coin. If you don't wish to pay income taxes, quit using the currency of the country you're living in!

Jesus then uses that same leverage of ownership and the argument to give God what belongs to Him doesn't fit if this were about money. Why? Because there is no image or likeness upon any Jewish money. It would be blasphemy. Therefore, if Jesus is arguing for Caesar's ownership of coinage based on his image upon it, He is arguing for God's ownership of the Herodians who bare the image of God.

12:18[211]

18 Then Matthew says "the same day" *some* **Sadducees, [k]who say there is no resurrection, came to Him; and they asked Him, saying:** the question they are about to ask is to place the person who believes in the **resurrection** in a camp where they would be seen as absurdly silly as believing in such a thing can bring about some really awkward situations.

12:19-23

23 Therefore, in the resurrection [which we don't believe in], **when they rise, whose wife will she be? For all seven had her as wife."** See this Deuteronomy 25:5-10 principle lived out in the book of Ruth—see appendix. Really, though, these are those guys who take what we believe and twist it into ridiculous scenarios like "Can God do anything? If so, can He make a rock so big He can't lift?" I mean, who saw a scenario where there are 1. 7 brothers; 2. Six of them die before the

---

[211]See more on these verses 18-27 in the appendix on bibliology.
[k]Acts 23:8

woman does; 3. They die only during a marriage with her; 4. None of them have good enough chemistry with her to have a pregnancy; 5. They all occur during her childbearing years. In their mind, "Surely nobody is dumb enough to believe in the resurrection when they can't explain our really deep and smart and well-thought questions?"

This 3rd question showcases not the "chief priests, scribes, elders" and not the "Pharisees and Herodians", but the Sadducees, and in their attempts to show the absurdity of biblical truth they show themselves to be ignorant of their own self-contradictions. So rather than this question becoming a discussion about their lack of authority concerning heavenly things; rather than this being a discussion about their lack of servitude to God Almighty; this question focuses—whether they intended it or not (which they did not)—on their lack of coherence; their lack of consistency; their lack of self-agreement. They believe the Bible—sort of, but they don't know it and don't consider the 2nd and 3rd order effects of what they say they believe: watch Jesus' argument.

12:24-27

Jesus answered and said to them, "Are you not therefore mistaken, because you do not know the Scriptures nor the power of God? Their devaluation of the power of God is related to their ignorance of Scriptures like Genesis 2:7.[212]

25 For when they rise from the dead, they neither marry nor are given in marriage, but are like angels in heaven. This does not mean that angels cannot have sex, for it seems that Genesis 6:1-3 teaches the opposite. This also doesn't mean angels are genderless for mostly every time they are mentioned, they have a male denotation. "The text does not say angels cannot have sexual intercourse; it says they *don't*."[213]

It could be that they **are like angels** in that there will be no more people created as there are no **angels** reproducing even now. All angels

---

[212] This seems to be a string of Genesis arguments going all the way back to the opening verses of Mark 10 (Matthew 19 in that Gospel).
[213] Michael S. Heiser, *Reversing Hermon: Enoch, The Watchers & The Forgotten Mission of Jesus Christ* (Crane, MO: Defender, 2017), 18.

that there are now have always been since they were created and therefore, there will be no more. This reproduction issue seems obvious since the Deuteronomy 25:5-10 is for the purpose of reproduction (in the deceased brother's name).

26 But concerning the dead, that they rise, have you not read in the book of Moses, in the *burning* **bush** *passage,* **how God spoke to him, saying,** º*'I am the God of Abraham, the God of Isaac, and the God of Jacob'*? By the time Moses is told this by the Lord, it has been around 300 years since **Abraham** has died. **God** said to Moses that **I am the God of Abraham** rather than "I was the God of Abraham." No, **Abraham** was alive when God spoke to Moses. At this point, for over 1500 years these men have lived somewhere.

the God of Isaac, and the God of Jacob'? **God is not the God of the dead, but of the living."** In Genesis 2:7, God picked up a pile of dirt and breathed into it and made a human being. We are souls who have bodies since we are human beings. Never will a human being be intended to exist without a body. Therefore, even though spirits may exist without a body (assumed to be impossible by Sadducees since they don't believe in spirits called "angels"), they have an innate expectation to be fully human again (with bodies).

    This "power" problem—coming from ignorance of the Scriptures—is the indictment of Paul of those before him in Acts 26:8. If God did this once, then how hard is it for Him to do it on resurrection morning? Genesis 22 shows that Abraham may have believed God could do this with his dead and burnt-up son when he told his servants "we're going to worship and return."

27 He is not the God of the dead, but the God of the living. You are therefore greatly mistaken." Once again, these "Sadducees" are the type, like the "scribes and chief priests and elders"; like the "Pharisees & the Herodians" are the type that will, rather than dealing with the Christ that is in front of them and answers provided to them by God, they are going to deaden their senses and salve their consciences by asking mindless questions. Instead of facing the Christ that is clear to them and

---

º Ex. 3:6, 15

the Bible they do understand and the truths that are obvious—they are going to ask silly questions and desire to have more answers from questions full of ethical dilemmas and situational "what if's."

12:28-34[214]

Then one of the scribes came, Matthew says this was a lawyer, and leads the reader to believe that he was sent as a last ditch effort. This was not a fact-finding mission but the quality of Jesus' answer leads us to believe that this man's fourth question (after the "scribes, elders, and chief priests" of the first question; after the "Pharisees and Herodians" of the 2nd queston; after the "Sadducees" of the 3rd question), finds that he had a love problem—for if He did not, Jesus would have assessed him differently. So, perhaps not an authority issue (question 1); perhaps not a worship issue (question 2); perhaps not an ignorance issue (question 3), but a love issue is what this man had because we see what Jesus told him.

perceiving that He had answered them well, asked Him, "Which is the first commandment of all?" "if you can't be stumped on taxes or the afterlife, let's talk about the law."

29 Jesus answered him, I would have probably picked a "favorite" from the Decalogue. That would have been a substandard answer.

30 *And you shall* **love** The totality of God's character is spelled out in the commandments, but…apparently…this same character can be hung on God's **love.** It certainly doesn't mean that my **love** replaces my obedience, but rather that my obedience is enabled by my **love.** Deuteronomy 6:1 is the beginning of this discourse, and we see that God gives us the command to **love** so that we can be "well." God is interested in our wellness, and our wellness springs from our **love.**

the LORD your God with If you want to know whether or not you're giving to God the things that are God's, here's your checklist right here. Now Paul used a trichotomy (1 Thessalonians 5:23). Moses used a dichotomy (Gen 2:7). Here, Mark records a four-way division from the

---

[214] I cover this more in the Matthew commentary (22:34-40).

mouth of Jesus. So what's the point? Are we supposed to be able to say, "All right! Here are the parts of a human being." No, I think this is God's way of saying, "All of you." But He gives us three in this passage.

31 And the second, like *it, is* **this:** ˢ*"You shall love your neighbor as yourself.'* Jesus wasn't asked about this one. It is at this point where Jesus gives more information than what was requested. He gave the "lawyer" more than what he wanted; He gave him what he needed. This is found first in Leviticus 19:13-18. We don't get to just say, "I love God and I am not going to obey God in any regard if it involves you." No, this one is **like it.** As seen in Leviticus, all the requirements that involve your countrymen were acts of loving your neighbor.

33 And to love Him with all the heart, with all the understanding, with all the soul, and with all the strength, and to love one's neighbor as oneself, is more than all the whole burnt offerings and sacrifices." We know this man knows at least the spirit behind Isaiah 1 and Isaiah 40—maybe even his peer Micah (Micah 6:1-8) or Psalm 50. It does a person well to remember that Gospel-centered living is the only thing that makes this **love** possible in any person's heart. In other words, a full appreciation—which implies actual impartation—of this Calvary **love** is the only motivator.

> Near the cross! O Lamb of God, Bring its scenes before me;
> Help me walk from day to day, With its shadows o'er me.
> In the cross, in the cross, Be my glory ever;
> Till my raptured soul shall find Rest beyond the river.[215]

34 Now when Jesus saw that he answered wisely, He said to him, "You are not far from the kingdom of God." A very relieving and yet sad statement: One is **not far from the kingdom:** One is **not far,** and yet is **not** "in." Are you in this **kingdom** or merely **not far?** This man knew questions; knew answers; but did not know that he was not in the **kingdom.**

ˢLev. 19:18; Matt. 22:39; Gal. 5:14; James 2:8
[215] _____ *The Cokesbury Worship Hymnal* (New York/Nashville: Abingdon-Cokesbury, ____), hymn #34.

But after that no one dared question Him. Everybody is leaving Jesus alone; they are leaving Him alone because the talking is over and his death is three short days away.

12:35-36[216]
36 For David himself said ʸby the Holy Spirit: Jesus says that God wrote through **David** in Psalm 110:1. Get to where you can trust what Jesus says—specifically, here—concerning the Old Testament. You can trust His words if you can trust that He arose from the dead. A man Who rises from the dead can be trusted.

'The LORD said to my Lord, we might notice that Jehovah (all caps) said to David's "Sovereign" (not all caps).[217] We do, in this context see an Old Testament conversation between God the Father and His Son, Jesus. The command from the Father to the Son which follows has much to do with 12:10-11 (which is a quotation of Psalm 118) and the listeners would see these as implications of their murder of Him and His exaltation (anyway).

"Sit at My right hand, *Till I make Your enemies Your footstool."* ' mentioned again to the high priest in Mark 14:62. It is as if the Father told Jesus, "sit here and watch." Jesus' submission, therefore did not end at Calvary. *Till I make Your enemies Your footstool"'?* referring to a culture (as in Nebuchadnezzar and Zedekiah) when a conquered king would be made to wallow under the throne of a conquering king. What a beautiful difference in the life of a son of a king. We get to sit at His table and are not treated as a conquered and bitter enemy. The implication here is that these Pharisees are the enemies of both Son and the Father, and that they will be under the **footstool** of the Son. This passage is quoted by Peter in Acts 2:34, by Paul (1 Corinthians 15:25), and mentioned in Hebrews 4 or 5 times.

12:37

---

[216]More on this in my commentary on Matthew (22:41-45) and in my commentary on the Psalms (Psalm 110).

ʸ 2 Sam. 23:2

[217]See appendix in my commentary on Matthew on "finding the Father in the O.T."

Therefore David affirmed twice as the author of this Psalm. **himself calls Him *'Lord'*; how is He *then* his Son?"** Why is this strange? Because usually the **Son** calls the Father **Lord,** but here David calls his **Son Lord.**

12:38-44[218]

Here Jesus shows the scribe that He is the one who is a part of the guild which persecutes widows (verse 40) and are much further from the kingdom ideal than those very widows (verses 42-44). The scribe, therefore, comes face to face with the fact that he is outside the kingdom ("not far from the kingdom" verse 34), and that his question about the greatest commandments (and so forth) are misleading—shrouding his corrupted view of Christ (verse 36) and self (verse 40).

---

[218]See much more on these verses in my commentary on Matthew (23:1-14).

Chapter 13

13:1[219]

Then as He went out of the temple, towards the Mount of Olives (13:3).

13:2

And Jesus answered and said to him, "Do you see these great buildings? [b]**Not** *one* **stone shall be left upon another, that shall not be thrown down."** The standing wall that remains to this day does not seem to qualify as **these great buildings.** I would therefore not allow the remaining wall to thwart the obvious sense in which the siege/destruction of A.D. 70 is in view here.

13:3-4

Now as He sat on the Mount of Olives opposite the temple, Peter, James, John, and Andrew the first time these four have been found together in this Gospel since the first chapter when they were called. **asked Him privately, 4 "Tell us, when will these things be?** The promise of 13:2 that the temple and its buildings (13:1) would be destroyed. **And what** *will be* **the sign when all these things will be fulfilled?"** Jesus gives much more information than what they are asking without telling them…or, He is really about to answer the question with only the necessary information and it occurs around the time when the temple would be destroyed.

The fact that we have talk concerning the end of the world (13:31) inhibits our adoption of what we might call the "full Preterist" view (the view that all things are to be fulfilled in only the first century around A.D.). We have already talked about the reality "dual interpretation" and we see 13:14 was already fulfilled before Christ and

---

[219] See more in my commentary on Matthew (24:1-4).
[b] Luke 19:44; this verse is so powerful that only my preaching philosophy keeps me from using it to nail the lid on the coffin in this series.

yet Jesus says it will occur again. In other words, in Jesus' time, Daniel 11:31 was history and prophecy.

If one is familiar with the 1st/2nd coming confusion of the Old Testament prophets (1 Peter 1:10-12), then assuming the New Testament apostles could have experienced the same between the A.D. 70 "coming" and the 2nd coming is also understandable. The chart (constructed primarily by my old boss, Pastor Sean Harris) shows that Paul was expecting a non-Judean specific final coming judgment for all those on the earth at the "day of the Lord". To Paul, there was a final fulfillment of Jesus' words.

13:5-8[220]

It seems this would be a good time to show that Biblical prophets used extravagant language which was only poetically fulfilled. One example would be Haggai 2:6-9 where heavens shaking (and so forth) must be fulfilled in Christ's first coming (because it had to precede the destruction of the 2nd temple in A.D. 70)[221] even though it was literal in the "first Moses" (Exodus 19:10-20). Hebrews 1:1-2 and 12:25-29 (quoting Haggai 2) very clearly confirm this "heavens shaking" in Christ's first coming. It seems reasonable, then, that as poetic language was used on this magnitude with Christ's first coming, that it is also overstated in the times of his coming in judgment[222] in A.D. 70 when the "buildings of the temples" were made flat.

And Jesus, answering them, began to say: "Take heed that no one deceives you. 6 For many will come in My name, saying, 'I am *He*,' and will deceive many.[223] There is ample value in quoting commentaries of today and long ago to show that we are not crazy for believing this occurred on some level in A.D. 70, but we should

---

[220]More can be found in my commentary on Matthew (24:4-26).
[221]More on this passage in my commentary on Matthew (chapter 12).
[222]Much was made of this in my commentary on Matthew (10:23).
[223]Believe it or not, there are people today who claim that they are the Messiah. Here's an example:
https://www.sermonaudio.com/sermoninfo.asp?SID=9412849160 [accessed 1/9/18].

probably discipline ourselves here to the simplicity of the passage.[224] After all, 1 John 2:18 records an apostle saying it was occurring by the time he wrote that epistle—as does 2 Thessalonians 2:3-7. We could also talk a great deal about world religions and their "false christs," but that is again outside the place of this text.[225]

7 But when you hear of ʰwars and rumors of wars, [226] **do not be troubled;** when we become "unsettled" **(troubled)** we become impetuous in doing things to "settle" ourselves.

8 For nation will rise against nation, or rather "ethnicity against ethnicity"

and kingdom against kingdom It need not be a large **kingdom** (Genesis 13-14) to be considered a **kingdom** or have a **king.**

13:9-13

"But watch out for yourselves, for they will deliver you up to councils, and you will be beaten in the synagogues. Those who demand an "only literal and only futurist" perspective on these verses must deal with the very Jerusalem/Jew-centric feel this has. If this is the proposed "world-wide" Revelation drama then why does it seem so focused? It's as laughable as saying "World Series" in MLB when it's Canada and US teams only. Or "World Champions in NBA" when it's only Canada and US teams.

10 And the gospel the reader has to admit this is no different a **gospel** than Mark 1:15 where Jesus' listener is told to "repent and believe" it. See notes under Mark 16:15 and the appendix from Genesis where we

---

[224] If one wishes to see some good sources saying "false Christs occurred in the first century", they can review the falling sermon where I enclose many; https://www.sermonaudio.com/playpopupvideo.asp?SID=2171619485010 [accessed 1/9/18].

[225] Ibid.

ʰRev. 6:2–4

[226] Did these things take place in A.D. 70? https://www.sermonaudio.com/playpopupvideo.asp?SID=32161949482 [accessed 1/15/18].

discuss all creation being restored through the Creator/King coming to earth to die.

must first be preached to all the nations. It seems as though this statement isn't concluded. We see the word **first** as if it belongs on a timeline with other events; perhaps it is before the "these things" contextually (if we didn't have Matthew we would have to lean on the context Mark has provided. Matthew certainly helps). It could also be "the end" of verse 13. One glimpse of this word **nations** and we see that this could be taken generically and found fulfilled (see Colossians 1:23); if taken figuratively it was also found fulfilled (Acts 17:6). If taken literally, we know it was not fulfilled before the end of the generation, but if dual fulfillment is in mind, it will indeed be fulfilled (Revelation 5:9; 7:11-15).

13 And you will be hated by all for My name's sake. But he who endures to the end shall be saved. In what way? By "flight" (verse 18).

13:14-20

"So when you see the [s]**'*abomination of desolation,'* spoken of by Daniel the prophet, standing where it ought not" (let the reader understand),**[227] Matthew 27:25 and Luke 23:28 seem to give us license to look for a fulfillment for both those listening to Jesus and to those who qualify as their "children," but the immediate fulfillment is to those in answer to the question of 13:4 being fulfilled in Jesus' generation (13:30).

> The events of 13:14–23 concern the Roman campaign against Judea. "Never to be equaled again" in verse 19 suggests an event

---

[s]Dan. 9:27; 11:31; 12:11

[227]When we know Jesus didn't say this parenthetical phrase and yet it appears in Matthew's record (Matthew 24:15), then we know that it is virtually out of the question that Matthew and Mark acquired their information from Jesus Himself—for how can we expect that they would have both "felt led" at the same time to say "hey, reader, pay attention." So this is a small token of how we know that either Matthew copied Mark or Mark copied Matthew or that they both copied a different source. The idea of an eyewitness of Jesus' teaching (Matthew) would copy a non-eyewitness seems a little far-fetched.

within human history rather than its conclusion. The "abomination that causes desolation" (v. 14) refers to the defiling of the temple.[228]

"then let those who are in Judea flee to the mountains. There are **mountains** to the east and the southeast of Jerusalem where one can certainly live in homes on the sides of these **mountains.**

15 Let him who is on the housetop not go down into the house, nor enter to take anything out of his house. these were often "2nd stories" to which one could resort in the hot evenings to catch a breeze.

20 And unless the Lord had shortened those days, no flesh would be saved; but for the elect's a word used only in this passage (13:20, 22, 27) **sake, whom He chose, He shortened the days. those days** the **days** of "tribulation" mentioned in verse 19.

those days…shortened. So I would suggest that Daniel's 70th week is designed to be seven years long, lasting seven years. It says that they are 360 day years because that is how many days are in a Jewish year. So it has a place holder for seven 360 day years, but I would suggest that the great tribulation will be shy of that by a few days, maybe a few weeks, a few months. It is a guess. It could mean, I guess, that the daylight hours of the day are **shortened.** This could be how there are no people that know when He shall come (13:32).

13:21-23

"Then if anyone says to you, 'Look, here *is* the Christ!' or, 'Look, *He is* there!' do not believe it. see 13:6 & 13:22 as well. **22 For false christs and false prophets will rise and show signs and wonders to deceive, if possible, even the elect.** It is not **possible** (John 10:5).

they shall deceive the very elect. So all over the place, even in the time of what we would call "the antichrist" you have many **false Christs.** Isn't that something? So when you read Revelation 13 and you get this

---

[228] David S. Dockery et al., *Holman Bible Handbook* (Nashville, TN: Holman Bible Publishers, 1992), 582.

picture in your mind that the antichrist is slaying the whole world and no one else has anything to do but walk around in a trance and worship the beast…But that is not the picture given to us from the Scripture.

>While the **elect** are not immune to "sorrow" (verse 8-12), they do have a special promise here: they will endure (13:13) and not be **deceive**d.

13:24-25

"But in those days, after that tribulation, Please notice the only thing Mark said about the tribulation was what? False christs and false prophets (13:19-23). The only thing worth writing about was the onslaught of false prophets and false christs in **that tribulation**. That is significant.

25 the stars of heaven will fall, and the powers in the heavens will be **ᵃshaken. Do we automatically assume these were fulfilled literally or do we simply cast our palms skyward in desperation?

> Exactly what is meant [by what is contained here] we do not know…We do not venture even to conjecture what these things may mean.[229]

We absolutely do not fling out such careless agnostics. Rather, we search the Old Testament for precedent.

>Isaiah 13:1-17 sounds a lot like this, and it describes the Medo-Persians "turning out the lights" on Babylon.

> [Regarding verse] 10. stars, &c.—figuratively for *anarchy, distress,* and *revolutions* of kingdoms (Is 34:4; Joe 2:10; Ez 32:7,

---

ᵃHeb. 12:26; Rev. 6:13
[229]Alivah Hovey, ed. *An American Commentary on the New Testament, Commentary on the Gospel of Mark* (Valley Forge: Judson, 1881), 199-200.

8; Am 8:9; Rev 6:12–14). There may be a *literal* fulfilment *finally,* shadowed forth under this imagery (Rev 21:1).[230]

This took place in the time of Daniel, around 500 years before Jesus (Daniel 5:1-12). These are then poetic figures of speeches saying "not even the heavens are looking at us."

Also Isaiah 34:4-5, regarding to Idumea (Edom), sounds the same. This was nothing more than their destruction at the hand of Nebuchadnezzar in the days of Jeremiah:

> When Judah was captive in Babylon, Edom, in every way, insulted over her fallen mistress, killed many of those Jews whom the Chaldeans had left, and hence was held guilty of fratricide by God (Esau, their ancestor, having been brother to Jacob): this was the cause of the denunciations of the prophets against Edom (Is 63:1, &c.; Je 49:7; Ez 25:12–14; 35:3–15; Joe 3:19; Am 1:11, 12; Am 1:11, 12, Ob 1:8, 10, 12–18 Mal 1:3, 4). Nebuchadnezzar humbled Idumea accordingly (Je 25:15–21).[231]

Why do we expect Jesus to use these figures of speech as a literal usage in regards to the future of planet earth? Would He use them so? Maybe, but not primarily so.

It's probably being used (as pertaining to Egypt in Ezekiel 32:2-8) by Jesus regarding Jerusalem's destruction in A.D. 70.

> 'So far as Egypt is concerned,' [accompanies the] remark that the darkness consequent thereupon is a figurative representation of utterly hopeless circumstances[232]

---

[230] Robert Jamieson, A. R. Fausset, and David Brown, *Commentary Critical and Explanatory on the Whole Bible*, vol. 1 (Oak Harbor, WA: Logos Research Systems, Inc., 1997), 445.

[231] Robert Jamieson, A. R. Fausset, and David Brown, *Commentary Critical and Explanatory on the Whole Bible*, vol. 1 (Oak Harbor, WA: Logos Research Systems, Inc., 1997), 467.

[232] Carl Friedrich Keil and Franz Delitzsch, *Commentary on the Old Testament*, vol. 9 (Peabody, MA: Hendrickson, 1996), 267.

Ezekiel lamented the destruction of Pharaoh Hophra and Egypt (cf. 29:8). The date was March 3, 585 B.C., one year and seven months after the fall of Jerusalem (32:1).[233]

Amos 5:1-20 uses this language regarding Israel's fall to Assyria.

Amos's prophecy was fulfilled in 721 BC when the Assyrian king Sargon II destroyed Samaria and exiled the survivors… Indeed, when a nation and its cities are destroyed and burned, the lights go out for those people when the smoke from the burning city blocks out the sun. That day is the end of the world for them.[234]

After seeing the truth regarding Babylon, Edom, Egypt, and Samaria, should we assume that Jesus used this same kind of language, but in a literal way, for future states of planet earth? Perhaps, but not primarily so (see table).[235]

Zephaniah 1:12-15 places this language at the destruction of Jerusalem.

What do the figures of darkness and gloominess mean? Yahweh declares his intention to "bring distress upon men." The calamity would cause those men to "walk like blind men," i.e., in total confusion. In the case of Josiah's son Zedekiah, the last king of Judah, this prediction received a physical fulfillment. After forcing him to witness the execution of his sons, Nebuchadnezzar had Zedekiah's eyes pierced. He spent his last years in blindness in Babylon.[236]

---

[233] Robert B. Hughes and J. Carl Laney, *Tyndale Concise Bible Commentary*, The Tyndale Reference Library (Wheaton, IL: Tyndale House Publishers, 2001), 304.

[234] Gary V. Smith, *Isaiah 1–39*, ed. E. Ray Clendenen, The New American Commentary (Nashville: B & H Publishing Group, 2007), 301.

[235] crafted originally by my friend and boss previously, Pastor Sean Harris of the Berean Baptist Church (Fayetteville, NC

[236] James E. Smith, *The Minor Prophets*, Old Testament Survey Series (Joplin, MO: College Press, 1994), Zep 1:14–18.

Mark expects his reader to know this as language for the destruction of a city. Are we surprised, now, that this language being used the first time concerning the fall of Jerusalem to the Babylonians is being used again by Jesus regarding the fall of Jerusalem to the Romans? With Jesus promising the buildings of the temples (13:1-4) had to be toppled and all the accompanying "signs" had to occur before the end of His generation (13:30), it seems to make perfect sense that 13:25 is speaking of the simultaneous destruction of Jerusalem in A.D. 70.

13:26

Then or, "at this time";[237] this gives the idea that there are three different events here (Mark only uses the word thusly): 1. Chaos in the cosmos; 2. **Son of Man coming;** 3. Gathering of the elect. This would mean, then, that we are not at liberty to give the same interpretation to both the darkening of the skies in the previous verse and to the **coming of the Son of Man.** To say that the destruction of the city is the darkening of the sky (verse 25) means that the **coming of the Son of Man** cannot be the same event.

they will see the Son of Man coming in the clouds with great power and glory. Deuteronomy 33:24-27 already described the God of "Asher" as "riding the clouds." This was normal, poetic language for an active God continually judging. In Psalm 18:6-10, Psalm 68:1-5, and Psalm 104:1-3, the Psalmist likewise describes His God as one Who rides a cherub and also, the wind. Isaiah 19:1-3 speaks of it in regards to a nation being destroyed.

> The political situation will deteriorate into civil war, bringing one Egyptian against another. God's act of stirring up this trouble (19:3) does not refer to the Assyrian attack of Sargon, but the period when four different dynasties struggled to take control of the nation a few years before 711 BC. [238]

---

[237] "G5119 - tote - Strong's Greek Lexicon (KJV)." Blue Letter Bible. Web. 2 Feb, 2018. <https://www.blueletterbible.org//lang/lexicon/lexicon.cfm?Strongs=G5119&t=KJV>.

[238] Gary V. Smith, *Isaiah 1–39*, ed. E. Ray Clendenen, The New American Commentary (Nashville: B & H Publishing Group, 2007), 356.

> "It cannot be determined whether this passage refers to the anarchy that followed the expulsion of the Ethiopians (DIODOR., I. 66) about the year 695, or the contests that preceded Psammetichus' ascending the throne (between 678–670)."[239]
>
> The disintegration of Egypt commenced about B.C. 760–750, towards the close of the twenty-second dynasty. About B.C. 735 a struggle began between Piankhi, King of Upper Egypt, and Tafnekht, King of Sais and Memphis, in which the other princes took different sides. Ten or twelve years later there was a struggle between Bocchoris and Sabaco. From this time onwards, until Psamatik I. re-established the unity of Egypt (about B.C. 650)…[240]

It may seem disheartening to see guesswork like this with dates decades apart, but what they have in common is that they are not literal expectations of seeing a bodily form of God riding on the clouds (Isaiah 19:1).

"So what?"

After these considerations, we see Jesus using the same language and, therefore, we assume He also speaks of the destruction of Jerusalem during which the temple is flattened (13:2) in Jesus' generation (13:30).

> It is a principle of biblical interpretation that when the Bible consistently uses a given type of language in a given context, whenever we see that language, we should look for that context. In the case of Mark 13, then, the language seems to be speaking of divine judgment. Certainly the destruction of the temple and the city of Jerusalem were acts of divine judgment. Therefore, the coming of Christ that Jesus spoke about here may be understood as His coming in judgment on Jerusalem in AD 70.[241]

---

[239] John Peter Lange et al., *A Commentary on the Holy Scriptures: Isaiah* (Bellingham, WA: Logos Bible Software, 2008), 223.

[240] H. D. M. Spence-Jones, ed., *Isaiah*, vol. 1, The Pulpit Commentary (London; New York: Funk & Wagnalls Company, 1910), 312.

[241] R. C. Sproul, *Mark*, First Edition., St. Andrew's Expositional Commentary (Orlando, FL: Reformation Trust, 2011), 351.

Daniel 7:13 is the very Scripture being here referenced by our Lord, and it does not, as some suspect have the **Son of man coming** to earth, but rather **coming** to the One on the throne (Mark 14:62).[242] This variation or slight adjustment, then, should allow the reader to see that Jehovah shares His power and prominence with the **Son of Man** and that they both will be coming on **the clouds.**

> It would be easy to multiply examples of this characteristic quality of prophetic diction. Prophecy is of the nature of poetry, and depicts events, not in the prosaic style of the historian, but in the glowing imagery of the poet. Add to this that the Bible does not speak with the cold logical correctness of the Western peoples, but with the tropical fervour of the gorgeous East.[243]

After reading Daniel 7 we realize that: 1. The Son of man comes to the one on the throne (much like Revelation 5, but I digress); 2. He is given a kingdom (after being seated fulfilling Psalm 110:1); 3. It occurs in and around the 4th beast; 4. It occurs around the time of the temple's destruction (Mark 13:1-4); 5. It also occurs after the destruction of Jerusalem (Mark 13:24-25); It happens during the generation of Jesus (Mark 13:30).

Again then, with the Old Testament language as the backdrop for Jesus' audience, we see this as more language for a judgment to come upon Jerusalem in Jesus' generation (13:30) in answer to the question of the disciples (13:3-4).

Now then, how does anybody **see** this (13:25; 14:62)? When you see that the "Son of Man" in Daniel 7:13 He is seen as receiving a

---

[242] The only "hang up" one might see (as I did) was the "sitting on the right hand of God" before the "coming with clouds [to God on His throne" (Daniel 7:9)] until you realize there are other times when things mentioned in pairs are not necessarily chronologically in order (Acts 5:30). In other words, we acknowledge that Christ is seated (Daniel 7:26) after He is brought with the clouds of Heaven (Daniel 7:13).

[243] James Stuart Russell, *The Parousia: A Critical Inquiry into the New Testament Doctrine of Our Lord's Second Coming* (London: Daldy, Isbister & Co., 1878), 81.

"never ending kingdom" (Daniel 7:14), and as such, the observer would "see" this **coming with the clouds** when they saw His kingdom (Mark 9:1).[244]

> Comparing this with our Lord's words, He seems to us, by "the Son of man coming in the clouds with great power and glory," to mean, that when judicial vengeance shall once have been executed upon Jerusalem, and the ground thus cleared for the unobstructed establishment of His own kingdom, His true regal claims and rights would be visibly and gloriously asserted and manifested. [245]

But with His statements in 9:1 and 14:62 (in the context of 14:53-65) we should have no issues with seeing it as such here and, once again, saying that either Jesus was wrong in all three situations or He was right and it occurred in a manner in which 2018 Americans would not be readily aware. We take this forward, shockingly, even more: Mark 13:32-37 are not a comfort to the ready other than the watchman of the house will not be furious with them for sleeping. The function of these verses is to strike fear in the hearts of those who get comfortable in Jerusalem and are not ready, then, when **the Son of Man com**es to judge that wicked city, and they are consequently trapped in that city (13:15-20).

13:27[246]

And then He will send His angels, Jesus is here claiming to be the "LORD of hosts." Here is an obvious claim to deity. **and gather together His elect from the four winds, from the farthest part of earth to the farthest part of heaven.** First of all, there is nothing secret here where any **elect** are being removed. Preceding context does not allow for that

---

[244]This is easy to see when we realize the "four beasts" of Daniel 7:1-12 are "kings" (Daniel 7:17) and as such were "literally" seen only when the "kings" they represented arose.

[245] Robert Jamieson, A. R. Fausset, and David Brown, *Commentary Critical and Explanatory on the Whole Bible*, vol. 2 (Oak Harbor, WA: Logos Research Systems, Inc., 1997), 88.

[246]Here is another reminder to reference my commentary on Matthew (24:31).

> *2 Maccabees 2:18 We trust in God, that he will soon have mercy on us and gather us together from everywhere under the heavens to his holy Place, for he has rescued us from great perils and has purified His Place.*
>
> Consider the fact that this apocryphal passage (which predates Jesus) includes: 1. The gathering in the same phraseology as in verse 27; 2. The temple; 3. Great perils (tribulation); 4. And abomination (thus requiring "purify"ing.

We have similar phraseology in the Scripture. Some seems to help us with **from the farthest part of earth to the farthest part of heaven** by showing us it is like our modern-day "from sea to shining sea" (see Deuteronomy 4:32, for example).

Still other places help us see a backdrop to Jesus' words in their depth.

> *Deuteronomy 30:1-5 "Now it shall come to pass, when all these things come upon you, the blessing and the curse which I have set before you, and you call them to mind among all the nations where the LORD your God drives you, 2 and you return to the LORD your God and obey His voice, according to all that I command you today, you and your children, with all your heart and with all your soul, 3 that the LORD your God will bring you back from captivity, and have compassion on you, and gather you again from all the nations where the LORD your God has scattered you. <u>4 If any of you are driven out to the farthest parts under heaven, from there the LORD your God will gather you, and from there He will bring you.</u> 5 Then the LORD your God will bring you to the land which your fathers possessed, and you shall possess it. He will prosper you and multiply you more than your fathers.*

As in 2nd Maccabees, we see a clear promise of God to re-gather the Israelites to their land. It seems like there should be some thought given as to whether the "elect of New Testament", those in Christ, are in view in Mark 13:27.

Jeremiah 49:36-39 tells us this has already occurred to Elam[247] while Zechariah 2:6-12 says it has already occurred to Jerusalem. The pattern is that this is the gathering of the dispersed Jews.

It must be, then, that this is not automatically speaking of the supernatural catching away of those who belong to Christ to Himself (as in 1 Thessalonians 4:16-18). Rather, the comfort was to those who were by the time of this writing, scattered.[248] As a matter of fact, the time limitations placed on this verse keep many a scholar from fancifully leaping to a far-off end-of-age:

> "When Jerusalem shall be reduced to ashes, and that wicked nation cut off and rejected, then shall the Son of man send His ministers with the trumpet of the Gospel, and they shall gather His elect of the several nations, from the four corners of heaven: so that God shall not want a Church, although that ancient people of His be rejected and cast off: but that ancient Jewish Church being destroyed, a new Church shall be called out of the Gentiles." But though something like this appears to be the primary sense of the verse, in relation to the destruction of Jerusalem, no one can fail to see that the language swells beyond any gathering of a human family into a Church upon earth, and forces the thoughts onward to that gathering of the Church "at the last trump," to meet the Lord in the air, which is to wind up the present scene. <u>Still, this is not, in our judgment, the direct subject of the prediction; for Mk 13:28 limits the whole prediction to the generation then existing.</u>[249]

Yes, this sounds as if it may be referencing the second coming of Christ and the ingathering of believers, as pictured in 1 Thessalonians 4. However, the Greek word translated as "angel"

---

[247] It seems there are no non-Jew connotations to "Elam;" "H5867 - `Eylam - Strong's Hebrew Lexicon (KJV)." Blue Letter Bible. Web. 5 Feb, 2018. <https://www.blueletterbible.org//lang/lexicon/lexicon.cfm?Strongs=H5867&t=KJV>.
[248] James A. Brooks, *Mark*, vol. 23, The New American Commentary (Nashville: Broadman & Holman Publishers, 1991), 215.
[249] Robert Jamieson, A. R. Fausset, and David Brown, *Commentary Critical and Explanatory on the Whole Bible*, vol. 2 (Oak Harbor, WA: Logos Research Systems, Inc., 1997), 88.

here, *angelos*, literally means "messenger," so it is also possible that Jesus was speaking of the gospel going forth by human messengers who would be God's instruments to gather in His elect following the fall of Jerusalem.

There is no question that this passage is difficult to interpret in its context. It has been a source of disagreement among Christians for centuries and will continue to be so. <u>Yet, I contend that it need not be interpreted as referring to the end of history.</u> It can be understood as referring to the cataclysmic events that occurred in A.D. 70.[250]

Well, if this is, in fact, the gathering of "Israel" in the generation of Jesus after the destruction of Jerusalem (13:24) and after He receives His kingdom (13:25),[251] then the question is how did Jesus gather the Jews from their dispersion in His generation? There are primarily two answers:

1. Christ gathers ethnic Israel:
    a. This gathering of Israel back to their holy land is indeed ethnic Jews being gathered to Israel in the years immediately following A.D. 70. I know of no such source.
    b. This gathering of Israel back to their holy land is indeed ethnic Jews being gathered to Israel, but that the only thing that was required in the generation of Jesus was **send**ing **His angels** to do so [whether these **angels** are heavenly beings or human messengers (which is the meaning of the Greek word *angelos*)], and that this **gather**ing took longer and is still happening.
2. Christ gathers "true" Israel.[252]
    a. This gathering of Israel is really Christ's gathering of spiritual Israel (the believers, also called "elect"

---

[250] R. C. Sproul, <u>Mark</u>, First Edition., St. Andrew's Expositional Commentary (Orlando, FL: Reformation Trust, 2011), 353.

[251] "Founded on the ruins of Judaism; Alvah Hovey, ed., *An American Commentary on the New Testament, Commentary on the Gospel of Mark* (Philadelphia: American Baptist Publication Society, 1881), 190.

[252] See Appendix on Dispensationalism, Israel, and the Church.

throughout the remainder of the New Testament) to a physical location (from the entirety of the land and into the mountains, 13:14).

b. This gathering of Israel is really Christ's gathering of spiritual Israel into Christ as they are saved and that the only thing that was required in the generation of Jesus was **send**ing **His angels** to do so [whether these **angels** are heavenly beings or human messengers (which is the meaning of the Greek word *angelos*)], and that this **gather**ing may take longer and could still happening (Ephesians 1:10 uses this language).[253]

So then why do we even believe in a second coming of Jesus today? If you see the table below you will notice that the apostles saw Jesus' sermon in this chapter as a pattern for what would indeed take place, and give us an ultimate fulfillment.[254]

Biblical Text	Mark's Gospel	1 Thessalonians	2 Thessalonians
Warning about deception	13:5		2:3
Pregnancy	13:8	5:3	
Tribulation/Persecution	13:9		1:4
Abomination Desolation	13:14		2:2-3
Coming of Christ (*erchomai*)	13:26		1:10
Visible Descent	13:26	4:16	1:7

---

[253]There are even those who feel as though this gathering of Israel is really Christ's gathering believers into a Heavenly Jerusalem, another term for the Kingdom (Galatians 4 uses this language) and that the only thing that was required in the generation of Jesus was **send**ing **His angels** to do so [whether these **angels** are heavenly beings or human messengers (which is the meaning of the Greek word *angelos*)], and that this **gather**ing may take longer and could still happening. The problem, of course, is that John 3:3 and Colossians 1:12 place this as a reality at the conversion of a sinner.

[254]Another fantastic example of "dual fulfillment" is Isaiah 6. Verse 10 speaks of the nation of Israel rejecting Isaiah's message while John 10:27-30 says it is speaking of the nations' rejection of Jesus during His Passion week.

Clouds	13:26	4:17	
Great Power/Glory	13:26		1:7, 9
Angels	13:27	4:16	1:7
Gathering	13:27	4:17	2:1
Souls from Heaven Coming	13:27	3:13; 4:14	1:10
Watching Required	13:35-37	5:6	

Because of the apostles who were a ways away from Jerusalem and in some cases after A.D. 70, we do see an ultimate fulfillment.

> *Acts 1:11 Ye men of Galilee, why stand ye gazing up into heaven? this same Jesus, which is taken up from you into heaven, **shall so come in like manner**.*

Zechariah 14 says He will come back and put his feet on the Mount of Olives, and the apostles saw this happening, ultimately, as it occurs in 13:24…after the tribulation. Please notice the four things we talked about there:

1. Tribulation in those days,
2. Sun darkened,
3. Moon darkened,
4. Falling stars, powers shaken.

So where does Revelation fit into this?

> *Revelation 6:12-14 And I beheld when he had opened the sixth seal, and, lo, there was a great earthquake; and **the sun became black as sackcloth of hair, and the moon became as blood;** And **the stars of heaven fell unto the earth**, even as a fig tree casteth her untimely figs, when she is shaken of a mighty wind. And the heaven departed as a scroll when it is rolled together; and every mountain and island were moved out of their places.*

What chapter of Revelation does Jesus return to earth? 19. So Revelation is not laid out in a chronological fashion, because all of the sudden you have the end of the tribulation happening in chapter six.

Acts 2:16 But this is that which was spoken by the prophet Joel...

And remember what did they do? They spoke in tongues, and 3000 were saved. Before that Peter preaches a sermon. After the tongues, before the sermon that is recorded in Acts, Peter begins his sermon by saying that this is that which was spoken by the prophet Joel in whose 2nd chapter (verse 28-31) he describes these signs as occurring "before the day of the Lord."

Mark says this occurs "after that tribulation." Revelation six tells us that all of this is the sixth seal of Revelation. We don't know how much time elapses in here, but it does appear that it after the sixth seal of Revelation. Then we find out from Acts 2 that Mark 13:24 happens before the day of the Lord. The day of the Lord doesn't take place until after Revelation's 6th seal which doesn't take place until **after** the great tribulation.

Jesus is talking to His disciples (13:3) and using the 2nd person plural as if to say that they are going to see much of what He has described here. What about chapter 14 where the disciples are getting the Lord's Supper? This is only 12 hours before His death and 48 hours after this passage in chapter 13. If "Israel" is the **elect,** are we going to say that "Israel" was given the Lord's Supper? If so, why does the church practice it? If the disciples are the church in chapter 14 on Thursday, why would they be "Israel" 48 hours earlier on Tuesday? What about chapter 16? Did "Israel" get the Great Commission—including baptism? How does it make you feel to hear that "God didn't give His Great Commission to the church?" or "The church doesn't have authority to baptize from Jesus?" If that's hard to believe, then imagine saying that the disciples are "the church" in chapters 14 and 16, but in chapter 13 they are "Israel."

13:26 sounds much like Revelation 1:7 so this is definitely not the "secret rapture" or which we hear in today's popular eschatology. Given the similarities between Paul and the Olivet Discourse (1 Thessalonians 4, 5 & 2 Thessalonians 2), we see not only is this what

Paul would call the coming of Christ for His believers, but it is still future from Paul's perspective.

13:28-31

"Now learn this parable from the fig tree: Other than the account of the cursing of the **fig tree** in chapter 11, this is the only place where it is mentioned and there it speaks of the **fig tree** being cursed for the rest of the age (11:14).[255] If I didn't have Luke 21:29 which speaks of this **parable** as unrelated, I would say this is the promise of a fruit-bearing Israelite religious economy again.[256] **When its branch has already become tender, and puts forth leaves, you know that summer is near. 29 So you also, when you see these things happening, know that it is near—at the doors! 30 Assuredly, I say to you, this generation** a phrase used in 8:12, 8:38, and 9:19. It simply cannot be confused with any other **generation** than the one living in Jesus' time. "Elsewhere in Mark the term means people who are contemporaries of Jesus, and I am rather disposed to accept this commonsense meaning, even though it seems to place an unfulfilled prophecy on the lips of Jesus."[257]

I try to never go outside the book, but one cannot help but go to Matthew (which contains a version of Mark 8:12, 9:19, and 13:30) to see how he first uses **generation** in his 1st chapter: the birth of a father to the

---

[255] I understand this is debatable given the strange translations overall, but a look at the four places in the Gospel in their original script will certainly confirm this; "G165 - aiōn - Strong's Greek Lexicon (KJV)." Blue Letter Bible. Web. 9 Jan, 2018. <https://www.blueletterbible.org//lang/lexicon/lexicon.cfm?Strongs=G165&t=KJV>.

[256] Luke 21:29 has Jesus pointing to a number of trees of which the **fig tree** is but one. To assume that Israel must make a comeback is to assume that the "other trees" in that verse must also make a comeback. It surely would be nice to act as though this fine point doesn't matter, but in fact it is the difference between a purely Preterist viewpoint (since the tree is for the generation of Jesus) or a futurist viewpoint (where "this generation" refers to those who see a budding Israelite religious economy).

[257] Bonnie Bowman Thurston *Preaching Mark* (Minneapolis: Fortress Press, 2002), 149-150; Thurston is a N.T. Professor at Pittsburgh Theological Seminary.

birth of the son. "It seems best…to understand **[this generation]** to mean Jesus' own generation."[258]

This is profoundly different than "that." There's even a different Greek word for "that" if Jesus intended on speaking concerning a different generation—like the one that would occur around a future coming of Christ. When you are outside of something geographically, and you are referring to something in the geography in question, you refer to it as "**that** place." It must be, therefore, that Jesus was referring to the **generation** in which He resided. See my commentary on Luke 21:32 where I discuss another consideration on this passage—albeit not the safest in our perspective of Jesus' veracity (in my estimation).

will by no means pass away till all these things take place. One simply must decide if this is true or not. It's at least true in a sense, but if it's true "in a sense," then it is also still future "in a sense" probably (since this is linked to verse 31 and the obvious end of everything present) and there goes our necessity to discuss, again, dual-fulfillment.[259] Don't forget their question (13:3-4) and Jesus' answer (13:5-29) in these verses confirmed by the fact Jesus thought His answer was to be fulfilled in His generation (13:30). Either Jesus was mistaken, Mark (and therefore, Matthew) was mistaken (Jesus really didn't say these words), or Mark was correct in recording Jesus' fulfilled prophecy. We acknowledge, then, that the perfect problem of "the Roman haughty contempt for Jewish pride" led to their "slaughter and dispersion."[260]

It would be a grand thing to remember that the Jews over-literalized the Scripture. They were told to love the Lord with their minds and hearts (and so forth, Deuteronomy 6 quoted in Matthew 22:37), but this became straps on the arms and phylacteries on the head.

---

[258]Frank E. Gaebelein, ed. *The Expositor's Bible Commentary with the New International Version (Matthew, Mark, Luke) volume 8* (Grand Rapids: Zondervan, 1984), 751.
[259]If you'd like more information on this, see https://www.sermonaudio.com/sermoninfo.asp?SID=729151943587 [accessed 1/15/18].
[260]William Steuart McBirnie *The Search for the Twelve Apostles, revised edition-special TBN Edition* (Carol Stream, Ill: Tyndale, 2004, 2.

Chapter 14

14:1-2

After two days it was the Passover and ᵇ*the Feast* of Unleavened Bread. Mark says more in verse 12 about this day. **And the chief priests and the scribes sought how they might take Him by trickery and put *Him* to death.** Chapters 8:31, 9:31, and 10:33 all contain this news as well…from the lips of Jesus. **2 But they said, "Not during the feast, lest there be an uproar of the people."** Just as they had previously feared the **people** in 11:32. This tells me it wasn't the people who "all of the sudden" turned on Jesus and cried "crucify Him."

14:3-5

And being in Bethany at the house of Simon the leper, So we know this is not the same episode of Luke 7. How? Because that was Simon the Pharisee's house and the woman there was disdained as a "sinner."

This is, however, something that occurs a few days earlier (John 12:1). Mark is, therefore, flashing back to show us how Judas got to this point.[261] In other words, the "thing" that occurred on "the Passover and the Feast" (14:1) was the conversation between the priests and Judas who had been previously turned at the episode to which we are flashing back. In other words, the purpose of this episode is to show us how Judas made the decision to betray Jesus.

Also, John's version calls Judas, the son of **Simon** (John 12:4). Perhaps this is why Judas is so bold: he's in his father's house.

as He sat at the table, a woman came John tells us it is Mary, Lazarus' sister. **having an alabaster flask of very costly oil of spikenard. Then she broke the flask and poured *it* on His head.** Since Jesus said it was the anointing of His body in verse 8, we can assume this was quite volumes and ran down our Lord's body in some fashion.

ᵇEx. 12:1–27

[261] And since Matthew and Mark both flashback at the same time it is natural to assume one used the other's material or they both used a 3ʳᵈ party's material.

5 For it might have been sold for more than three hundred ᵈdenarii and given to the poor." And they criticized her sharply. Of course we could now answer the question of **"Why"** with the amendment of the question to "Why was this fragrant oil poured out? Or why was this costly, year's wage poured out? We do understand that this is probably not the purpose of this passage but it doesn't mean that it isn't a teaching point by the Holy Spirit. Some are becoming disenfranchised and bitter. When somebody outside a group worships the Lord they become a target to the bitter. It's as if they were shaming the woman who: 1. Crossed the bridge and broke the box of ointment; or 2. Would have nothing to show for all she had poured out to the Lord, and further—to say that He was not worth more than the poor. Or, "the poor are more than the Lord."

Did she waste her offering on the Lord…with nothing to show for it? Of course, we see there was a return for it (14:9), but even so? Do we feel as though our time of worship with the Lord is wasted because we can tell little of it? Our Lord's Day services? Our personal devotion times? This episode tells us we have wasted nothing. A trip to the altar where you know you had an experience with the Lord? You've wasted nothing and He has not forgotten your sacrifice of honor and adoration. This is not about utility; it is about generosity. It wasn't about "what good does this do" or "what does this do for the kingdom?" She did not leave this room saying "what do I have to show for this evening?"

As a preacher, there are times when you leave thinking "what did I accomplish from the pulpit?" Perhaps the better question is "Was there an impression made? On the Lord? On the people?" I've wasted nothing. We make commitments because we love the Lord. Not because anybody remembers it, but because the Lord remembers it. Hebrews 6:10 says God does indeed notice our works. Let Him remember it…if nobody else does.

Don't forget the needy always need and know they need.[262] And just as they will have their proper season to help (and we should help them, verse 7), there are times when Jesus bids you to lose it all at His feet and sometimes…sometimes when we drop things at the feet of

---

[d] Matt. 18:28
[262] Jesus even sites Deuteronomy 15:11 with the expectation to help!

seeming **waste**—and others will tell us we **waste**d resources and energy and time—we remember the closeness of how we felt to Jesus in those moments and we allow Jesus to look at the naysayers and answer: "that's **why**."

You see, Jesus is worth losing everything over. Do you think in this context of losing our precious cargo connected with the "Gospel" is a surprise when we remember

> *Mark 8:35 For whoever desires to save his life will lose it, but whoever **loses his life** for My sake **and the gospel's** will save it.*

Why indeed, people? **Why** was this poured out? Because Jesus is impeccable and we pour out our best upon Him instead of pouring out our doubts about Him in the dark; not having the answers to our deepest questions we pour out our best adoration of a King we cannot always explain. **Why?** It seems fitting for a King.

14:6-9

6 But Jesus said, "Let her alone. Why do you trouble her? Jesus answers their **why** question with one of His own. What do these two **why** questions have in common? Perhaps it's because the very thing with which they were charging this woman is that which they are experiencing: waste. They waste their breath accusing one they don't understand, and they don't understand her or her actions because, contextually, they don't understand the Gospel (verse 9)—His atoning death and resurrection. And this, this is why Judas is turned. He realizes now that Jesus was merely announcing a dreadful possibility of His death, but that He is now all but ensuring it.

8 She has done what she could. This passage seems to be grabbing the last three chapters and culminating them here. We have our tie to chapter 11 with the chief priests and scribes' fear of the people (14:1-2) and our tie with chapter 13 and the Gospel (14:9). Here, though, we have a tie with the end of chapter 12 and the widow (12:44).

> *Mark 12:44 for they all put in out of their abundance, but she **out of her poverty put in all that she had**, her whole livelihood."*

So in comparing this wealthy lady with a poor widow, we find that those in the house were being compared with the scribe of chapter 12 who had an incomplete understanding of who Christ was and who was without Christ. He found that he was close to the kingdom, but not in it. Is this the point of the passage? Perhaps not, but it is good the way the Holy Spirit wrote the lesson. Exactly how far were the disciples from being scribes? One group "devours" the poor (12:38-44) and the other group criticizes the "rich" and we find out from both contexts that a disciples who doesn't understand the Gospel is as good as a scribe—and by extension, a Pharisee, Sadducee, Herodian, chief priest, and temple elder.

She has come beforehand to anoint My body for burial. This is a very strange comment. We seem to see a custom to do this. Apparently she had an ointment she did not need for another burial. John tells us she didn't need to do a re-anointing for her now living brother (the ladies came to the empty tomb to anoint and already dead Jesus).

9 Assuredly, I say to you, wherever this gospel which is apparently related to His death because He spoke of His own "burial" in verse 8, and used the word **this** which would make no sense if there were not some correlation between what Jesus just said in verse 8 and what He is now saying in verse 9. So, the Gospel which Jesus Himself preached in 1:15 and then told His disciples to preach in 16:15 has something to do with His death and His death—we hear again and again—is an act of His will to free others from their sin (10:45).

14:10-12

[i]**Then Judas Iscariot, one of the twelve** You almost don't need verses 3-9 (check out the flow). It's as if Mark is saying, "let me tell you what turned Judas." Both of these episodes have much to do with money, and both involve Judas (John says it was Judas who objected to the woman's actions).

---

[i] Ps. 41:9; 55:12–14; Matt. 10:2–4

12 Now on the first day of Unleavened Bread, One need only to go through Exodus 12 or Leviticus 23 to see that households needed to remove all leaven from their homes. It seems that this stressing of the removal of the leaven before the killing of a Lamb at the Passover remembrance emphasizes the removal of all impurities from one's home, from one's life before the very sober partaking of the Lamb. Since we find that 1 Corinthians 5 calls Jesus our Passover, then it seems logical to purify our hearts and souls and lives before we partake of Christ.

when they [4]killed the Passover *lamb,* This was called a "feast" in verse 1.

14:13-15[263]

And He sent out two of His disciples same **two** as went after the donkey in chapter 11? **and said to them, "Go into the city, and a man will meet you carrying a pitcher of water;** usually a woman's task. This is why he would sort of stand out. Maybe there was "secret handshake" afore planned? **follow him.** Once again, it seems as though Jesus has done some planning (as He did in the processional requiring a colt. A person does wonder how this **man** would have recognized the **two disciples.**

It seems fitting to see that this **man** who would **meet** the **two disciples** at least lived at this home or was a servant. It seems reasonable to assume that this "large upper room" (verse 15) is also the "upper room" used in Acts 1:13[264] since it is in the same city and would have been prominent in the minds of the apostles who first met Jesus in this same "room."[265] It furthermore seems reasonable that this is the same house where Peter visited, breaking up a prayer group meeting on his behalf. This house was known as the house of Mary, the mother of

---

[4] sacrificed

[263] More can be seen in my commentary on Matthew (26:17-19).

[264] In meaning, it is equivalent to ὑπερῷον [found in the Acts passages], upper room, place for prayer, and assembling together."; John Peter Lange, Philip Schaff, and William G. T. Shedd, *A Commentary on the Holy Scriptures: Mark* (Bellingham, WA: Logos Bible Software, 2008), 140.

[265] The family would have had a special bond with Jesus already, and therefore, His followers after His departure.

Mark. This would mean, if these reasonable assumptions were true, that the young man in this episode is Mark, who happens to be the writer of this Gospel.

This gets even more interesting when we look at 14:51-52. This is probably Mark implying his presence: "for some the only explanation is that it is the author's allusion to himself, his 'signature in the corner of his work' or something comparable to a medieval artist painting his own face on one of the crowd.[266] This would be comparable to John referring to himself five times as "the disciple whom Jesus loved" in the Gospel bearing his name. In other words, it seems that since the other Gospel writers left this mystical man out of their accounts, it must be that this is Mark.

So what? Well, whether Mark or not, the young man probably is the same one that led the **two disciples** to the house with the upper room and then followed them (unbeknownst probably to those who were following Jesus) to the Garden of Gethsemane where 14:32-49 take place.

Furthermore, it is probably only Mark that provided us an eyewitness account of the prayer of Jesus in the garden since Judas was gone, the three who were with Jesus were sleeping, and the rest were left behind away from the time of prayer while this unnamed man is close by enough to hear and then be almost arrested—leaving behind his garment. That would mean that Matthew and Luke later get their information from this young man for their own Gospels.

On top of that, we have a "young man", mentioned only in the Gospel of Mark awaiting the women at the empty grave on the morning of the resurrection. It seems, then, that the first person recorded as finding the empty tomb was this "young man" mentioned only in the garden previously.[267]

---

[266] James A. Brooks, _Mark_, vol. 23, The New American Commentary (Nashville: Broadman & Holman Publishers, 1991), 238.

[267] I will be the first to admit that the words spoken by this "young man" have a striking resemblance to the words of the angel who rolled the stone away in Matthew 28:6. They even wear the same clothing. I would say the safer interpretation is that it was the angel, appearing as a young man, who told these women of the resurrection.

15 Then he will show you a large upper room, furnished *and* prepared; there make ready for us." This was a reclining table (usually on your left side)[268] in a "u" shape with the opening towards the door of the room.

> The food consisted of roasted lamb, unleavened bread, and the dish of bitter herbs (Exod. 12:8–20). The lamb reminded the Jews of the blood that was applied to the doorposts of their homes to keep the angel of death from slaying their firstborn. The bread was unleavened to remind them of the haste in which they left Egypt (Exod. 12:39). The bitter herbs spoke of their suffering as Pharaoh's slaves. The drinking of wine was added later to the ceremony.[269]

14:17-18[270]

18 Now as they sat and ate, This, coupled with verse 22 with the same phrase, help us to see that the episode beginning here and ending at verse 21 occur at least somewhat simultaneously with the episode between verses 22 and 24. If you're not quite sure, look at Luke's account to see where these two little episodes are recorded in reverse order.

14:19

And they began to be sorrowful, and to say to Him one by one, "*Is* it I?" And another *said*, "*Is* it I?" Can you hear the heartbreak? "Surely I am not he, am I, Lord?"[271]

---

[268]If the place of honor is to one's right, then John must have been on his right as he was laying upon Jesus' bosom—otherwise Judas was to the place of Jesus' right. By the way, this is how Lazarus and Abraham appeared to the rich man—eating (Luke 16:23-24), and how the Father and Son appeared to John the Gospel (John 1:18). See my commentary on Matthew (chapter 8) or my commentary on Revelation (chapter 19) about how the kingdom of God IS a meal (Matthew 22:1-7 as well). It's a shorthand way of saying "it is a place of festive fellowship" (rather than a very narrow understanding that there is an endless "eating.")

[269] Rodney L. Cooper, *Mark*, vol. 2, Holman New Testament Commentary (Nashville, TN: Broadman & Holman Publishers, 2000), 236.

[270]More to be found in my commentary on Matthew (26:20-25).

14:20-21

21 The Son of Man indeed goes just as it is written of Him, but woe to that man by whom the Son of Man is betrayed! It would have been good for that man if he had never been born." Much could be made about whether this is saying that life does or does not begin at conception or rather at birth. It seems natural and easy at this point to leave it simply as "it would have been better for Judas if he had not even begun his life."

14:22-26

See comments on Mark 3:13-19, comments on Mark 12:1-12, my commentary on minor prophets (Hosea), and the appendix on the Psalms.

14:27-30[272]

Then Jesus said to them, "All of you will be made to stumble because of Me this night, for it is written: 'I will strike the Shepherd, *And the sheep will be scattered.'* There is no question that this is involved and there is much I am missing in the writer's intent of Zechariah 13—particularly since we have not exegeted the book of the prophecy of Zechariah. One thing is sure: forgiveness of sins is a gushing reality (Zechariah 13:1) where there was once a wounding of hands (Zechariah 13:6), and this reality is the scheming of the One Who said He would wound His shepherd (Zechariah 13:7). One thing is equally as sure, the Shepherds wounding is related to the forgiveness of Zechariah 13:1. Sadly, sheep do not understand the confusing methods of their shepherd by the hand—the Roman hand, the Jewish hand, the Herodian hand, the Imperial hand, the Satanic hand, the Iscarian hand—of Jehovah Who speaks in this passage.

---

[271] W. Hall Harris III et al., eds., *The Lexham English Bible* (Bellingham, WA: Lexham Press, 2012), Mt 26:22.

[272] More to be found in my commentary on Matthew (26:30-35).

Just as the feeding of the 5000 (Mark 6:32-44) is a forecast of the marriage feast (Revelation 19:9), and the hymn after the Lord's supper (Mark 13:26) is a forecast of the singing of Christ and His people around the throne toward the Father (Hebrews 2:11) so is the anointing of Jesus (Mark 14:3-11) a foretaste of the anointing of Christ by His Father upon His return to His Father (Hebrews 1:9). The hand of the broken woman with the broken bottle, then, is a shadow of the hand of the Father, and if a shadow, then the representative of the hand of the Father. It is no great marvel, then, that as the woman anointing Jesus was the anointing hand of the Father so also is the hammering hand of the Roman soldier the hammering hand of the Father. This is Scandalous or Marvelous; Horrible or adorable; frightening or delighting. Song writer Wes King said it thus:

> *A tool of torture becomes a sign of hope*
> *The measure for the love of God*
> *The intersection of eternity and time*
> *Did ever such love and sorrow meet*
> *Or thorns composed so rich a crown*
>
> *The hand that held the hammer*
> *Was the hand of God*
> *The hand that took the nails*
> *Was His only Son*
> *The doors of heaven opened*
> *As He opened up His hands*
> *And it rained down mercy*

If, then, this is true concerning Jesus—receiving the good from the Father's hand as well as the bad—how much more is it for we who have been accepted into God's family (Ephesians 1:6)?

And many of us are recipients of the "oil of gladness" through the service of others to us, and it stuns us and we love how the aroma fills the room. We feel appreciated by God Himself; relished by God Himself; love by God Himself…it's as if we belong to Christ's body. If we step back from this story we have no issues believing that the woman in the room is the agent of God—extending His hand over the head of His Son, but…a rod?

Yet when we go back to the passage Jesus is quoting in Zechariah 13, it is clearly—according to verse 6 of that chapter—the words of God: He is the "I" Who is **striking the shepherd.**

How would you do it? Would you have a Father Who merely allowed His Son to be victimized? Would you desire a scheme where the scheme was temporarily out of the control of the Father? Isaiah 53:5,10; Acts 2:22-24; Romans 8:32; 1 Peter 1:20 attest to this profound truth that, somehow, mysteriously, this was the act of God.

14:31

But he spoke more vehemently, "If I have to die with You, I will not deny You!" And they all said likewise. So here on this walk from the upper room to the garden of Gethsemane we have two very difficult topics: God's involvement in killing His Messiah, and Peter's overwhelming confidence in Himself. I suppose this is why so many of us are careful to tell what "we would do" in a situation if we were the ones under pressure.

Shouldn't Peter sit back and think…"maybe I should ask, 'Lord can I avoid this?' Isn't there a way to posture myself so that I don't run away from the Lord? Isn't there a way I can keep from being a coward, Lord?" But we see nothing but an ill-mannered, unfriendly, misguided disagreement that majors on will power and speaks almost nothing of God's power. Since Peter doesn't understand about his failure in the big moments with the big things, I guess it's time for him to learn from his failures in the small things…

14:32-34

33 And He took Peter, James, and John which He had done many other times. **with Him, and He began to be troubled and deeply distressed.** Probably the source for the following information is the young man who leaves the scene during the arrest. **34 Then He said to them, "My soul is exceedingly sorrowful, even to death.** It is at this point that we see that sorrow itself, maybe even depression, is not necessarily sinful. **Stay here and watch."** It seems as though **watch** included prayer (verse 38).

14:35-36

36 And He said, "Abba, Father, all things are possible for You. Take this cup away from Me; nevertheless, not what I will, but what You will." This is the #1 lesson of Jesus: Prayer is mostly bringing ourselves to the point where we align with God. This prayer habit of Jesus should not surprise us. It is the focus of the model prayer (Matthew 6): "thy; thy; thy; thine."

14:37-38

Then He came and found them sleeping, and said to Peter, Mark doesn't mind singling him out, it seems (as in the last chapter), both good and bad. **"Simon, are you sleeping? Could you not watch one hour?** See, here is Jesus posing a question that finds its power in the minimizing of that which Peter is unable to accomplish! Praying an hour; staying awake one hour! Add to that a comment to Peter about his "willing spirit", his "willing attitude and fortitude" and his "weak flesh" appears to hearken back to the previous discourse on the way to the Mount of Olives—the garden of Gethsemane: "Peter, how in the world can you be so sure you'll be strong enough to withstand stumbling, to avoid stumbling, when you can't even stay awake one lousy hour to talk to the Father for me? Think about my 'sorrowful, death-filled soul.'"

38 Watch and pray, lest you enter into temptation. The spirit indeed is willing, but the flesh is weak."
One might consider this an excuse for flippant humanity or so-called carnal Christianity, but on the heels of this unpleasant rebuke to Peter it is very clear that this is a desperate reminder of how badly sons of Adam need the power of prayer and a lack of faith in their own, innate ruggedness.
    Unless anybody thinks Paul wrote using these terms and meant something differently while he did so (Galatians 5:16-17), we are not simply talking about "attitude" (**spirit**) and "bodies" (**flesh**). By the way, the usage of "Abba" by Jesus greatly influenced Paul's Galatians 4:6.

1. There is a connection between these disciples' prayers and their **temptation**.

2. These is a connection between these disciples' prayers and their **spirit** and their **flesh.**
3. In this case, the test to sleep is an invitation to sin and there are, therefore, no distinctions between a simple test or an invitation to sin.

Have there been any times when you viewed your prayer life as a protection against failure…not the failure of the task but the failure to serve the **spirit?**

14:39-40

Again He went away and prayed, Here's the 2nd lesson of Jesus' prayer life: When your friends disappoint you, you are not deterred from your Father. You do not see the failings of a few as the failings from the Father. He has never failed you. You do not let your exasperations with your neighbor be your disillusionment with the Master. Oh, how He loves us. Draw near to Him.

The connection of these sleeping disciples' prayerlessness with the warfare in which Jesus engages has much to do with the relief He desired would result from their toiling with Him in prayers. It really makes this pastor wonder: if Jesus desired the corporate prayer of men, how much more am I in need of such assistance from my earthly companions? It is a wonder, is it not, that Jesus needed to pray at all? If He, then, needed to pray as the Only Begotten Son of God, how much more does this son of Adam, cumbered about with not only a human nature, but a sinful human nature, need the same prayer? Yes, infinitely more prayer!

40 And when He returned, He found them asleep again, for their eyes were heavy; and they did not know what to answer Him. Now, I don't know why this is so hard. Have I slept standing up? Yes, but that is not happening here, I am sure. Why don't believers do those seemingly small things to simply stay awake?   We can, as these disciples could have done, blame the circumstances for their weariness: "the night is late." "Normal people are asleep at this time." "A warrior has to get his rest." "I've got a full belly from the Passover meal." We can blame all kinds of factors, but standing up is not a hard thing to do.

14:41-42

Then He came the third time and said to them, "Are you still sleeping and resting? It is enough! The hour has come; behold, the Son of Man is being betrayed into the hands of sinners. Herein a sober reminder that it will not always be time to pray. As a matter of fact—even more soberly—there is not always time to pray. Sometimes, it is too late to pray. Sometimes, the hour has passed where you and I can affect the transpiring of certain events. I do not know what would have been different, other than the experience of Jesus, had the disciples been faithful to "watch and pray." I say this because of the next phrase. There was a time when something would occur.

14:43-44[273]

And immediately, while He was still speaking, Judas, one of the twelve, with a great multitude with swords and clubs, Isn't this laughable? The one who is controlling weather patterns in Matthew 5 is now going to be subdued with soldiers? It seems that Judas should have known better. Remember, we believe the text says that he did. We could let the **chief priests and and scribes and elders** off the hook for seeking to bind Jesus if they were nowhere around during his miracles. We would even let them off the hook if they arrested Him already. Oh, no, We find right away that Jesus speaks to the whole lot of them—calling them to bear witness that there are reasons why they did not do it before, and now they are doing it under the darkness.

14:46-47[274]

47 And one of those who stood by drew his sword and struck the servant of the high priest, and cut off his ear. It is s strange action this man, identified by John as Peter, takes. What is he doing? What Peter is doing? Was he expecting to be martyred here? Was he expecting to somehow survive a flurry with a multitude of soldiers and but 2 fellow—and at the best case 10—fellow freedom fighters? Was he

---

[273]More can be seen in my commentary on Matthew (26:47-56).
[274]See more on 14:47-49 in the appendix on bibliology.

expecting Jesus to bail them out by flashing some of that "Son of Man" power?

14:51-52

See comments on 14:13.

14:53-65

Regarding verse 62, "Jesus was claiming that he would ascend to the throne of Israel's God and share God's very glory. To students of the Old Testament, this was the height of blaspheme, thus 'they all condemned him as worthy of death.'"[275] Other than this, see my commentary on Matthew (26:56-68).

14:66-67

Now as Peter was below in the courtyard, since verse 54 where he "warmed himself by the fire."

14:69-70

70 But he denied it again. And a little later those who stood by said to Peter again, "Surely you are *one* of them; for you are a Galilean, and your speech shows *it*." You might notice this phrase is not in every version. The good news is that if this phrase doesn't belong the reality still probably exists as they identified him as a **Galilean** somehow—and this phrase occurs in Matthew.

14:71

Then he began to curse and swear, people under pressure to hide their Christianity say some pretty awful things to not appear weak.

14:72

---

[275]Hank Hanegraaff *The Apocolypse Code* (Nashville: Thomas Nelson, 2007), 26.

A second time *the* rooster crowed. Then Peter called to mind the word that Jesus had said to him, "Before the rooster crows twice, you will deny Me three times."[276] This was in verse 30. The other Gospel writers seemed interested in the actual "cockcrowing"—an event that ended the 3rd watch of the night (Mark 13:35) while Mark speaks of an actual single **rooster crow**ing some time earlier, probably at the confusing lights in the late night/early morning hours in the court of the high priest (as well as the conclusion of the 3rd watch known by the same name).

And when he thought about it, It is better said "he cast Himself down"[277] **he wept.** This is a Peter who is wondering if "this is all real." Is Jesus supposed to die like He said? That's easier to believe than the news that He has given that He will rise again (8:31; 9:31). Peter simply did not want his life to go down as a waste, and he did not want his life to end on such an awful possibility that Jesus' words were the embellishment of a teacher, and then give his life simply for following what would amount to as a simple premature death for the crime of partaking in an insurrection.

    A follower by Bible definition is one who, according to Mark 8, takes up His cross, and the reason why believers are so distracted is because they put eggs in all the baskets…just in case…

    Christians have to say better and believe better than saying this is all just a blind leap. I mean, this is a good start, but it is not the limit of who we are. Those would be lyrics written by a biblically shallow church who thinks that their pastor is a community leader or entertainer or an optional add-on if there isn't anything else of higher priority. This Christianity takes minor keys in the Scripture and makes them symphonic majors and it springs out in some of the "Christian music industry."

---

    [276]Other than this very slight difference in the account with Matthew, one can see that the follow on passage (just as many others) is that chosen by Matthew and this, once again, proves that one was copying the other or that both were copying another source.
    [277] "G1911 - epiballō - Strong's Greek Lexicon (KJV)." Blue Letter Bible. Web. 5 Feb, 2018. <https://www.blueletterbible.org//lang/lexicon/lexicon.cfm?Strongs=G1911&t=KJV>.

No, we are not hoping Christianity is true. We are faced with facts of history. Jesus did die. Jesus did rise again. Jesus did speak in Scripture. His words can be trusted, and by extension, all the words of the Old Testament because He constantly quoted them, fulfilled, them, and referenced them. It also means the words of His apostles because He commissioned them.

Now, I don't want to minimize the pain that Peter is enduring. This is not a win-win or a win-lose; this is a lose-lose from Peter's perspective, and Peter is concerned that the pain of dying with Jesus is more than the pain of losing his significance and comfort. He has, for all intensive purposes, lost the last 3-4 years of his life following a false hope of a new political power in which he was to be a major shareholder. To him, in those moments, he was losing a friend, a hero, a life, and probably his freedom, his business, and his wife. He felt as though he lost it all; and to him, the pain of denying a friend and hero and starting over as an embarrassed business owner was a little less than the pain of losing everything else.

So, now what? Off into the night he runs a loser who is disoriented; a coward who left a friend after pledging his life. They would die together…until they had to die together.

Is this the end? We know it is not the end for Jesus.

Peter is wondering at the news of the empty tomb given him by some ladies that found "a young man" therein. Peter is shocked at the idea of a tomb without the body of Jesus, but the news from the one in the tomb is what Peter needed to hear. Perhaps now that the Lord is alive again He will begin again with a man more worthy; a man or woman who didn't misplace priorities; a man or woman or adolescent who has a better record of putting all the eggs in the basket of Jesus.

Jesus told the one in the tomb who told the ladies to tell Peter "make sure you tell Peter (Mark 16:1-7) that the party isn't complete without Him (Mark 16:7). Tell Him that this train's not moving on without Him getting aboard. You tell him to get on that caravan to Galilee. Don't let him hang his head. Don't let him play super modest.

You tell that miserable failure and I'll make a believer out of him yet." Jesus knows the frailty of humanity, and He said "I've been singling you out when you opened your mouth! I've been singling you out when you overcommitted yourself! I've been singling you out when you fell asleep doing a simple task. Now, I'm singling you out to make sure you're still wanted, and you're still needed!"

Chapter 15

15:1-2[278]

Immediately, in the morning, This is really a time on the clock, so to speak, according to Mark 13:35. **the chief priests held a consultation with the elders and scribes and the whole council;** It was of greatest necessity that they handle **Jesus** since His adult ministry brought Him here only during feasts, and that would mean that this perfect set-up would have to wait another 7 weeks until Pentecost and that was way too long for them to wait. He was gaining popularity way too fast.

and they bound Jesus, Again, this is hilarious in its irony: Jesus, the binder of the stars in their orbits and the wind to its currents, is being willingly bound. This really seems to have taken place on the heels of a legitimate, legal pronouncement of guilt—having now reached morning.

led *Him* away, and delivered *Him* to Pilate. This must mean, then, that the Jews could not kill Jesus on this particular day (see John's Gospel for the reason). **2 Then Pilate asked Him, "Are You the King of the Jews?"** Given the fact that Jesus had already told the High Priest that He had en eternal kingdom (his alluding to Daniel 7:13-14 in His "trial" before the High Priest), this seems like a fair question. The whole crowd seemed, once again, to be misunderstanding the very Scriptures they "believed." **He answered and said to him, "*It is as* you say."** This is not "yes" or as some say "you said it!" Jesus' answer…is deliberately ambiguous in the Greek. The NIV "Yes, it is as you say" obscures this ambiguity, which was necessary because if Jesus had answered with a simple yes the trial would have ended immediately with conviction.[279]

15:3-5

---

[278] See more in my commentary on Matthew (27:1-2; 11-23).
[279] James A. Brooks, *Mark*, vol. 23, The New American Commentary (Nashville: Broadman & Holman Publishers, 1991), 250.

And the chief priests accused Him of many things, but He ᵈanswered nothing. Tell me this isn't powerful! Jesus is not trying to clear His name? This is so strange.

4 Then Pilate asked Him again, saying, "Do You answer nothing? See how many things they testify against You!" "Don't you want to answer for yourself? Don't you know what's at stake?" It's as if **Pilate** doesn't think Jesus knows that it is in His best interest to be understood. There is a fascination all of us would have with this Jesus Who is not preoccupied with saving His Own life.

5 But Jesus still answered nothing, so that Pilate marveled. Here is a magnificent reminder to those of us who follow Christ: we owe the world precious little in the area of explanation. Maybe believers should remind themselves that their audience is primarily in Heaven. While we're at it, perhaps we should remember that our primary hope is the resurrection (1 Peter 1:3-4; 1 Peter 3:15) of Christ—it is not this obsession or preoccupation with answering every misunderstanding the world has with us.

This is a huge deal, and Pilate **marvelled.** Other than Jesus' "you said it" response to the question of His claims to be King, He said precious little. Surely, a man who is about to die would declare his innocence, right? We would expect frantic avoidance of death—especially if we are dealing with a painful death. "He knew that self-preservation is of enormous importance to all human beings, and now he was giving Jesus the chance to preserve his life."[280]

The reality is that Mark 8 already made a connection between the Lord's death and ours. We are reticent to embrace this…yet we've been singing it for years:

> *Faith of our fathers, living still*
> *In spite of dungeon, fire and sword,*
> *O how our hearts beat high with joy*

ᵈIs. 53:7
[280] Jim Bishop *The Day Christ Died* (New York: Harper & Brothers, 1957), 263.

Whene'er we hear that glorious word!
Faith of our fathers! holy faith!
We will be true to thee till death!

Often we desire opportunity to answer, not because it is the Father's will, but because we fear death. We just want to be understood, when we are confronted the Pilates and priests of this life, so we can make it all make sense to the lost of this world. I am sorry, we are in two separate worlds. Look at Genesis 19:4 and you will find insane people who don't want to hear simple math. They are not interested in evidence leading to logical conclusions. They hear that "transgendered women are 49 times more likely to contract HIV" and the Elton Johns of modern day Sodom say things like "well, of course they are; they are rejected from the normal work place and forced into sex-related lines of work."[281]

Then, one must consider that Jesus could have given Pilate the correct answer after He gave him the correct question, but if He did this…how do we find a Gospel? When one says "God wants all to be saved," we immediately come back and delicately remind the person that "Yes and no, He does." There are certain things He did not do to procure the salvation of some. This is the Greatest. Do you see a Man? One Who does not feel the need to answer a world when He already knows the will of the Father? He fears no death and so He fears no man! Is this the One you follow? Are you willing to go to the ends of the world for one cause, and that is the fame of this Mighty Son of God?

15:6-10

Now at the feast he was accustomed Maybe it was to counter his otherwise very unpopular reign (Luke 13:1-5). **to releasing one prisoner to them, whomever they requested. 7 And there was one named Barabbas,** A man whose name means "son of a father." This could be a pseudonym, but perhaps we should remember that "the Son of Man" substituted Himself for "the son of a man." **who was chained with his fellow rebels; they had committed murder in the rebellion.** There they are, held in a cell perhaps, and **chained** together. This is you

---

[281] http://www.cnn.com/2016/05/18/entertainment/elton-john-bathroom-bill-essay/ [accessed May 30, 2016].

and this is me: **murder**ous **rebels.** Perhaps we should quickly admit that finding ourselves in here is not the intent of Mark probably, but it is hard to miss Mark 10:45 as the backdrop where there is a swap here—and worse, those who were released were not immediately thankful. 1 Peter 3:18 stresses this great reality of the great exchange with "just for the unjust."

10 For he knew that the chief priests had handed Him over because of envy. Here is our hint that Pilate is out of control (see verses 15-20 especially), and hoping that rather than making a hard decision that may cost him his position should news travel back to Rome, it's just less painful to suffer in his conscience regarding Jesus than it is to suffer in his loss of all things. In other words, we could easily see that Pilate is being placed besides Peter by the Holy Spirit as those who conveniently place Christ aside when it could cost them their livelihood. It is, then, hard to miss Mark 8:34-35 as backdrops to these two men.

15:11-13

But the chief priests stirred up the crowd, whatever this might consist of at the trial (which was not in Pilate's judgment hall, verse 16).—certainly not the entirety of those who greeted Him on "Palm Sunday" or those who constituted the "common people" of 12:37 (Tuesday afternoon). **so that he should rather release Barabbas to them. 12 Pilate answered and said to them again, "What then do you want me to do *with Him* whom you call the King of the Jews?"** He knew what their crowd had been calling Jesus earlier in the week no doubt, and he was perhaps appealing to their own words as a way to at least avoid killing this gentle man. This was, obviously, to no avail.

15:14

Then Pilate said to them, "Why, ʲwhat evil has He done?" But they cried out all the more, "Crucify Him!" Genesis 19:11 speaks of those Sodomites who groped for the door to get to those who struck them with blindness. Certainly these were insane men—blinded by their blood lust. Perhaps even Romans 1:21 where those who reject the knowledge of

---

ʲ Is. 53:9

God have "darkened hearts." Moreover Ephesians 4:19 which speaks of those who have "blind hearts" being "past feeling."

15:15-20[282]

So Pilate, wanting to gratify the crowd, released Barabbas to them; This was not about what is moral or right. This was not about merit or judicial findings.

and he delivered Jesus, after he had scourged *Him,* **to be [1]crucified.** It should be pointed out promptly here that Barabbas goes free because Jesus remains silent. Christ suffers when He did not need to. Why? In the small picture: so he could die. In the larger picture…so the guilty go free. Certainly, we understand that we guilty ones go to Heaven rather than suffer the wrath of God because Jesus did not talk His way out of this calamity. 1 Peter 2:21-25 speaks of His perfect faith in the Father when being faced with absolute injustice.

16 Then the soldiers led Him away into the hall called [3]Praetorium, and they called together the whole garrison. Hundreds of soldiers to handle one man? This is that awful surrounding of the "bulls of Bashan" in Psalm 22. **17 And they clothed Him with purple; and they twisted a crown of thorns, put it on His** *head,* We do not surmise these to be any particular type of thorns just for the sake of making the crucifixion more gory—even if it makes the sacrifice of Jesus more awe-inspiring. The fact is that there were many types of thorns. Couple this with the idea that the overall theme here is mockery—yes, cruelty, but primarily mockery, and then add to that the reality from Psalm 34:20 and you have a good case for these being nearby, thorny branches from which they made a mocking victor's crown. It need not be any more or less.**18 and began to salute Him, "Hail, King of the Jews!"** Otherwise translated in the NT as "be glad", and is even used in the next chapter when He sees women coming from the empty tomb: "all hail." So we see a sort of mocking "Long live the king"

---

[282]More in my commentary on Matthew (27:26).
[1]Is. 53:8
[3]The governor's headquarters

19 Then they ⁿstruck Him on the head with a reed and spat on Him;
This is a repeat of 14:65: more beatings and more spitting, and they persisted in this unholy act.

> Another example is Jesus' trial. In Mark 15:19 we read, "And they were striking his head with a reed and spitting on him and kneeling down in homage to him" (ESV). You get the sense from the English that they beat him over and over again, but you may not get that they spit on him repeatedly. ἐνέπτυον is explicitly continuous; they did it over and over again, which is expressed in the TNIV as, "Again and again they struck him on the head with a staff and spit on him."[283]

and bowing the knee, they worshiped Him. 20 And when they had mocked Him, they took the purple off Him, Scourged earlier in the passage this would have been quite painful given the coagulation already taken place.

put His own clothes on Him, and led Him out to crucify Him. Finally, after verse 15, the mob has decided to carry on with Pilate's directive. People often do awful things in a crowd they would not do by themselves. It would do well for the believer to "observe the masses and do the opposite." At this point, one wonders why this must occur, and we realize it was as Jesus stated twice in chapter 14, "written of Him." More to the point that interests us, though, is that He was "giving His life a ransom" (10:45).

15:21-22

Then they compelled a certain man, Simon a Cyrenian, Here's a black man. **the father of Alexander and Rufus,** It seems that these were known to Mark's audience—probably the Romans (Romans 16:13) **as he was coming out of the country and passing by,** Here's a man who honestly didn't ask to be there. He was simply **passing by.** What exactly did this man have to do with this drama? He's just being a good

---

ⁿIsaiah 52:14; 53:5
[283] William D. Mounce, *Basics of Biblical Greek: Grammar*, ed. Verlyn D. Verbrugge, Third Edition. (Grand Rapids, MI: Zondervan, 2009), 127.

Jewish man, with his boys. He is going to be both: 1. A helper of Jesus, and 2. an unwilling participant in Christ's sufferings. This was, in the mind of **Simon,** no doubt, The Grand Mistake. He was caught at the wrong place at the wrong time, and was by God's grand design, a piece of this story of the Gospel. Have you every looked around in the middle of an apparent mess and thought "how did I get here?" God could have had another man **compelled**, you know.

to bear His cross. The Latin Scripture leaves room for this to be simply the "crossbeam" and this would simply be shorthand for that piece of wood (versus an entire "criss-cross") **22 And they brought Him to the place Golgotha, which is translated, Place of a Skull.** Some have said it was because that was the way the hill was shaped and others say it simply referred to the many who died there—whose remains were then left without burial.

15:23-24

See my commentary on the Psalms (Psalm 69).

15:25-28[284]

It shall be pointed out that this death of Jesus and His resurrection is the Gospel, and that it was done in answer to prophecy (8:31; 9:31; 10:33) and to serve as an exchange to free us from our sin (10:45). **Now it was the third hour,**[285] Or around 9a.m., perhaps. Just as there was four watches of the night (13:35) there were four sections of the day and these were sometimes named after the hour which concluded them (just as the night watches). **and they crucified Him. 26 And the inscription**

---

[284]More from this passage on my commentary from Matthew (chapter 26).

[285]Of course, John says it's the 6th hour, but it may have been more than a mark on the clock to John and that can be discussed elsewhere, perhaps; Gerald L. Borchert, *John 12–21*, vol. 25B, The New American Commentary (Nashville: Broadman & Holman Publishers, 2002), 258.

Probably, the easiest answer is that the "actual time" was somewhere between the technical 3rd or 6th hour and that it was rounded down by Mark and up by John; Ted Cabal et al., *The Apologetics Study Bible: Real Questions, Straight Answers, Stronger Faith* (Nashville, TN: Holman Bible Publishers, 2007), 1612.

of His accusation what kind of crime was it to be **THE KING OF THE JEWS**? Both Matthew and Mark call this the **accusation.** His offense is that He is an opposing **KING.** It doesn't take much Bible study to see that the crime for Jews seeking His death was blasphemy (previous chapter). This is a Roman concern directly. Indirectly, it is a Jewish concern because it caused consternation with the Roman appointed **KING** 6:14 would say this was Herod, perhaps, but the understanding would be Rome and it's declared ruler Pilate; or perhaps Ceaser himself (John 19:15).

Is there anything more ridiculous than being a **KING** with no **KING**dom? Is Jesus simply a loser who cannot admit that He is without a **KING**dom? If so, then why is He a threat? What's so threatening about a man who is delirious? If He causes insurrection, then fine—kill Him for insurrection. But what is so criminal about being a **KING**? Again, we have to decide whether Mark thinks you know the answer or whether Mark doesn't think you need the answer. We have to decide if there was a different Gospel than Mark floating around that gives us the backdrop for this **KING**ship idea, but Mark does not. For brevity's sake we will assume that since Matthew and Mark are so similar that Mark does not assume that his readers already had Matthew. We are well assured that neither Luke nor John were written yet and we need not assume that the many Gospels Luke references (1:1-4) were actually any older than Mark. With a theme as rich as Jesus being the **KING OF THE JEWS**; with the abrupt interrogation by Pilate using this title for Jesus (15:2,9,12,18) it seems that Mark's readers already understood this grand truth about the subject of Whom he was writing.

So, again, what's wrong with being a **KING**? Probably nothing. One gets the idea that Pilate didn't wish to crucify Jesus and that he himself was wondering the same thing: "Jewish leaders, what's the problem with being a **KING** with no **KING**dom? He doesn't have an army. He doesn't have a throne. He may be crazy, but if He isn't you can't fight Him anyway. And if He is crazy, then where is the threat?"

Pilate understood this contradiction of the Jews more than they did and simply feared too much to call them on it for fear of his own job; his own kingdom; his own peace. Perhaps we should ask the same question Pilate was asking when he posted this sign above the head of Jesus: What's so harmful about Jesus being a **KING**?

If He is a healing **KING,** then what healing would you lack? What pains would you endure endlessly? What sins would you serve if you spirits and souls were unchained? How much pain would having a healing **KING** bring?

If He is a feeding **KING,** then what would your stomachs lack? What urges and impulses for your life would attack? What needs of your soul would you find reverting back? How much hunger would having a feeding **KING** bring?

If He were a teaching **KING,** then what would your minds do without? What desire to know and what knowledge to grow would evade your soul if a **KING** were your sage and royal His page? How much ignorance would a teaching **KING** bring?

If He were a demon-bashing **KING**, then with what would your fears run about? When would your courage give out? When would your glory run out? How much Hell would pour out? How much terror would a demon-dumping **KING** bring?

If He were an equalizing **KING**, then how would your feelings be hurt? Why would you struggle to find the right words? How would you count this world of such worth? If God's only Son finds level ground then what could be wrong, and how much pain would be wrought, and what harm could this woman-exalting and slavery denouncing **KING** bring?

The answer is your answer, and the answer is mine. We want a healing **KING**; a feeding **KING**; a teaching **KING;** a demon-destroying **KING;** a equality-bringing **KING**. But the crime of Jesus wasn't any of those in the eyes of the High Priest. His crime; His **accusation** was that He was a **KING** with a **KING**dom, and He decided who entered (not the religious necessarily, chapter 7; not the rich, chapter 10; but the child-like and those who "automatically" bring good seed (4:35).

His crime; His **accusation** was that He was a **KING** with a **KING**dom, and He decided the conduct of those who would be a part: They could not be the rebellious, or the reserved ("take your life"; "give yours in exchange for mine", both in chapter 8). Ruling among those who don't vote and dying for those who don't know; that is our **KING**, and it was a crime for which He died.

Perhaps we should at this point say Jesus is "guilty" of this "crime." He is…He is "**KING**." Psalm 24 and Hebrews 1:3 and Colossians 1:18 speak plainly of this truth while Revelation 19 cranks it up and little by saying He is the **KING of KINGs**.

27 With Him they also crucified two robbers, one on His right and the other on His left. 28 So the Scripture was fulfilled which says, *"And He was numbered with the transgressors."* So Jesus the **King** is numbered with the **transgressors** so that we as **transgressors** (quoting from Isaiah 53 here) could be numbered among the **King**'s sons at His table (2 Samuel 9).

15:29-30

And those who passed by indicating that He was probably crucified near a road. **blasphemed Him, wagging their heads and saying, "Aha! *You* who destroy the temple and build *it* in three days, 30 save Yourself, and come down from the cross!"** A person would wonder if John, being the only one who mentions Jesus' saying here referenced, knew that Matthew & Mark's crowd would know of this accusation—thus leaving it out himself. Meanwhile, Matthew & Mark's audience would have known—being less removed from the occurrence—about John 2's record of this prophecy here ridiculed by the passers by (and thus needed not mention it). Here again, we seem to have a second situation in this chapter (along with Caesar's kingship affirmed by the Jews, discussed under 15:26) where Mark assumed his reader knew what John's audience could not have known, being too far removed from its occurrence.

15:31-32

Likewise the chief priests also, mocking among themselves with the scribes, said, "He saved others; Himself He cannot save. For the second time in two verses, these folks actually mock the idea that Jesus could **save** Himself. **32 Let the Christ, the King of Israel, descend now from the cross, that we may see and believe."** "We will entrust ourselves to Him as our King if He can save Himself." Of course, if He had come down, He would not be worth trusting for He would have been contrary to the will of His Father, in sin, and unqualified to save anybody.

Even those who were crucified with Him reviled Him. Were they hoping that doing so would make the Master act? Or, were they (for the time being) so enraged that this man thought He were better though His condemnation was no different than their own?

15:33-36

See my commentary on the Psalms (Psalm 71).

15:37

And Jesus cried out with a loud voice, and breathed His last. It seems as though Mark was fine with us not knowing what was said.

15:38-39[286]

Then the veil of the temple prescribed by Moses and dividing the semi-accessible area from the seldom-accessible area of the tabernacle first; then, the **temple.**

> *Exodus 26:30-34 ...you shall raise up the tabernacle according to its pattern which you were shown on the mountain. 31 "**You shall make a veil** woven of blue, purple, and scarlet thread, and fine woven linen. **It** shall be woven with an artistic design of cherubim. 32 You shall hang **it** upon the four pillars of acacia wood overlaid with gold. Their hooks shall be gold, upon four sockets of silver. 33 And you shall hang **the veil** from the clasps.*

---

[286]See my commentary on Matthew (27:50-53).

*Then you shall bring the ark of the Testimony in there, behind **the veil**. **The veil** shall be a divider for you between the holy place and the Most Holy. 34 You shall put the mercy seat upon the ark of the Testimony in the Most Holy.*

was torn in two This did a number of things:

1. It was an invitation to enter the throne room. This obviously makes no sense if one doesn't realize that the tabernacle of Moses and the temple of Solomon were made after a heavenly reality (Acts 7:44).

    A. In our position as belonging in His presence (Hebrews 10:19-23).

    B. In our prayers (Romans 5:1; Ephesians 2:17-18; Hebrews 4:14-16).

    C. In our prospect. It was an assurance that Heaven was to be expected (Hebrews 6:19-20).

2. It showed that there was no ark present (it had departed centuries earlier).[287] Psalm 141:2 & Acts 3:1 speaks of the afternoon "hour of prayer" taking place at this same ninth hour (Mark 15:33-34). Imagine as the priests light those many altars of incense within the holy place.[288] Imagine as that veil ripped open at the hour of prayer and they saw…nothing. There was no hope in the old system. God was no longer simply living in a building like they had thought—rather, like they had presumed (which was never the intent of the builder of that system, Acts 7:44-51). They felt as though there was a part of their lives that could not be touched by God…'cause He was in the box. Perhaps we could say that we had treated a room like God as these folks had done.

3. It was an act of grief to provide a bookend toward the end of the book to coincide with Jesus' partaking of a "baptism or repentance" (Mark 1:4): tearing a cloak was a display of agony over the existence of sin. At the baptism, Jesus was "in the name of the Father" "repenting"/turning

---

[287] This is assuming, of course, they didn't construct a duplicate. By the way, the apocryphal book of 2nd Maccabees 2:4-5 speaks of Jeremiah hiding the ark at Mount Nebo.

[288] Contrary to the tabernacle, the temple of Solomon did not have just one altar of incense. This was to be a temple for all nations and as such… the traffic would be, at times, incalculable.

towards His people while at the end, the Father seems to have deep-seated remorse over the death of his Son. In that day, there was an expectation to "bear the heart" by the seven closest person to the victim, and there were even rules in this Jerusalem Talmud as to who was allowed to "tear their garments" and to what extent they ought to do so.[289] This seems like that. This seems like God expressing great grief.

God took great pleasure in "all that He had made" (Genesis 1:31). When Adam sinned and creation was cursed—bringing a lack of efficiency and fruitfulness (Genesis 3:16-17; Romans 8:21-24)…who suffered the most? When the watchers came forth and bred with daughters of men (Genesis 6:1-4)[290]…who suffered the most? When the earth was flooded and billions died (Genesis 6-9)…who suffered most? God did.

Who suffers the most when creation acts in a way consistent with being cursed? God does.

Who suffered most when His only Son was killed to restore His creation (John 3:16)? God did. Contrariwise, who gained the most in the work of Christ? God did (Colossians 1:20).

4."At the moment the veil in the temple with embroidered cherubs on it was rent from top to bottom, symbolizing that **those angels could step aside** so that the people of god could approach the throne of grace with confidence."[291] I guess I wish I would have come across that before I preached this message. It's' a great idea.

39 So when the centurion, who stood opposite Him, saw that He cried out like this and breathed His last, he said, "Truly this Man was the Son of God!" This is marvelous in view of the fact that the **centurion** knew nothing of the veil being torn.

15:40-41

---

[289] http://www.chabad.org/library/article_cdo/aid/281558/jewish/keriah-the-rending-of-the-garments.htm [accessed 12/26/17].
[290] See appendix in my commentary on Revelation.
[291] Allen P. Ross *Recalling the Hope of Glory* (Grand Rapids: Kregel, 2006), 116.

There were also women looking on from afar, among whom were Mary Magdalene, Mary the mother of James the Less and of Joses, apparently not the siblings of Jesus as listed at the end of chapter 13. **and Salome,** in Matthew's parallel account, this is the "mother of Zebedee's sons." What is also glaring is the absence of men. Where are all the tough men? Ah, the "shepherd was smitten and the sheep were scattered (14:31). If it were not for John's reference to himself we would have no record that any of the disciples were at the cross at all.[292] Mark seems, as do the other Gospel writers, intent on telling you that the women carried the weight when it came to abiding by the Lord. After all, he speaks of women watching Jesus at His death, His burial, and what they would have thought was in His death on resurrection morning. This is probably intended to teach their readers that Christianity ought to be the great equalizer of worshippers because there would be virtually no adoration without women. On a literary level, it was to prove that they had in fact properly identified the tomb on Easter morning.[293]

41 who also followed Him and ministered to Him when He was in Galilee, and many other women who came up with Him to Jerusalem. We find an even more complete list in the opening verses of Luke 8. What do they see? What did they hear? The last bellowing out of a dying man (verse 38). The only man we see adoring this now dead Savior is a man who knew nothing of faith in this Messiah moments before. May we learn and relearn the lesson that Mark's reader first learned: Never despise the undervalued. The brother of James said this in James 2:1-5 and Paul in 1 Corinthians 1:18-30. The stage is set for those who have what we might call gender-based privilege and religious-based privilege to get the upper hand and to use those privileges for the good of the kingdom, but instead of faith-filled apostles standing around their temporarily dead Savior, we find a profane Gentile and a band of women.

Perhaps this is why neither Matthew nor Mark mention the thief that repented: It would draw away from this centurion that repented.

---

[292]Peter seems to say He was there (1 Peter 5:1), but it's hard to argue.
[293] James A. Brooks, *Mark*, vol. 23, The New American Commentary (Nashville: Broadman & Holman Publishers, 1991), 264.

15:42-46

42 Now when evening had come, because it was the Preparation Day, that is, the day before the Sabbath, This is a subtle hint for the reader that the man of whom we are about to read was virtually alone, and that he didn't need to fear the Jews being out and about. **43 Joseph of Arimathea, a prominent council member,** Luke removes the notion that **Joseph** was complicit with the **council.** He was probably not invited to the midnight trial (14:64).

who was himself waiting for the kingdom of God, If somebody was wondering what this meant exactly, Matthew says "he became a disciple." Mark's opening summary of the message of Jesus gives us a good idea that this Joseph was the closest thing to a convert that then existed (Mark 1:14-15).

"The early church would not have invented a story about Jesus being buried by a Jewish leader, who at most was a secret disciple."[294] Rather we would have had one of the male heroes coming through in the final moments to redeem Him. A Gentile, a group of women, and a secret disciple come along and steal the show. Nobody makes up stuff like this. These Gospel accounts were either never intended on convincing anyone or they were intended on conveying life-changing truth and convincing everyone.

coming and taking courage, Look at this wonderful phrase and don't hurry by. **went in to Pilate and asked for the body of Jesus.** This provides at least three main "Josephs" in the Bible: 1. The son of Jacob; 2. the husband of Mary; 3. This one.[295] This was a sign of honor: a burial before sundown (Deuteronomy 21:22-23 required this). This **Joseph** seems to have much in common with **Pilate:** They believe Jesus is more than a criminal, and thus should receive a burial.

---

[294] James A. Brooks, <u>Mark</u>, vol. 23, The New American Commentary (Nashville: Broadman & Holman Publishers, 1991), 265.

[295] The other Gospels are much more explanatory about this character and his accomplice (Nicodemus) and their standing among the Sanhedrin.

44 Pilate marveled that He was already dead; apparently, crucifixion was a much longer death.

and summoning the centurion, he asked him if He had been dead for some time. Isaiah 53:9 is beautiful in this regard. That Scripture shows that the reason He was allowed to be buried was because of His purity. In other words, it was normal to allow the criminals to be stripped from crosses and thrown in the city dump in the Valley of Hinnom. Pilate, though, reminds me of Darius the Mede in Daniel 6—walking all night to see if one He was forced to imprison would live through a lions' den. This man, **Pilate,** allowed this "criminal" Jesus—whom He felt forced to condemn—to be buried.

Here, then, we have fourfold witness of the death of Jesus: the Centurion, Pilate, Joseph, and these women. This combats the ancient heresy that Simon of Cyrene died in his place[296] or the sect of Islam that Judas was made to suffer in the place of Jesus who did not die, but rather ascended to Heaven without death.

45 So when he found out from the centurion, he granted the body to Joseph. Pilate was not aware of the debate that would ensue in later centuries as to whether Jesus had actually died.

46 Then he bought fine linen, took Him down, he was not alone in doing so, says John.

and wrapped Him in the linen. And he laid Him in a tomb John keeps us from thinking he was alone. They treated this body with such admiration.

> How Beautiful the hands that served
> The Wine and the Bread and the sons of the earth
> How beautiful the feet that walked
> The long dusty roads and the hill to the cross

---

[296] Irenaeus of Lyons, "Irenæus against Heresies," in *The Apostolic Fathers with Justin Martyr and Irenaeus*, ed. Alexander Roberts, James Donaldson, and A. Cleveland Coxe, vol. 1, The Ante-Nicene Fathers (Buffalo, NY: Christian Literature Company, 1885), 349.

How Beautiful, how beautiful, how beautiful is the body of Christ

How Beautiful the heart that bled
That took all my sin and bore it instead
How beautiful the tender eyes
That choose to forgive and never despise
How beautiful, how beautiful, how beautiful is the body of Christ.[297]

which had been hewn out of the rock, This implies what is explicit in the other Gospels: Joseph had a tomb and he was giving it, at least in part, to Jesus. Jesus has no place to lay His head—not even in death.

and rolled a stone against the door of the tomb [and departed, says Matthew]. Imagine even supposing it was permissible to burn Jesus' body in a sort of convenient gesture.[298] Burial was the honor Joseph sought to bestow on Jesus.

---

[297]https://www.azlyrics.com/lyrics/twilaparis/howbeautiful.html [accessed 2/19/18].

[298]There are, perhaps, other debates to have…like whether a family should have a funeral or memorial service for their loved one; or whether the church and its leadership should have something to say in these family processes; or, whether a church should have its own cemetery to the exclusion of unbelievers…but those debates will have to wait for another time.

We do have families that have been faced with deaths and they are concerned about budgeting and they are concerned about debt and you can save 60% of costs by having a loved one cremated, We don't think it's because they love their loved one any less. We don't think it's because they don't want their loved one to be cared for or honored. In some cases, most of the time, it is nothing but expedient either financially or even to the point where many people are not even having funeral services because it's emotionally expedient. Here are some reasons that we, the pastoral staff, feel like you should not choose cremation for your loved one.
1. It seems that there is an honorable way to care for that which God gave to be the temple of His spirit while on earth. 1 Corinthians 6:15-20 indicates that the reason we behave ourselves while living is because we are the house of God. Perhaps it is a stretch, but **it seems there are better ways to dispose of that which was the house of God than burning.** There is a biblical stewardship of this body, it seems. Why not make stewardship decisions now that your children or others behind you would otherwise have to make? Moreover, this is a decision that the community of faith should be able to approve. If weddings should be that which the church observes, how much more the funeral? How much more the burial of the loved one?

This is a major opportunity to show respect for the contribution this person made in your life. It is hard to imagine burning someone's remains as being this "show of respect."
2. Burning, in Leviticus, was a demonstration of God's consuming wrath poured out on the specific sacrifice, and the finality of God's consuming fire. The priests are to burn these sacrifices up completely. That's what the Roman Catholic Church did with John Wycliffe at the Council of Constance. They exhumed his bones and burned them and through them in the river. He was still haunting them even after his death so they said, "Dig up his bones and burn them." That was a way of communicating finality. "We're done with him. He will never bother us again." Burial, however, does not speak of finality. **Burial is a witness to an enduring reality**—such as in Ecclesiastes 3:14. Burial grounds become resurrection grounds.
3. John 19:40 speaks to the fact that **it was the custom of the Jews to bury**. Paul said, "To the Jews was committed the oracles of God," (Romans 9:1-4) so certainly the method by which the Jews took care of bodies should be an example to Christians if the oracles of God were committed to them. They become for us very foundational and we need a legitimate reason for abandoning a Jewish custom.[298] Lazarus was buried, at great expense, as seen in John 11.

    How many guys did it take to carry Joseph from Egypt in a box? How many times did they think, "this is getting a little old. He's not going to know. Let's just burying him right here?" There is no way Joseph wanted to wake up in Egypt. He wanted to be in the Promised Land. Since we are recipients of the relationship of the Covenanting God, perhaps we should adopt some of those old practices if they reflect the God of the Covenant until, like Peter regarding their diet, we receive further revelation.
4. **Burning is usually a treatment God uses for His enemies.** It is as if He is forecasting their future after death. We get an account of Moses being buried. However, God burnt Korah.[298] He burned up the sons of Aaron, Nadab and Abihu.[298]
5. **We are most like Christ in burial, not burning.** Some accounts on the linens and the perfumes and the ointments were almost 50 pounds of weight, a considerable cost. Earlier in Passion Week, Mary anointed Jesus with a <u>very costly</u> perfume and Jesus said that she anointed His body <u>for burial</u>. They loved him Jesus. "Yes, he's gone but we can still manifest our love for Jesus."
6. **We have a place to respect the departed.** While we understand one can still go to a mausoleum to see a collection of ashes in an urn, this more speaks to the idea of an outright "cremation and sprinkling the ashes somewhere" sort of scenario. Being able to visit and rethink God's work in the life of a loved one is a privilege that we feel honored in which to partake in view of our increasingly busy world. It's a place to plant flowers, to clean headstones, to tell stories, to prompt questions, etc.... God's people are consistently required to build monuments for His glory, and we can always go and remember and tell stories at a marker.
7. **It is a traditional, Christian practice to bury one's dead.** It is not that we only have two options: be archaic; or, be progressive. No, it is possible to enjoy both

15:47

And Mary Magdalene and Mary *the mother* of Joses observed where He was laid. They had been following Him since Galilee (verse 41) so this was not only natural; it seemed like all there was to do.

---

technological advancements and to preserve some meaningful norms that depict Christian consensus. In other words, sometimes we do things because "we have always done it that way" and our identity as Christians is important. 2 Thessalonians 3 says "We command you, brethren, in the name of our Lord Jesus Christ, that you withdraw yourselves from every brother that walks disorderly, and not after the tradition which he received of us. For yourselves know how you ought to follow us..." We don't want to reduce this to his merely bringing us some sort of extra-canonical body of truth that we're supposed to follow, but certainly there were some things that were not on the level with doctrine but were still important enough to be observed.[298]

If we're going to be Christian, let's be distinctively Christian. "Learn not the way of the heathen" (Jeremiah 10). While some brethren think that means you shouldn't have a Christmas tree in the context, it seems there are some more weighty matters, especially in the church today.

Conclusion: If you have had your loved one cremated, you may be wondering how that affects the resurrection. In Genesis 22nd chapter, Abraham believed that God could resurrect a cremated body or he would not have had the mind of burning his son, a burnt offering, and then promising their companions that they would be back after worship. Knowing that he was about to kill his son if God didn't intervene, he was willing to "offer" his son and yet he made the promise, "We'll be right back." Abraham believed that God could raise up his son from ashes on rock, if necessary, to fulfill his promise through the seed, Isaac. I leave you with this little nugget: get some life insurance.

Chapter 16

16:1-7

Discussed under 14:13-14 and 14:66-72. More can be found in my commentary on Matthew (chapter 28).

Sabbath was past We need to quickly admit that Mark did not have two **Sabbath**s in mind (see 15:42). This needs to be said in light of the idea that Jesus somehow died earlier than Friday.[299]

16:8

So they went out quickly and fled from the tomb, for they trembled and were amazed. And they said nothing to anyone, for they were afraid. They were, therefore, quiet on their journey through the streets. They did eventually report their findings to the disciples with some immediacy as seen in both Luke 24 and John 20.

for they were afraid. Some believe in a longer ending merely because this seemingly strange defeatist tone to the passage. Let us not forget, though, the same response to those who knew Jesus was alive in the calming of the storm (Mark 4:41), a demon-possessed man (5:15), an anxious woman (5:33), and those who followed Him to Jerusalem (10:32).

16:9-11

[3]**Now when *He* rose early on the first *day* of the week,** we shall readily admit that this summary seems like a break in the flow. See my summary below.

---

[299]Luke 24:21 has a phrase that usually bothers me ("three days since") but that verse merely requires that the killing of Jesus begun on Thursday; "G1096 - ginomai - Strong's Greek Lexicon (KJV)." Blue Letter Bible. Web. 19 Feb, 2018. <https://www.blueletterbible.org//lang/lexicon/lexicon.cfm?Strongs=G1096&t=KJV>.

[3] Vv. 9–20 are bracketed in NU as not in the original text. They are lacking in Codex Sinaiticus and Codex Vaticanus, although nearly all other mss. of Mark contain them.

I have always had a problem with what is generally coined as "textual criticism" which is hardly "textual criticism" at all in my view. Consider the following two quotes as a first-time inquisitor of the topic:

> Thus ends the Gospel according to Mark. <u>At least it does in the two earliest and generally regarded most reliable</u> Greek manuscripts,[300]

> <u>Most of the Greek manuscripts have the inferior, medieval type of text</u>, but some have a text of medium value. Some of the manuscripts that have the long ending, however, mark the passage as suspect. Among the early Christian writers supporting the longer ending are Justin(?) (d. ca. A.D. 165), Irenaeus (d. ca. A.D. 202), and Tertullian (d. ca. A.D. 220). <u>The KJV and NKJV have vv. 9–20 because they are based on the medieval type of Greek text.</u>[301]

Do you see this difficulty? 1. Most of the existent manuscripts have it, but 2. Not the best ones. Herein lies the battle, honestly: Is the earliest manuscript the best one?

1. Could it be that the reason it is found in a well-kept status as the two under investigation is because they were seldom used? Could it not rather be that the "earliest" ones are simply not in existence anymore because of their being much copied (as evidenced by the preponderance of the manuscripts containing the contested reading)?
2. Might it be that the ones that are found were found to be corruptions quite early and left unused?
3. Shouldn't the early quotations of the writers, dating prior to the "earliest and most reliable," tell us that there were in fact earlier manuscripts than the "earliest" ones we have now?

And sometimes it could be something much easier: Maybe the manuscripts with the short end mirror the journal feel of the rest of the

---

[300] James A. Brooks, *Mark*, vol. 23, The New American Commentary (Nashville: Broadman & Holman Publishers, 1991), 272.
[301] Brooks, *Mark*, vol. 23, 272.

book and the copies containing the end of this Gospel were made from the completed version of Mark.

He appeared first to Mary Magdalene, out of whom He had cast seven demons. The second time this is mentioned (Luke 8:2).

16:14-18

Later He appeared to the eleven as they sat at the table; and He rebuked their unbelief and hardness of heart, because they did not believe This is key, in my opinion, in relieving some of the pain of the following verses—particularly those who are promised salvation in verse 16 and those who will have signs follow them in verses 17 and 18:

1. Regarding verse 16, Jesus is speaking to those who have been baptized (by John the Baptist) and yet do not believe what we would define today as the Gospel: The Christ Who was killed for our ransom (10:45) is alive. In other words, these disciples are being both scolded for unbelief and told to preach the "gospel" (verse 15) they did not believe a minute ago. So we have non-believing, baptized disciples, and Jesus I think is saying it is not baptism that saves you, but belief.
   Perhaps it is easier to see if the verse is read aloud with the emphasis on "he that believeth" (v. 16a) and on "but he that believeth not" (v. 16b) rather than on "and is baptized." It could be read as "your baptism is good, but your belief is required."

2. Regarding verses 17 and 18, it seems that the passage lends itself to addressing those of **the eleven** who would actually **believe.** In other words, the promises of verse 17 and 18 shouldn't be statically read in some sort of limitless promise to all types in all generations, but rather to those in Jesus' audience primarily, and perhaps…through some levity those whom they would reach.[302]

---

[302]We should be really careful here. If I were to walk into the sanctuary of my church next Sunday morning and say, "anybody wishing to have a free copy of my commentary on Mark should see me after this service," nobody would think "that offer is good forever to everyone regardless of the year or the supply of said

If there's anything the reader of Acts and Hebrews (2:1-4) should get, it is that these disciples had their works confirmed with these signs.

15 And He said to them, "Go into all the world ⁿand preach the gospel to every creature. Interestingly, the author is the only one of Gospel authors that uses this word which is related to "creation" as it is understood in Genesis 1:1. As a matter of fact, **creature** is the very same word as "creation" in Mark 10:6.[303] So, Mark had at his disposal both the word for mankind (*anthropos*) and the words for the genders within mankind (*andras* and *gyne),* and he chose to use the word **creature.** The bottom line is outstanding: 1. The disciples are being commanded to be the image bearers of the King throughout His domain, that is the whole earth; 2. The disciples are to subjugate all people (called **creatures** here) on the earth as the first man was commanded to subjugate all the creatures in Genesis 1. There is no question that this parallel was to be ascertained.

See my commentary on Genesis (1:26) for the connection with Genesis 1:26-28 and the rest of Mark through the scope of Genesis 1:26-28. There are two corollaries for the believer today who believes they carry the faith of the apostles: 1. Christ is the King of the whole world, and we are to make it clear by being His reflections the world over. In other words, He is the King, yes, but he is the King in His Greatest Glory when His reign is evident throughout the whole world. 2. We are to subjugate and take dominion by being proper reflections of His image, preaching the Gospel.

17 And these signs will follow those who believe: In My name they will cast out demons; Seen in Acts 16:8. **they will speak with new tongues;** Seen in Acts 2:4. **18 they will take up serpents;** Seen in Acts 28:4.

---

commentaries." There are comfortably understood limitations by nature of the content.
    ⁿCol. 1:23
    [303] "G2937 - ktisis - Strong's Greek Lexicon (KJV)." Blue Letter Bible. Web. 7 Aug, 2017.
<https://www.blueletterbible.org//lang/lexicon/lexicon.cfm?Strongs=G2937&t=KJV>.

and if they drink anything deadly, it will by no means hurt them; Probably the only phrase in these last verses that appear difficult in order to accept the whole.

they will lay hands on the sick, and they will recover." Seen again in Acts 28:8 (healing of Publius' father on Melita).

16:19-20

So then, after the Lord had spoken to them, Not right after. Acts tells us there was 40 days between His resurrection and the ascension. **He was received up into heaven,** Seen again in Acts 1:9-11. **and sat down at the right hand of God.** Seen again in Acts 2:33. **20 And they went out and preached everywhere,** Seen in Acts 17:5-6. **the Lord working with *them* and confirming the word through the accompanying signs. Amen.** Seen again in Acts 4:9-10 and 5:12.

Appendices

Appendix 1: Review of E.M. Bounds' "Necessity of Prayer"
Appendix 2: A Discussion on Suicide
Appendix 3: A Discussion on the doctrine of "Scripture"
Appendix 4: Some Positions on Israel and the Church

Appendix 1: Review of E.M. Bounds' "Necessity of Prayer"[304]

The life of E.M. Bounds extends from the 1830's until August of 1914. After desiring to study law, he felt the call to be ordained as a Methodist preacher. Furthermore, he served as a chaplain in the confederate army wherein he was spent some time as a Prisoner of War.

He cared for the souls of men through prayer during his time as a pastor, and editor, and an evangelist. He passed away in Washington Georgia.

Purpose/Thesis of This Book
The main idea herein is that prayer is essential for every part of any one desiring to be a person who walks with God. There are no shortcuts in the believer's life. Bounds goes even further to state that if there is no inclination to pray, there is no indwelling Holy Spirit. Hence, this person is lost without Christ.

Summary of the Book
Since these were mere notes that were edited by another individual, it would be somewhat inappropriate to assess Mr. Bounds' ability to layout a book. However, the book begins with three chapters discussing the role of faith and trust (which I think are synonymous) in prayer (Chapters 1-3). These are indispensable elements.

Then, there is a progression to the role of "desire" (Chapter 4)—then, of "fervency" in prayer (Chapter 5). Then, profoundly, one finds the bar raised even higher to find two chapters on "importunity" (Chapters 6 &7), and the importance of endurance in prayer. Later on, there is a further progression of "vigilance" of prayer in one's perspective (Chapter 11).

Then, there are a series of elements that are both instigative and responsive of a prayer life such as "character and conduct" (Chapter 8), "obedience" (Chapters 9 & 10), rich knowledge of the Word of God (Chapters 12 & 13), and church attendance (Chapter 14).

---

[304]Originally Written in Pursuance of M.R.E. from LBTS (2010).

One does not see an overemphasis on things the writers of today may have written concerning career enhancement, financial prosperity or self esteem. One might assume that these were concerns in Dr. Bounds' day, but that these would "take care of themselves" in the process of putting things in their proper order.

Assessment of the Book
Exegetical and Hermeneutical Skills
These two terms allude to the questions, "What is there?" and "What does it mean?"

Obviously, the man has great ministerial credentials. Furthermore, it can be said that he held a prayerful discipline with which few can share company. What is certain is that He believes in the authority of Scripture as there is, in every one of the fourteen chapters, repletion of Holy Writ.
There is, by and large, an apparent adherence to the Word of God. Care must be given in going from Scripture to Scripture lest we fall into hasty interpretation (exegesis).

There is an example, however, of just the opposite in the chapter three: Dr. Bounds deals with "Prayer and Trust". He says, "Trust is not a belief that God can bless, that He will bless, but that He does bless, here and now." One may take great exception to this since he just dealt with Mary and Martha in the aftermath of Lazarus who felt as though "God's blessing" would be revealed in a brother who would not have died. As Bounds shows, God's blessing "here and now" was revealed in letting Lazarus die so a greater miracle could be performed (John 11).

Concepts and Principles reflected in the article
Of course, one does not need to rehash fourteen chapters to get the sense that prayer permeates each part of the believer's life. One even gets the idea that he mentions those most crucial themes in their order of importance as they thrive throughout the writing of this book. There are some prevailing themes, however, that should be pointed out:

1. Prayer is both a result and a source of most spiritual traits and disciplines.

Take, for instance, the idea of "Prayer and Faith" covered in chapters 1 and 2: In chapter one, he says, "when faith ceases to pray, it ceases to live". Dr. Bounds is saying that the exercise of prayer is one that strengthens the inner man. He goes on to say "faith is kept alive by prayer".

However, he also says that effective prayer is impossible without faith. In chapter two, he says, "Doubt and fear...usurp the place of faith, and although we pray, it is a restless, disquieted prayer that we offer, uneasy and often complaining". He then goes on to use Philippians 4:6 quite effectively.

What is apparent from his writing is both the mutual benefit which prayer and faith share, and the resultant progression of faith within prayer. Faith also sparks desire to pray which strengthens the new man to new heights of faith.

2. A prayerful life must have a militant posture.

This militant posture bears fruit in the traits of "fervency" (Chapter three) and "desire" (Chapter four). There is an emphasis placed on declaring a war of sorts against frivolous thinking ("the menace of prayer—wandering thought"- Chapter four), an emphasis placed on zealous declaration of one's needs as before a king ("God requires to be represented by a fiery church"), and an emphasis placed on the need for a living man to keep praying to stay alive spiritually ("it stays and pleads and persists, and refuses to let go until the blessing has been vouchsafed").

Dr. Bounds has it right: we are to emulate the "Author and Finisher of our Faith" (Hebrews 12:2) in "striving against sin" (Hebrews 12:4). One cannot read these Scriptures without remembering the picture of a battling, praying Christ in the wilderness, in the garden, on the cross, and in the grave.

3. Prayer cannot be paid forward or paid back.

Dr. Bounds is a champion of the idea that you cannot pray for today's needs tomorrow. The fact that it is a militant issue (point 2) gives the element of appropriateness and urgency. One cannot pray for tomorrow's needs today. There is the overwhelming Sovereign hand of God which knows all and sees all, but to pray effectively, one needs as many details as possible to "ask and receive".

He drives this point home throughout, but says in chapter one, "As every day demands its bread, so every day demands its prayer. No amount of praying, done today, will suffice for tomorrow's praying". We have not, "because we ask not" (James 4:2). We have no "reception" because we have done no "asking"- no doors open, because we have not "knocked" (Matthew 7:7). So, it is certainly difficult to pray for as we ought when the situation has not developed fully enough for us to pray intelligently.

Conclusion
You don't get any more utilitarian than taking part in the action of prayer. Bounds has shown its relevance to every part of the Christian endeavor—from faith to church attendance.

Understanding that this book was a labor of love and work of editing done by his good friend Homer Hodge, one wouldn't leave the seeming overabundance of devotional material upon Bounds. There does seem to be much more of a "deeper life" emphasis, and less of a "nuts and bolts" feel. In other words, though this book could be split up even further than it is already in the chapter divisions, the real answer, once again, is editing.

I would not recommend this book to anyone who is already convinced that the Scriptures are the authority on prayer simply because I believe it is much more readily defined in the pages of the Gospels, in about as many words.

Appendix 2: Some thoughts on Suicide out of Mark's Gospel

The opportunity for this message came on the heels of the death of our town's mayor. He took his life. Of course, I felt like I needed to deal with the issue and I didn't want to handle it insensitively at all; nor did I wish to make the text fit the topic.

I had a legitimate fear of which I prayed love would cast out (1 John 4:18). I feared being misunderstood, and I feared disappointing folks by not providing answers.

Let's first say that depression is not the same as suicide. Many have been depressed without having to do certain things like….kill one's self.

Also, a desire to die is not the same as suicide ideation (as will be seen later in Mark 8). Job (Job 3), David (Psalm 55), Elijah (1 Kings 19), Jonah (Jonah 4) all wished for death.

Genetic propensity toward depression or suicide does not remove cognitive decision making. It may make things more difficult, yes, but it doesn't make things impossible.

3:23-29

1. **Suicide is a moral issue.** While the topic here is about the "blasphemy of the Holy Spirit," Christ gives, in no uncertain terms, the reality that there are but two forces in the world and they are consistently active. One must, therefore, decide whether their suicide is that which causes God to shrug. In other words, does God have an opinion about it? If so, it's a moral issue.

   Suicide involves the unauthorized taking of a human life, and as such **violates the sixth commandment (Ex 20:13);** *God does not sanction it…The biblical narrative records examples of several individuals who took their own lives. In each case the* *circumstances of the suicide were inglorious and regrettable. Samson, tortured and humiliated by the Philistines, took his own life with theirs after a ruinous career of disregard for the Lord (Jdg 16:30). Ahithophel committed suicide after being publicly humiliated by having his advice rejected, and in order to avoid being executed for treason (2 Sm 17:23). Zimri, after murdering an Israelite king, ended his life to avoid being killed by his pursuers (1 Kg 16:18). Judas committed suicide after his betrayal of Jesus (Mt 27:5). There are no biblical examples of honorable suicide. An examination of the Bible's accounts of these lives and deaths suggest two primary scriptural observations about suicide: first, it is an option that some deeply troubled people will choose when facing desperate circumstances; and second, it is a pathetic and tragic end to a human life.*[305]

Myth: "Suicide is not a spiritual issue." Some corollaries would be "some suicides are mental issues" or "some suicides are simply depression-caused."

Nothing we do is secular. All things are to be done to the glory of God (Colossians 3:17). Every person the earth either glorifies God or does not glorify God with all actions. If we find one who is outside their faculties when they commit a crime—due to their choices or not do to their choices, their life changes forever (consider involuntary manslaughter).[306]

Moreover, a believer should never stop thinking like a believer (Romans 12:1-2; Ephesians 4:23).

There are two important groups of emotions: positive faith-based emotions and negative fear-based emotions. Each of these groups has its own set of emotional molecules attached to it. It is vital to understand the

---

[305] Ted Cabal et al., *The Apologetics Study Bible: Real Questions, Straight Answers, Stronger Faith* (Nashville, TN: Holman Bible Publishers, 2007), 454.
[306] Carries 13-16 months as a Class F Felony in NC; http://statelaws.findlaw.com/north-carolina-law/north-carolina-involuntary-manslaughter-laws.html [accessed 5/19/17].

> *difference between these two polar opposite groups. Faith and fear are not just emotions, but spiritual forces with chemical and electrical representation in the body.[307]*

2. **Suicide is forgivable.** Notice the idea in this passage, as already defined, is that when you reject Christ's Words and Christ's Works (to include redemption), you are committing the most heinous sin. This means, that somehow, someway, in some manner, if a person hasn't rejected Christ, forgiveness is obtainable for suicide.

   > **Myth: "All sins are equal."** This is the kneejerk response to those who insist that "suicide" is worse because you can't ask forgiveness, yet this very prooftext shows that this statement is not true. There is a sin that is unforgiveable; so to say that God sees all sins the same is simply not true. Perhaps we should remind everyone that there are many sins that can cause you to not have time to "ask forgiveness:" drunken driving, for example; eating one's self into coma, etc…

5:4-15

As far as suicide is concerned, here is a man who wishes to inflict pain on Himself (5:5) and would have killed himself if the demons had full reign—as it says they finally did kill their host in verse 11.

3. **Suicide is not God's idea (5:5).** Perhaps not all suicides are demonically-influenced as in this portion of Scripture, but you better know that Demons were self destructive. Consider Jesus' response to the question about "killing a marriage" in Mark 10. He appeals to "what Moses said at the beginning." What did Moses say at the beginning? Among other things that Moses said at the beginning, Genesis 2:7 says God "breathed into man's nostrils life's breath." Life is God's idea. Abundant life is God's idea. Nobody can look at Ahithophel or Zimri or Judas in the despair-driven suicides and say "their suicide was of God!"

---

[307] Caroline Leaf *Who Switched off My Brain? Controlling Toxic Thoughts and Emotions* (Dallas: Switch on Your Brain USA LP, 2009), 19.

Myth: "It was their time." Be very careful about this. That assumes that people never die early, and the fact is Scripture does not say that. As a matter of fact we keep pointing out that Scripture says the opposite for something as simple as taking the Lord's Supper unworthily (1 Corinthians 11:30).

4. **Jesus is the cure for suicide (5:12).** This man was driven to Jesus. Whether we are demon possessed or demon oppressed, our cure for the demons of life, whether demons of angelic origin or demons of mental illness are all found lying prostrate before the King. None others will assist in this manner (5:4).

8:34-36

5. **Suicide is not merely a willingness to die.** Willingness to die is not the problem. An unabashed, deliberate planning for death is not the issue.

There are honorable ways to give one's life [as in war or in a medical emergency where a mother gives up her life for her baby to live (Rachel in Genesis 35)].

As a matter of fact, saving your life as an "end" to itself is a problem; fear of death is a problem. We want to stress "Giving one's life;" this is an honorable action.

9:20-22

6. **People are its survivors**. In this case, a father and a son, with little thanks to the disciples. Furthermore, it was a father who had been with his son **from childhood.** Perhaps the greatest part about foster care is that when fathers and mothers for some reason cannot dwell with their troubled children, one will find help from a father who will find Christ.

10:45[308]

7. **Jesus Died for the sin of suicide (10:45).** Sin is the master. It owned us. We do no favors by downplaying the willful act of taking a life…even if it's our own. It is a fearful thing to cause one's own death through willful, cognitive action, and to wake up in the face of God. Yet, we must make it clear that Christ paid the ransom to rescue us from the bondage to sin.

Do we create another category of sin for which Jesus only died if sinners confess their particular sins? Salvation is by the death of Jesus + prayer then? If so, it's not just suicide that is unforgivable. Everybody who dies in rebellion of any kind is no longer saved.

Did Jesus only die for those sins that don't lead to one's death? If so, what about carelessness like drunk driving or daredevil entertainment like downhill skiing?

Closing words to the Christian:
1. Keep a high opinion of "life." Keep a high opinion of godly life.
    a. ½ of all transgendered peoples attempt suicide (UK study in 2012).[309]
    b. Those in late teens and early twenties are 18% more likely to have suicidal ideation with each casual sexual encounter (OHSU study from 2013).[310]
    c. 80% of suicides may be reduced if we can keep folks from romanticizing about methods to do so.[311]
2. Keep some honest foresight and suspect that anybody could be heading in the direction of suicide.
    a. Think about your regrets ahead of time so that your recollection of your relationship is honest and helpful
    b. Begin relationships and maintain rates of interaction that you can maintain.

---

[308] See Matthew 20:24 and following and their treatment in the author's commentary on Matthew.

[309] http://www.sermonaudio.com/sermoninfo.asp?SID=213151346321 [accessed 5/18/17].

[310] http://researchnews.osu.edu/archive/casualsex.htm [accessed 5/18/17].

[311] https://world.wng.org/2014/07/hello_darkness? [accessed 5/18/17].

3. Be committed to a truth that exceeds your own opinion. There is a connection:
   "A survey by the Barna organization in 2002 found that only 22 percent of American adults believe there is absolute truth. For born-again Christians the figure is 32 percent. To get a sense of how people view moral issues today, take a look at some that the Gallup research organization asked people to judge as right or wrong. Percentage of Americans who think these are morally wrong: Divorce 23%; Gambling 34%; Having a baby outside marriage 40%; Gay or lesbian relations 43%; Doctor-assisted suicide 46%; Abortion 50%; Suicide 77%"[312]

4. Find something to give your life for. <u>This is the way of Our Master (John 10:18).</u>

---

[312] North American Division Corporation of Seventh-day Adventists, <u>Adventist Men's Ministries Curriculum</u> (Lincoln, NE: AdventSource, 2011), 75.

Appendix 3: A Study on the Scriptures in Mark (Bibliology of Mark)

This is especially salient to a Baptist Pastor in a Baptist Church:

> *The Holy Bible was written by men divinely inspired and is God's revelation of Himself to man. It is a perfect treasure of divine instruction. It has God for its author, salvation for its end, and truth, without any mixture of error, for its matter. Therefore, all Scripture is totally true and trustworthy. It reveals the principles by which God judges us, and therefore is, and will remain to the end of the world, the true center of Christian union, and the supreme standard by which all human conduct, creeds, and religious opinions should be tried. All Scripture is a testimony to Christ, who is Himself the focus of divine revelation.*[313]

There are basically four passages of Scripture in the Gospel of Mark where the term *graphe* (Scripture) is found in this book.[314]

12:1-12

9 "Therefore what will the owner of the vineyard do? Matthew tells us that Jesus' listeners provided the answer contained in the rest of this verse:

11This was the LORD's doing, And it is marvelous in our eyes'?" What are the timeless and indispensible principles of this Scripture about Scripture in verse 10? What is Jesus saying when He asks them "have you not read this Scripture?"

He was at least playing to the fact that they should have known the Scripture. Further, that they were expected to be reading the

---

[313] http://www.sbc.net/bfm2000/bfm2000.asp [accessed August 30, 2017].
[314] "G1124 - graphē - Strong's Greek Lexicon (KJV)." Blue Letter Bible. Web. 30 Aug, 2017.
<https://www.blueletterbible.org//lang/lexicon/lexicon.cfm?Strongs=G1124&t=KJV>.

Scripture. His question to them in verse 10 is almost insulting. As a matter of fact, it was downright inflammatory since they would soon be singing this Psalm[315] during the upcoming Passover Feast as it is a "Hallel Psalm"—a group of Psalms sung during the Feast beginning on the day of Christ's death.[316] Think about it, many in among their own countrymen would be singing this very Psalm on the day that the head of the corner was rejected—and they didn't even know it. He was saying that the Psalms are at least part of the Scripture. He quotes from Psalm 118. As a matter of fact, this is the "hymn" the disciples sang with Jesus following the Lord's Supper (Mark 14:26).

As it pertains to this topic, He was saying that it was inevitable that the Scripture must be fulfilled. "Why didn't you see this coming?" or "Why weren't you warned against being a part of this?" Like Judas, these men looked up one day and saw they were fulfilling the very prophecies that they had read their entire lives. And if the Scriptures are treated the same, as is supposed by Jesus' generic reference to them, then all Scriptures must come true. And if all Scriptures must come true, then all Scriptures are completely foreknowing and accurate. And if all Scriptures are perfectly foreknowing and accurate, their source can only be God.

"Scripture," then, up to this point in the Biblical narrative had a chief function of testifying to who Christ may be. From Genesis 3:15 until John the Baptist's ministry, there is a question "who is it?" From John the Baptist until Revelation 22:21, there is a statement: "That's Him!"

12:18-27

24 Jesus answered and said to them, "Are you not therefore mistaken, because you do not know the Scriptures nor the power of God? So, our analysis says that Jesus' statement in verse 24 reveals the

---

[315]Mark Blitz *Blood Moons: Decoding the Imminent Heavenly Signs* (Washington: WND, 2014), 51-52; Blitz believes Psalms 113-118 were the "hymn" Jesus sung with his disciples in Mark 14:26.

[316]Hughes, 284; while singing the "rejection" clause on the day of His death would have been Providential enough, imagine singing the "has become the head" clause on the day of His resurrection!

Sadducees lack of trust in the **power of God,** yes, but also in the **Scriptures**.

Now, The **Scriptures** are, in fact, coupled with the **power of God.** This gives us the understanding that the Scriptures testified of what God was able to do, but that they did not **know** them. Why did the Sadducees not know them? Because they only saw **Moses** as authoritative. They did not see the other writings as authoritative, and therefore, did not see the potential of the **power of God** in raising the dead (see verse 18 again; reference against Deuteronomy 25:5-6). It seems that there is no telling of the **resurrection** in the writings of Moses (other than perhaps Job which can be seen in "the authorship of Job" in an appendix in my commentary on Job). Jesus is perhaps referring to Job 19:25 or Isaiah 26:19 or Ezekiel 37 or Daniel 12:3. The point is that while they wanted to concentrate on the writings of Moses, Jesus points out they did not **know the Scripture** and therefore, were not convinced of **the power of God.**

Once again, the prophets we named are **Scripture** as much as Psalms or the writings of Moses (12:25). We have, then, the threefold witness spoken of by Jesus in Luke 24:44.

The **Scriptures** give us the answers to the questions we seek. Sometimes, they are in plain sight although not in plain language (12:25-26). Since they spell the **power of God,** they must therefore be an accurate representation of God, and therefore, trustworthy. Since it is trustworthy concerning the resurrection, it must be trustworthy concerning the principles of how one may obtain the resurrection of the just unto salvation. Since it is trustworthy concerning the understood and well-known qualifications of obtaining the resurrection of the just and salvation, it must therefore provide solid bases for camaraderie among those who have been assured to have obtained it.

14:47-49

49 I was daily with you in the temple teaching, and you did not seize Me. But the Scriptures must be fulfilled." We see from this passage that Jesus expected the entirety of Scriptures to be fulfilled. Mark doesn't bother to discuss whether Jesus had any control in this at this juncture. However, since we know from other Scriptures (Acts 1) that Judas was unwittingly a part of fulfillment—as were the scribes and Pharisees (Mark 12:10)—it seems reasonable that Jesus was going to be a part of the fulfillment (see the 4th reference in Mark 15:29) according to the Father's will and that He would not attempt to stop its fulfillment. In other words, Christ's lack of desire to stymie their fulfillment is just as inconsequential as the others' ignorance of their fulfillment.

Appendix 4: Israel, the Church, and Dispensations

Once upon a time, I wrote the following statements for a position paper which was never used by the man under whom I served.

I. Concerning Israel

- WE AFFIRM that God favored the Jewish people above all other nations in the Old Testament.[i]
- WE AFFIRM that some of the covenants which He made with the nation of Israel were conditional.[ii]
- WE AFFIRM that salvation is received by faith alone under both the "Old" and "New Covenant."[iii]
- WE AFFIRM the guilt of the nation of Israel in their rejection of Jesus as their Mediator of the New Covenant.[iv]
- WE AFFIRM that "Israel of God"[v] is synonymous with "body of Christ" and is different than "national Israel."[vi]
- WE AFFIRM God's future fulfillment of His promises to Israel, "grafting them in" again to the "Israel of God."[vii]

II. Concerning the Church

- WE AFFIRM that the word "church" is an "assembly called out" in the original usage, rather than a building.[viii]
- WE DENY that the universal "body of Christ" was unknown to God prior to Israel's rejection of Jesus.[ix]
- WE DENY that church began at Pentecost as an "organization"; but rather it began in the time of Christ[x] having meetings,[xi] ordinances,[xii] officers,[xiii] membership acceptance,[xiv] membership rejection,[xv] and a tangible mission which included the starting of other regular local meetings with the same distinctives.[xvi]
- WE DENY that the church as an "organism" began in the time of Paul, but was merely recognized during his time,[xvii] and is made up of all who have been placed into Christ.[xviii]
- WE DENY that national Israel ever had salvation by virtue of their physical lineage;[xix] but rather the "Israel of God"[xx], made up of people

who had been justified by faith, have always been God's covenant people.[xxi]
- WE AFFIRM that God has one group of "elect", and that the church as an "organism" and the "Israel of God" is made up of both Jews and Gentiles.[xxii]

III. Concerning Dispensations

- WE DENY that God dealt with His people the same way in every "time", "age", or "dispensation."[xxiii]
- WE DENY that these variations in "economy" reflect a change in God's character which does not change.[xxiv]
- WE DENY that variations in "economy" reflect a change in His predetermined will which does not change.[xxv]
- WE DENY the "Kingdom of Heaven" in Matthew's Gospel and the "Kingdom of God" in Mark's and Luke's Gospels are to be understood as different ideas.[xxvi]
- WE DENY that the "kingdom" is presently fulfilled in its entirety;[xxvii] rather, it must be entered through the "New Birth"[xxviii], and in its future reality[xxix] will be brought to earth by the "King of Kings", Jesus Christ.[xxx]
- WE AFFIRM that the "saints", who are made up of the covenant people of God from all ages,[xxxi] will rule and reign [xxxii] with King Jesus[xxxiii] first from Jerusalem,[xxxiv] and then from the New Jerusalem.[xxxv]

---

[i] Deuteronomy 7:6-7; Romans 9:1-5.
[ii] Deuteronomy 7:9-12.
[iii] Jeremiah 31:31-34; James 2:23.
[iv] Matthew 27:25; John 19:15; Acts 2:36; Acts 3:14-15; Acts 5:28; 1 Thessalonians 2:14-15; Hebrews 9:14-15.
[v] Galatians 6:16
[vi] Romans 2:28-29; Philippians 3:3-5; Revelation 3:9.
[vii] Jeremiah 31:35-37; Ephesians 2:11-16; Romans 11:1-2; 17-32.
[viii] Matthew 16:18; Acts 19:39; 2 Corinthians 6:17; Hebrews 10:25.
[ix] Ephesians 1:4-5; 3:1-6.
[x] Matthew 4:18-22; Mark 1:16-20; Luke 5:1-11; John 1:35-45.
[xi] Acts 1:13; Hebrews 10:25.
[xii] Matthew 26:26-30; Matthew 28:19; 1 Corinthians 11:2.
[xiii] 1 Timothy 3:1-13.

[xiv] Acts 9:26-27.
[xv] 1 Corinthians 5:7-13.
[xvi] Matthew 28:19-20.
[xvii] Philippians 2:1; Ephesians 3:1-6.
[xviii] Romans 8:9; 1 Corinthians 12:13.
[xix] Jude 5
[xx] Galatians 6:16.
[xxi] Acts 7:38; Psalm 22:22 cf. Matthew 26:30.
[xxii] Ephesians 2:11-3:6.
[xxiii] or as the KJV sometimes translates it—"worlds".
[xxiv] Malachi 3:6; Hebrews 13:8.
[xxv] Hebrews 6:17-18.
[xxvi] Matthew 13 and Mark 4 with consideration of the parables of the "Kingdom"; Matthew's Gospel was written primarily to Jews—who were very reserved in using the name of "God". "Luke", on the other hand, was written to an individual who was probably not Jewish (Luke 1:3).
[xxvii] 1 Corinthians 15:24-28; Colossians 1:13.
[xxviii] John 3:3-5.
[xxix] Matthew 6:9-10.
[xxx] Psalm 24:8-10; 2 Timothy 4:1; Revelation 19:11-16; 20:4-6.
[xxxi] Ephesians 1:10.
[xxxii] Revelation 20:4-6; 2 Timothy 2:12.
[xxxiii] Daniel 7:13-14, 22.
[xxxiv] Psalm 24:7-10; Isaiah 7:14; 16:5.
[xxxv] Isaiah 2:2-3; 66:20; Revelation 21:2.

Made in the USA
Middletown, DE
05 June 2019